The New Great Game

THE NEW
GREAT GAME

Blood and Oil in Central Asia

Lutz Kleveman

ATLANTIC BOOKS
London

First published in revised and updated form in English
in the United States of America in 2003
by the Atlantic Monthly Press, an imprint of Grove/Atlantic, Inc.
841 Broadway, New York, NY 10003–4793

Published in Great Britain in 2003
by Atlantic Books, an imprint of Grove Atlantic Ltd

Originally published in German as *Der Kampf um das Heilige Feuer*
by Rowohlt Verlag GmbH in 2002

ISBN 1 84354 120 3

Atlantic Books
An imprint of Grove Atlantic Ltd
Ormond House
26–27 Boswell Street
London WC1N 3JZ

Printed and bound in Great Britain by MPG Books Ltd, Bodmin, Cornwall

In Memory of My Father
Udo Karl Theodor Kleveman (1929–1997)

Contents

The Devil's Tears: An Introduction

O n the afternoon of December 16, 2001, a black U.S. Air Force
C-17 transport plane begins its descent over the Central Asian
plains. Aboard the plane is fifty-year-old General Christopher Kelly.
His mission: to set up an American airbase in the small republic
of Kyrgyzstan, the first U.S. troops to be stationed on a combat
mission on the territory of the former Soviet Union. Their enemies
are the Taliban and the remnants of the Al Qaeda terror network
in Afghanistan, more than six hundred miles to the south in the
Afghan mountains.

At exactly 3:32 P.M. local time, the C-17 touches down at the
civilian airport of Manas, near the Kyrgyz capital of Bishkek. Two
days earlier, the worst blizzard in decades raged across Kyrgyzstan.
Airport workers toiled through the night with shovels to clear the
landing strip. "Who would have thought during the Cold War that
I would ever reach this place?" Kelly quips as he peers out at giant
mounds of snow. He has served in the Air Force for twenty-eight
years. In a matter of weeks, a base for three thousand troops is to
be established at the airport. "This is combat, this is the real deal,"
Kelly says.

General Kelly is a product of a new American alliance with a
former Soviet republic, a partnership that was unthinkable only a
few years earlier. The terror attacks of September 11, 2001 and
the U.S. campaign in Afghanistan have pushed Central Asia, a region that had been as obscure as the Balkans ten years ago, to the

forefront of world attention. The vast territories between the eastern shores of the Black Sea and the peaks of the Pamir Range were long known as the "black hole of the world." For more than seventy years of Soviet rule, the region around the Caspian Sea (the world's largest inland lake) was isolated from the West, virtually inaccessible to foreigners.

After the Soviet Union's collapse in 1992, eight republics in the Caucasus and Central Asia—Georgia, Armenia, Azerbaijan, Kazakhstan, Kyrgyzstan, Uzbekistan, Turkmenistan, and Tajikistan—obtained formal independence, opening their borders to their southern neighbors and to China in the east. The goal was to establish new political and economic relations to smooth the transition to capitalism.

Instead, almost all the ex-Soviet republics in the Caspian Sea region are still ruled by former communists and KGB generals who reluctantly adopted nationalistic rhetoric to retain dictatorial control over states still in search of their national identities. Most of the republics were created by Joseph Stalin, who paid no attention to each area's population mix—a legacy that continues to fuel conflict between the many ethnic groups of the region. At the same time, the new nominally independent states are striving to free themselves from Moscow's hegemonic grip, looking for new allies.

The war against Al Qaeda focused international attention on the Caspian region as an area of strategic importance. However, the Afghan campaign is only an episode, albeit an important one, in a much larger struggle: the "New Great Game." Coined in the early 1990s, the term describes an odd rerun of the first "Great Game" in the nineteenth century. As immortalized in Rudyard Kipling's novel *Kim,* the British Empire and Tsarist Russia were fighting then for supremacy in Central Asia.[1]

When the Tsarist armies conquered the Caucasus and subjugated the nomadic peoples of Turkestan, London and Calcutta saw this as a threat to the British Crown Colony of India. In turn, the Russian government in St. Petersburg feared that the British might incite the Muslim tribes of Central Asia to rebel against Russia.

The two empires jousted for control of Afghanistan, whose central location offered the most strategically viable base for an invasion of India or Turkestan. Lord George Nathaniel Curzon, viceroy of India in 1898, clearly knew what was at stake for the British in the Great Game: "Turkestan, Afghanistan, Transcaspia, Persia—to many these names breathe only a sense of utter remoteness or a memory of strange vicissitudes and of moribund romance. To me, I confess, they are the pieces on a chessboard upon which is being played out a game for the dominion of the world."[2]

Now, more than a hundred years later, great empires once again position themselves to control the heart of the Eurasian landmass, left in a post-Soviet power vacuum. Today there are different actors and the rules of the neocolonial game are far more complex than those of a century ago: The United States has taken over the leading role from the British. Along with the ever-present Russians, new regional powers such as China, Iran, Turkey, and Pakistan have entered the arena, and transnational corporations (whose budgets far exceed those of many Central Asian countries) are also pursuing their own interests and strategies.

The greatest difference in today's Great Game are the spoils. While in the Victorian-era struggle, London and St. Petersburg competed over access to the riches of India, the new Great Game focuses on the Caspian energy reserves, principally oil and gas. On its shores, and at the bottom of the Caspian Sea, lie the world's biggest untapped fossil fuel resources. Estimates range from 50 to 110 billion barrels of oil, and from 170 to 463 trillion cubic feet of natural gas. The U.S. Department of Energy comfortably assumes a 50 percent probability of a total of 243 billion barrels of oil reserves. Azerbaijan and Kazakhstan alone could sit on more than 130 billion barrels of oil, more than three times the United States' own reserves. Only Saudi Arabia, with 262 billion barrels, can claim greater resources. As recently as the summer of 2000, the giant Kashagan oil field was discovered off the Kazakh coast, believed to rank among the five largest fields on earth.[3]

People have known that there was oil and gas around the Caspian Sea for centuries. As early as the Middle Ages, members of

the Zoroastrian sect went on pilgrimages to the Apsheron peninsula in today's Azerbaijan to pray near gas-fed flames, worshipped
as "Holy Fire," that burst forth from its soil even today. At present,
transnational energy corporations, littoral states, and world powers
vie for the same holy fire, desperately searching for alternatives
to the Persian Gulf, which still holds two-thirds of the world's oil
reserves.

In industrialized countries' energy ministries, what would be
the last oil rush in world history has evoked a sense of euphoria.
Democratic governments are courting corrupt Caspian potentates,
while transnational companies have signed lucrative contracts
and invested more than 30 billion dollars in new production facilities. A further hundred billion dollars has already been earmarked
for additional investments. As post-communist Russia and the state-
owned Saudi oil fields offer few opportunities for joint ventures, the
Caspian boom is proving to be a blessing for the oil corporations.

The British and Russian officers of the nineteenth century
who encountered each other along the old Silk Road, often disguised as explorers and cartographers, have been replaced by a
new brand of adventurers: geologists and oil engineers. And yet,
the "Tournament of Shadows," as Tsarist foreign minister Count
Karl Robert Nesselrode once called the Great Game, is played out
not by courageous individuals, but by large corporations, bureau-
cracies, and military forces.

"I cannot think of a time when we have had a region emerge
as suddenly to become as strategically significant as the Caspian,"
declared Dick Cheney in a speech to oil industrialists in Washington, D.C. in 1998, when he was still CEO of the oil supply corporation Halliburton.[4]

Today, Vice President Cheney is one of the most influential
men in the coterie of President George W. Bush, himself a Texan
oil magnate who wrote in his 1999 autobiography, "I am fascinated
with the oil industry. All my friends have in one way or the other
been involved in the oil industry."

Immediately after taking office, the Bush administration made
oil politics a new priority in the United States, where 4 percent
of the world's population consumes more than one-fourth of all

energy. In May 2001, Cheney presented the National Energy Policy report, which addressed the issue of how to secure America's energy demands in the next twenty-five years. For the report, Cheney had met with American business leaders behind closed doors, with the Bush administration classifying the participants' identities and the minutes of the talks, a measure normally taken only if national security is at stake.

The report's official authors, members of a commission that included Secretary of State Colin Powell, recommended that "the President make energy security a priority of our trade and foreign policy." While acknowledging that the Middle East oil producers will remain central to world oil security and that the Gulf will be a primary focus of U.S. international energy policy, the report added that "our engagement will be global, spotlighting existing and emerging regions that will have a major impact on the global energy balance." The Caspian Basin was singled out as a "rapidly growing new area of supply," and the report advocated a deepened "commercial dialogue with Kazakhstan, Azerbaijan and other Caspian states to provide a strong, transparent and stable business climate for energy and related infrastructure projects."[5]

To be sure, contrary to initial expectations, there is less oil in the Caspian than in the Persian Gulf region. With a maximum oil production of six million barrels per day, by 2015 the Caspian region could reach a share of 5 to 8 percent of the world market, roughly equal to that of the North Sea. Most of the world's oil supply will continue to come from the Middle East, and yet that is precisely why the Caspian has become so important in the United States' effort to wean itself off its dependence on the Arab-dominated OPEC cartel, which, since the oil crisis in 1973, has used its near-monopoly position as a pawn and leverage against industrialized countries.

The hazards of Gulf oil dependency became all the more compelling in August 1990, when Iraqi dictator Saddam Hussein invaded Kuwait, giving him temporary control of one-fifth of the world's oil reserves. Only after an enormous military and financial effort did a U.S.–led international coalition expel Iraqi troops from Kuwait, and ever since then American troops have been

stationed in the unstable Gulf region, with the U.S. Navy's Fifth
Fleet patrolling the Strait of Hormuz, the world economy's Achilles'
heel. The cost of this permanent military presence, which has
effectively turned Arabic mini-states such as Kuwait into American protectorates, is estimated at about $50 billion a year. The
Bush administration's 2003 invasion of Iraq to remove the Hussein
regime and the threat it allegedly posed to the oil-rich region cost
the American taxpayers an additional $80 billion.

These efforts reflect American strategic interests in the Middle East, which is the largest oil supplier to the United States, followed by Canada, Venezuela, and Mexico. The Gulf region provides
about one-fifth of the eleven million barrels of crude the United
States imports every day and which roughly meet half the country's total energy needs. As America's own crude production is
going to drop by an estimated 12 percent over the next decade,
though, imports will have to provide for two-thirds of the total
energy demand by 2020. Additionally, the economic boom in such
countries as China and India is likely to cause global oil consumption to surge from today's seventy-three million barrels per day
to ninety million barrels by 2020, according to the International
Energy Agency. As many oil wells outside the Middle East are near-
ing depletion, OPEC will expand its share of the world market to
more than 60 percent.

This will increase the political clout of the Saudi oil sheikhs
in particular, whose possession of one-fourth of the world's reserves puts them in a unique position to dictate prices to the West.
Saudi Arabia is the only country in the world capable of acting as
a so-called swing supplier. To compensate for production losses
such as those caused by the recurrent political crises in Venezuela,
the Saudis are able, in a matter of weeks, to boost production from
eight to 10.5 million barrels per day. Alternatively, they could
choose not to act at all if a price hike is in their interest.

Many people in Washington are far from comfortable with the
Saudi power. The desert kingdom is increasingly perceived as an
embarrassing and potentially dangerous ally, even more so since
September 11, 2001, when nearly all the plane hijackers were
Saudis. There is a growing risk that radical Islamist groups could

topple the corrupt Saud dynasty. Inspired by Osama bin Laden, who has accused the U.S. troops stationed on Saudi soil since the Gulf War of 1991 of the "greatest theft in history" for allegedly keeping oil prices artificially low, those radical groups could stop the flow of oil to Western "infidels." The so-called petrol riots in Britain in the autumn of 2000, when tens of thousands descended into the streets to show their fury at fuel shortages, were an ugly preview of the chaos such an interruption of oil deliveries would cause.

Yet even without an anti-Western revolution such as the one in Iran in 1979—when 4.3 million barrels of crude disappeared from the world market overnight—Saudi oil is already, as it were, ideologically contaminated. In its efforts to stave off political turmoil, the corrupt regime in Riyadh funds the powerful radical Wahhabi sect that backed the Afghan Taliban and foments terror against Americans around the world.

In a bid to decrease its dependence on the Saudi oil sheikhs, the United States has for years pursued a policy of "diversifying energy supplies." This strategy seeks to secure and control oil resources lying outside the unstable Middle East. Bill Richardson, secretary of energy under President Clinton, described how the Caspian region fits into this strategy. "This is about America's energy security, which depends on diversifying our sources of oil and gas worldwide. It's also about preventing strategic inroads by those who don't share our values. We're trying to move these newly independent countries toward the West. We would like to see them reliant on Western commercial and political interests rather than going another way. We've made a substantial political investment in the Caspian, and it's very important to us that both the pipeline map and the politics come out right."[6]

The "pipeline map" Richardson referred to is one of the most controversial elements of the new Great Game, and over the past ten years has led to conflict and war in the Caucasus and throughout Central Asia—with no end in sight. The Caspian Sea is entirely landlocked. From the oil wells, it is a journey of nearly a thousand miles to the nearest high sea ports where tankers could ship the crude to market. Pipelines, umbilical cords for the industrialized

world, need to be constructed. But which route should the pipelines take?

Under communist rule, when a Soviet republic's infrastructure was directed entirely toward Moscow, almost all pipelines
were built northward across Russian territory. Today, Russia insists that new pipelines follow the same routes. In a strategic bid
to strengthen the new republics' independence from Moscow, the
United States is instead attempting to keep the precious oil beyond Russian grasp, while at the same time trying to thwart plans
for a pipeline leading south through Iran. To achieve both,
Washington in the mid-1990s supported plans by the U.S. energy
corporation Unocal to build a pipeline from Turkmenistan through
Taliban-controlled Afghanistan. Additionally, the United States has
championed a new gigantic pipeline project from Azerbaijan's
capital of Baku across the Southern Caucasus to Turkey's Mediterranean port of Ceyhan.

The U.S.–led Afghan campaign has fundamentally altered the
geostrategic power equations in Central Asia, which has become
the new focus of American foreign policy. This raises a fundamen-
tal question: Is there a link between the quest for Caspian oil and
the war on terror in Central Asia?

While Washington's military presence in Afghanistan appears
to be primarily targeted against international terrorism, it would
be naïve to assume that American decision makers are not also
pursuing other strategic interests in Central Asia. As early as 1997,
President Clinton's Assistant Secretary of State Strobe Talbott
argued that were the Caspian region to fall into the hands of religious or political extremists, it "would matter profoundly to the
US if that were to happen in an area that sits on as much as two
hundred billion barrels of oil."[7] While the Caspian energy resources may not be the casus belli, they certainly could be the
big price in the war on terror, which the Bush administration now
uses to dramatically extend American influence in Central Asia.

In my work as a journalist, I have long tried to examine how
the struggle for raw materials can lead to conflicts and wars. I first
investigated this fatal causality in West Africa, in the diamond
mines of Sierra Leone as well as in the Nigerian oil fields. The bit-

ter confrontation between the energy giant Shell and the Nigerian tribes about the Niger delta's oil made it clear to me why fossil wealth is often more of a curse than a blessing for a country and its people.

This book is the result of many research trips and interviews in the countries of the Caspian region, the Caucasus, and Central Asia. In exploring the various front lines of the new Great Game, I tracked down its players, observers, and victims. Meeting with oil executives, warlords, diplomats, refugees, oil workers, politicians, agents, and generals, I traveled for thousands of miles from the Caucasus peaks across the Central Asian plains down to the Afghan Hindu Kush and to Kashmir.

My journey began in Baku, the capital of Azerbaijan, which is both the center of the Caspian oil boom and the starting point for a U.S.–backed giant pipeline to the Turkish Mediterranean coast. I followed its projected course across the war-torn country of Georgia, where Western investors face rampant corruption and the constant threat of Russian military attacks. After an excursion by UN helicopter to the secessionist Caucasus republic of Abkhazia, I crossed the Caucasus mountains to reach Chechnya, where pipelines also play a role in the terrible war between Russian forces and Chechen rebels.

Following a brief return to Baku for a dramatic turn of events, I flew to Kazakhstan, the new "Wild East Oil Dorado," where massive corruption scandals involving American energy corporations mar the world's greatest oil discoveries in three decades. From there, I visited the Muslim Uighur people in Xinjiang, the westernmost province of China, which, by aggressively pursuing pipeline plans to transport Kazakh oil to Shanghai, is turning out to be one of the United States' main Great Game rivals. The other is Iran, part of George W. Bush's "axis of evil," whose oil bosses told me in Tehran of their plans to thwart the American pipeline plans by offering Iran's oil network to the Caspian states.

After a nocturnal boat trip across the Caspian waters I then reached Turkmenistan, one of the world's most isolated countries, whose eccentric dictator erects golden statues of himself while trying to play Americans and Russians against each other. Venturing deeper into Central Asia, I traveled to Uzbekistan, Washington's new and despotically ruled ally, to witness the arrival of thousands of U.S. antiterror troops, now stationed within a day's march of the Caspian oil riches.

After a visit to U.S. troops at another new base in Kyrgyzstan and to their potential adversaries, Russian troops in neighboring Tajikistan, I traveled to post-Taliban Afghanistan, the latest Great Game battlefield. There, I met with warlords, government members, and American officers to investigate new plans to construct a pipeline through U.S.-controlled territory. My long journey ended in Pakistan, the cradle of terrorism and the driving force behind the Afghan pipeline deal, where I tracked down Islamic militants who threaten to bring the American presence in the region to a violent end.

All the different countries and people in this story have a small part to play in the new Great Game. The actors may have changed since Kipling's time but its culmination in war and death remains the same, and the victims are nearly always innocent civilians. They know why oil is called "the Devil's tears."

Pipeline Poker: Baku's Oil Boom

Vagif Guseinov watches us suspiciously as our driver parks our black Volga next to a monument in the courtyard of his headquarters. "Long live the oil workers!" reads the inscription in Cyrillic letters on the monument, but the hammer and sickle have been removed. Mr. Guseinov, a colossus of a man, mechanically extends his right hand, a veritable bear paw adorned with four or five golden rings. Mr. Guseinov may be wondering why his bosses at central headquarters gave me permission to visit Sandy Island. In the old days, this would have been impossible.

This group of two dozen oil rigs off Azerbaijan's coast, one of the largest in the Caspian Sea, was once guarded like a state secret, and no unauthorized person ever made it across the 4-kilometer dam linking the artificially created island to the shore. In the early 1950s, Soviet engineers constructed a seemingly infinite maze of pipelines, pump stations, and drilling towers on wooden stilts, stretching from Sandy Island far into the open sea, held together by twelve kilometers of roads, likewise on stilts. Today, the giant site belongs to Socar, the state oil company of the former Soviet republic that became independent ten years ago.

Vagif Guseinov, Socar's general director on Sandy Island, has worked in the Caspian oil industry for more than thirty-five years. He has decorated his office, as is advisable for civil servants in today's Azerbaijan, with a total of eight portraits of President Heydar Aliyev. One painting of the former KGB general dates from

11

1976 and bears the inscription "Shining Son of the People" in Azeri.
Six telephones are lined up on the desk, each of a different color.

The building from which Mr. Guseinov rules over Sandy Island
is a wooden shack that has been hastily erected by his workers.
The director points out the window to a house about five hundred
yards away, half-submerged in water. "My old headquarters," he
admits. "We built it too close to the shore. Who could have known
at the time that the level of the Caspian would rise so much!"

Guseinov gives me permission to visit the drilling rigs, but
only at my own risk. "The installations are very old, do watch your
step!" The offshore production site is in utter decay. The roads
leading out to the open sea look like the aftermath of an intense
artillery barrage. Our driver has to steer the Volga precariously
around gaping holes, under which dirty, oil-soaked waves splash
against the rotting stilts. Pipelines and oil reservoirs have rusted
away, while crooked drilling towers of wood and steel are reminiscent of the first oil wells in Pennsylvania in the 1870s. Far off
on the shore, the high-rise buildings of Baku are visible through
the haze.

We stop in front of what looks like a derelict drilling tower.
A set of wooden stairs dangles off the iron bars, leading nowhere.
On the platform, surrounded by scattered debris, sits the "Christmas tree," which is what oil engineers call the well's central valve.
"Western investors have not shown much interest in Sandy
Island yet," Mr. Guseinov comments wryly. "Once some Russians
working for Lukoil showed up but they only looked around briefly
and never came back." Production has sunk to a level of 150,000
tons a year, a fraction of its one-time volume. However, some
1,600 people still work on Sandy Island. "We will never shut down
the rigs even if the wells are depleted. The people need work,
full-stop."

The pipes around the Christmas tree hiss and gurgle and
suddenly an engineer who accompanies us opens a valve. Out
gushes the slimy, brownish crude oil, accompanied by a sweet-
smelling stench. A few liters of an estimated 50 to 110 billion barrels that lie hidden beneath the bottom of the Caspian Sea and on
its shores form a growing puddle right at our feet. By the time the

engineer closes the valve, several liters of crude have already poured out, left to seep through the ground and into the seawater.

Before our departure Mr. Guseinov insists on treating me to lunch at the canteen. On our way there, every worker we pass takes off his hat and bows respectfully to the boss. Women step anxiously backward so as to not stand in our way. "It is payday," Guseinov snarls over his shoulder. In a separate room of the canteen, three waiters serve a *soljanka* soup, followed by fried "black ducks," shot by workers over Sandy Island the day before. The meat tastes unnervingly of oil. Soon, Guseinov orders three bottles of Russian vodka. He fills our glasses and, in a deep guttural voice, proposes a toast to the oldest man at the table, our Volga driver. Then a second toast, to the deep and unbreakable friendship between Azerbaijan and Germany, a third to international cooperation, and several more in the befuddling socialist phraseology of peace, understanding, and *drushba,* friendship. As a tribute to the post-Soviet Islamic revival in the Caucasus, Guseinov lifts his eyes briefly to the ceiling before every sip, mumbling a phrase. "I ask Allah please to look the other way when I drink," he explains with a grin. One of the engineers raises a toast—the seventh or eighth—to the general director, the "wisest, most humane, most just and far-sighted boss" that Sandy Island has ever had. Guseinov looks moved.

Then it is my turn. I toast in honor of all foreign companies that drill for oil in the Caspian Sea. Hesitating, the engineers look to Mr. Guseinov, who clears his throat. "It is good that the Americans are investing their money in Azerbaijan," he says curtly. Silence. Suddenly the old Volga driver, who has not spoken a single word all day, says, "Americans have no culture." To enthusiastic nods from his colleagues, one of the engineers adds: "If only they would help us lead a successful war against Armenia." At this point Guseinov intervenes: "Now, now, comrades! That is high politics which we had better leave to the president. We are just simple oil men."

It is already dark when we return to Baku. A cool breeze blows from the water, each gust laced with the odor of petroleum. The day before, the wind came from the south, overland from Persia, bearing the promise of an early spring. Now Siberia sends a cold reminder. The streets lie deserted in the pale moonlight, with only the odd Mercedes limousine or Jeep creeping past. Acacia trees line the rows of wealthy middle class houses from the turn of the century whose oriels and wrought-iron balconies evoke Paris or Marseille. During the day, the streets are busy with groups of men in black leather jackets and ladies in high-heeled shoes window shopping at Cartier or Versace boutiques.

Yet even the nouveau riches and their promenades cannot dispel the impression that boomtown Baku, the new Oil Dorado of the Caspian Sea, is scarcely more than an upmarket shithole. The glittering buildings, expensive boutiques, and picturesque minarets of the old town cannot mask the strong stench of oil that never dissipates, day or night, not even when the wind blows in from the sea. The writer Fitzroy Maclean, then a British diplomat accredited in Moscow who travelled to Baku in the late 1930s, found the town in much the same condition. "Even before you reach Baku, the derricks of the oil wells and the all-pervading smell of oil warn you that you are approaching the town. Oil is the life of Baku. The earth is soaked with it and for miles round the waters of the Caspian are coated with an oily film."[1]

To make matters worse, Baku's current mayor is a Koran-abiding guardian of public morality. Street cafés are closed and it is rumored that the police have begun to arrest foreign oil executives caught with local hookers. It was not always this way. Baku was once a city filled with promise. The Neftciler ("oil worker") Prospect along the seaside promenade is lined by tall *Gründerzeit* palaces, their richly ornamented facades decorated with pseudo-classicist pillars. The best architects from across Europe descended on the city during its first oil boom more than a hundred years ago, when more than half the petroleum on the world's markets came from Baku.

On the arid Apsheron peninsula that stretches into the Caspian Sea, petroleum has seeped from the soil for ages. On his journey to China in the thirteenth century, Marco Polo reported of a well near Baku whose outpour, while unsuitable for drinking, could easily be burned. Moreover, Polo wrote, the sticky stuff could be put to good use for cleaning wounds in his camel's skin.

Azerbaijan was originally known as the "land of fire" because of natural fires, fed by gas from the soil, that burned on the Apsheron peninsula. Today, a similar spectacle can be observed in a small village north of Baku. There, a bumpy dirt road leads to the Yanar Dag, the mountain of fire, where the air is heavy with the smell of gas and ten-foot flames shoot out from a sooty limestone cliff. Next to the fire, villagers have set up a couple of benches and tables, where they sit at night drinking vodka until someone throws a rock at the limestone, kicking up a new batch of flames.

From the early Middle Ages Zoroastrian pilgrims, who worship fire as a sign of God, came to these cliffs from Persia, erecting temples around the mysterious holy fires. One such *atashgah* (temple of fire) still exists north of Baku. Alexandre Dumas described the *atashgah* he saw during his visit to the Caucasus in the mid-nineteenth century: "We went inside the temple through the gates, which were entirely enveloped in flames. The prayer room with the cupola is erected in the middle of a large quadrangular court; the eternal fire is ablaze right in the middle of the prayer room."[2] The flow of natural gas to the fire altar in the temple's inner courtyard has long petered out, so a rather mundane municipal gas pipeline now feeds the eternal flames.

Oil was discovered in Baku in the early nineteenth century, when it was a recently annexed Russian duchy. People who dug up the soil with their hands scooped off the oil that seeped out. Around the early 1870s, a Russian entrepreneur was the first to use machines to drill for crude, and by 1873, some twenty small refineries belched black smoke into the Baku air. That same year, a Swedish chemist named Robert Nobel arrived in Baku. He was the older brother of the factory owners Ludwig and Alfred Nobel, who had become very rich producing arms and dynamite in St. Petersburg and Paris. Robert had gone bankrupt with several companies, and was now working for his brother Ludwig. He was sent to the Caucasus with 25,000 rubles to purchase Russian

walnut wood for the production of rifle butts. No sooner had
Robert set foot in Baku than he got carried away by oil fever and,
without consulting his brother, bought a small refinery.[3]

Ludwig soon followed Robert to Baku, and the two brothers
founded the Nobel Brothers Petroleum Producing Company. In the
course of only a few years it replaced America's Standard Oil,
owned by John D. Rockefeller, as the world's leading supplier of
oil. The Nobel brothers became the oil kings of Baku, and their
workers proudly referred to themselves as "Nobelites." By the late
1880s, Nobel wells yielded 23 million barrels of Russian crude
every year, more than four-fifths of the American production.
Then, as now, the greatest problem was how best to transport the
oil from the landlocked Caspian shores to Europe. Initially, it was
shipped across the Caspian Sea, up the Volga, then finally to its
destinations by train. This was both complicated and expensive.
Then, in 1883, a direct railway line was built from Baku across the
Caucasus to the Black Sea port of Batumi, which Russian troops
had only recently seized from the Ottoman Empire.

The project was funded by the Rothschilds, a family of French
bankers. They needed cheap crude for their refineries in Europe
and quickly became the Nobels' fiercest competitors. However,
when the line was finished, the locomotives were not powerful
enough to pull more than six tank wagons across a pass in the
Georgian mountains. The Nobels had a solution. With the help of
four hundred tons of dynamite from Alfred in Paris, they blew a
tunnel into the mountain pass in 1889 and laid a seventy-kilometer-
long steel tube. It was the region's first oil pipeline and marked
the beginning of the so-called oil wars over global markets among
the Rockefellers, the Nobels, and the Rothschilds that, in retro-
spect, almost appear quaint compared to today's geopolitical
struggle for Caspian oil.

Traces of this first oil boom can still be found in Baku. The
Nobel villa, a white manor of wood and glass, stands on a hill
above the port, in an industrial zone that came to be called "Black
City." The terrace from the Nobel estate afforded a landscape of
hundreds of refinery chimneys belching acrid black smoke into
the sky.

A few miles along the coastline from Black City, which still bears this name today, one reaches hundreds of old oil wells rusting on the shore amid giant pools of shiny black sludge and pinkish water. Several derricks grind painfully up and down while rubbish is strewn everywhere. The ghostly scenery calls to mind World War I photographs of the Passchendaele and Ypres battlefields. Not a single green plant or blade of grass can be found for several square miles in any direction.

At one of the derricks two workers with oil-smeared faces and boots full of holes labor hard to revive a defunct pump. Despite the biting cold, they absurdly use their bare hands to try to loosen a frozen apple-sized screw. Around them, the rolling hills open onto black lakes, surrounded by dead yellow sand. This is the scene of giant blowouts from a century ago, when valves broke under the pressure from below, sending fountains of oil high into the sky. Locals gave them names such as "Wet Nurse" or "Devil's Bazaar," while the biggest among them, a blowout from the mid-1880s oddly named *"Drushba"* (friendship), gushed oil for five months at a rate of 43,000 barrels a day. Most of it seeped back into the ground, scorching the soil.

Along with the nation's first oil barons, Russia's socialist movement also had its origins in Baku. When the Tsarist regime began to crumble in the early twentieth century, oil workers in Baku repeatedly went on strike to protest against working conditions. One of their leaders was a young Georgian agitator named Joseph Dzhugashvili, later known as Joseph Stalin. In 1901, Stalin, who then called himself by the nom de guerre "Koba" (the irrepressible), organized strikes in Batumi against the Rothschilds and was arrested by the Tsarist police. After his escape from a Siberian labor camp, Stalin continued with his secret revolutionary activities in Baku. "I first discovered what it meant to lead large masses of workers. There in Baku I received, thus, my second baptism in revolutionary combat. There I became a journeyman for the revolution," Stalin later wrote.[4]

In 1903, Stalin was involved in a massive workers' revolt that started in Baku and spread throughout Russia, leading to the first general strike in the empire. Two years later, during the first

Russian revolution, workers deliberately sabotaged industrial sites, setting many oil wells on fire. Bloody ethnic clashes broke out between Azeris and Armenians, and by the end of 1905, two-thirds of all oil wells in Baku were destroyed and the entire oil export business had collapsed. With international investors withdrawing from the city, production never recovered. On the eve of the First World War, the share of Russian oil in the global market dropped to 9 percent. Baku's oil boom was over.

The Great War became the first conflict in world history where oil reserves decided victory and defeat. Ultimately, the German Empire lost the war of attrition in the trenches of the Western front because its war machinery had run out of fuel. In early 1918, the military situation seemed auspicious for the German forces. In March, the Russian revolutionaries who had ousted Tsar Nicholas II but needed troops to combat Tsarist loyalists signed the peace treaty of Brest-Litovsk. The Bolshevik negotiator Vladimir Ilyich Lenin ceded to the Germans the Baltic territories, Finland, and Ukraine. For Erich von Ludendorff, chief of the German general staff, it was not enough. He wanted Baku's oil. Turkish troops, allied with the German army, were already moving toward the Caspian oil wells. Von Ludendorff offered to hold the Turks back in return for direct oil deliveries to the Reich. When Lenin agreed, Stalin sent a telegraph to the Baku commune that had chased out the oil barons and seized control of the city. Stalin's order was to start pumping crude oil. The communards refused.

In July and August 1918, the Turks laid siege to Baku and seized several oil fields. It was a short-lived victory, as a small British detachment pushed north from Persia and liberated the city, denying von Ludendorff desperately needed oil supplies. By the time the British left the city to the Turkish army in September, it was too late for the exhausted Germans, who surrendered on November 11, 1918. Lord Curzon, a member of the British war cabinet and future foreign minister, declared a few days later, "The Allied cause had floated to victory upon a wave of oil."[5]

The Caspian oil also played a significant role for the Germans during the Second World War. In early 1942 Adolf Hitler ordered his army into the Caucasus as part of "Operation Blue." In order for its motorized units to continue their blitzkrieg in the East and force the Soviet Union to its knees, the Wehrmacht desperately needed fuel supplies from the Caspian. The German offensive literally ran out of gas in the Caucasus mountains. Often the German vehicles were stuck for several days waiting for new supplies. As their tanker trucks were also out of fuel, the Germans transported fuel canisters on the backs of camels. When the Sixth Army was encircled by Soviet troops at Stalingrad in the winter of 1942–43, Hitler initially refused to withdraw his forces from the Caucasus. The dictator reportedly told Field Marshal Erich von Manstein, "It is a question of the possession of Baku. Unless we get the Baku oil, the war is lost."[6] Finally, in January 1943, the Caucasus troops were ordered to retreat. Two years later, Soviet tanks entered Berlin.

The end of the Second World War heralded the beginning of a new era for the Caspian oil industry. Soviet engineers constructed the first offshore oil rigs, right off the Baku coastline. This began the career of Khoshbakht Yussifzadeh, the grand seigneur among Baku's oil bosses. The seventy-two-year-old Yussifzadeh is vice president of Socar, Azerbaijan's powerful state oil company. Its headquarters are in an imposing white palace right on Neftciler Prospect, which previously housed the Soviet oil administration for the entire Caspian region before the communist empire's collapse.

The way to Mr. Yussifzadeh's office leads through glass corridors that link the various parts of the palace. The two secretaries in the anteroom ask for patience, as the vice president is still on the phone. Through the door a deep rolling voice can be heard, then a sudden burst of hoarse laughter, and the thunder of a hand smashing flat on a desk. The secretaries smile apologetically, shrugging their shoulders.

Moments later Yussifzadeh calls me in. Behind the huge piles of papers on his desk, he has the appearance of a Spanish don. Though his hair is not yet completely gray, age has drawn deep furrows across his face. Massive tear sacs drop from his warm and alert eyes. Large geographical maps cover all of the walls, most

of them of the Caspian Sea. On top of a cupboard stand dozens of
ampules filled with samples of crude oil.

"For forty-nine years I have been in this business, I have lived
for oil," says Yussifzadeh as he takes a sip of green tea from his
cup. "The Oily Rocks and I grew old together." The Oily Rocks were
the most daring offshore project in the Soviet Union after the Great
Patriotic War, as the Russians refer to World War II. About twenty-
five miles off the Baku coast, geologists had discovered evidence
of great oil resources. "We wanted to have them but, you see, we
had no experience in how to start drilling in water." The engineers
gathered seven old barques and linked them together with steel
bridges. These were the shaky beginnings of an offshore oil rig
that was to grow into a veritable city on the open sea. Soon, more
than a hundred kilometers of roads linked six hundred oil wells,
with thousands of workers moving into blocks of apartments. Following his geology studies, Yussifzadeh spent the first twelve years
of his career on the Oily Rocks. "For us, it was a brave new era.
We were pioneers, explorers. After work we went to the cinema
or bars. You see, there were also many women there who worked
in the laboratories or the canteen."

Yussifzadeh made money, the first good cash after many years
of poverty. He grew up without his father, who had been killed
during the Stalinist purges of the 1930s, while his mother raised him
and his two siblings single-handedly.

"Then I was allowed to go to university, and on the Oily Rocks
I earned 2,900 rubles, with benefits even 5,000 rubles. At the time,
that was fantastic!" Yussifzadeh climbed the career ladder, becoming chief geologist for the entire Caspian Sea by the 1970s. The
career move coincided, however, with a decision by the Soviet
leadership to neglect oil production in this region and instead to
focus on strategically more convenient resources in Siberia and
Kazakhstan.

Despite this change of policy, Yussifzadeh went ahead with
test drillings for new oil fields along the entire Caspian coast. "Most
of the oil fields off the Kazakh coast that are causing such brou-
haha these days were originally discovered by me." He jumps up
from his chair, walks over to a cupboard and opens it. An ava-

lanche of rolled-up maps spills out. Holding a particularly ruffled-looking map with a triumphant expression on his face, he wipes the dust off the northern half of the Caspian Sea. "Up here it says 'Kashagan,' does it not?" In the summer of 2000, geologists discovered a giant oil bubble in Kashagan, with an estimated volume of thirty billion barrels, presumably one of the five largest oil fields in the world. The find caused a sensation on the oil markets around the world, and lies at the core of all debates about pipelines in the Caspian region.

"I knew it at the time, that there would be a lot of oil down there." Yussifzadeh's problem was that the site was part of a nature reserve. Only the ministry of fishery in the capital was able to grant an exception for drilling. "So I flew to Moscow and applied for an authorization to do a test drilling at Kashagan. The lady colonel in charge of the matter declined the request categorically. 'Only over my dead body!' she said. Today the lady colonel is dead, and the foreign corporations are drilling at Kashagan. No one mentions the environment anymore."

With the Soviet Union's collapse in late 1991, Azerbaijan became an independent republic. The nation of seven million almost immediately slipped into chaos. Several governments ousted each other in a succession of coup d'états, and a totally demoralized Azeri army lost the bloody war with Armenia over the predominantly Armenian-populated enclave of Nagorno-Karabakh. In 1993, Azerbaijan, bereft of 15 percent of its territory, was on the verge of falling back under Moscow's control. That was when Heydar Aliyev stepped back into the political spotlight. A distinguished KGB general and member of the Politburo, the Azeri had for decades been one of the most powerful communist leaders of the Soviet Union. Nicknamed "the fox" by his friends and enemies, Aliyev saw that in nearly all post-Soviet republics, former high-ranking communist officials were back in power. So it came as no surprise when the sublime tactician was elected president of his home country in October 1993.

Aliyev quickly realized that the only chance for Azeri independence—and for keeping his power—lay in the oil business. He made his son Ilham, a notorious playboy, second vice president of Socar. With the oil business firmly in the hands of the presidential family, no decision in Socar has been made without direct consent of the Aliyevs.

In Yussifzadeh's office, just as in Vagif Guseinov's office, there are no fewer than seven photographs of Aliyev. In his eight years of rule, the autocrat has orchestrated a true cult of personality. Pictures of the leathery, sphinxlike Aliyev stare from the walls in every office across the country. The paintings with the caption "Shining Son of the People" show an amazingly rejuvenated president emitting red and yellow rays of light, while in actuality, the eighty-year-old Aliyev is suffering from cancer and has long since chosen his son Ilham to succeed him as president.

After Aliyev seized power, he wanted to free his country from a patronizing Kremlin that, with Aliyev's past in mind, had expected a pro-Russian policy. The Azeri had other ideas. The country lacked the money and the necessary technology to exploit its resources off the coast. So Aliyev opened the country's oil fields to foreign investors. This ensured that Western governments, in particular the United States, would have a continued interest in an independent Azerbaijan. As early as the spring of 1994, Aliyev nominated a team of experts, led by his son Ilham, to negotiate a good deal with interested oil companies.

Yussifzadeh, a longtime friend of Aliyev's, took part in the negotiations. "We made a public invitation to tender, and six, later twelve, companies showed interest, the most avid by the American company Amoco and by British Petroleum." A suitable venue had to be found for the talks, but at the time Baku could not offer a single hotel with Westernized amenities. There were also concerns for the security of the oil executives. "Many people in Azerbaijan were opposed to us reaching an agreement with foreigners. And of course, the Russians objected as well." In Moscow, the dispatches from Russian agents in Baku were read with growing concern. Instead of relying on his old Soviet connections, Aliyev revealed himself almost overnight as a glowing Azeri nationalist bent on snatching his country's raw materials from Russian control. Rumors of an impending Moscow-backed putsch spread throughout Baku.

The negotiating partners agreed to convene first in Istanbul during the summer of 1994. "We were all very excited," Yussifzadeh remembered. "After all, it was the first time ever that a delegation went abroad without Russian company—previously that had been unthinkable." The initial meeting, however, was spiked with great mutual distrust. "Across the table from us were suddenly the very same people who only a few years before had been our capitalist enemies," says Yussifzadeh, laughing out loud at the memory. "At first we felt insecure and had many doubts. To us, those oil bosses from America seemed like Gypsies who were only waiting for their chance to take us for a ride."

Before that meeting, Yussifzadeh had rarely dealt with Americans. "My idea of them was still very much influenced by all the propaganda. Once, in the 1970s, a delegation from the United States came on a visit to Baku, and I was surprised by just how nice and normal they were. They gave me a bottle of Buffalo whiskey." A second present still covers one of the walls in Yussifzadeh's office: a map of the world, several square meters in size. It is strictly geographical, without any political borders.

After the first contact the negotiations moved to Houston, Texas, the unofficial capital of the American oil industry. "Those skyscrapers made of glass, all that luxury in the city—it was somewhat different from home," Yussifzadeh recalls. The Baku delegation was booked into a five-star hotel. Yussifzadeh insists that, in spite of rumors of corruption, not one generous gift was offered to influence the Azeris' decision. "I wish somebody had given me some money! But all I got was souvenirs, pens and similar stuff." Yussifzadeh concedes that other members in the team may have had different experiences, but he had no knowledge of personal misconduct. A far more pressing matter than bribery was Moscow's insistence that the Azeris not conclude any treaty as long as property rights in the Caspian Sea remained unresolved. Aliyev would not be swayed. "He wanted this treaty at any price," Yussifzadeh remembers. "We had clear instructions from our president not to return empty-handed from the United States." Yet the negotiations proved extraordinarily complicated, as neither side had any experience of how to put

together a production sharing agreement (PSA) in a post-Soviet
country.

After forty-seven exhausting days, an agreement was reached.
On September 20, 1994, a triumphant Aliyev met with the CEOs of
the Azerbaijan International Operating Company (AIOC), an international consortium of about a dozen oil corporations, to form
what came to be called the "contract of the century." For the first
time since the foreign oil barons were dispossessed and expelled
in the October revolution of 1917, overseas companies were allowed to invest in Baku's oil industry. Several billion dollars flowed
into new production facilities, with a majority share secured by
the American company Amoco. British Petroleum, initially a sec-
ondary shareholder, later acquired Amoco and became the most
important corporation doing business in Baku.

Russia and Iran protested strongly against the contract, accusing Aliyev of handing out concessions for oil fields that Azerbaijan possibly did not own. No agreement exists among the five
Caspian littoral states—Russia, Kazakhstan, Turkmenistan, Azerbaijan, and Iran—on a territorial separation of the Caspian Sea.
Complicating matters further, both Iran and Turkmenistan laid
claim to oil fields that had been given to the Western consortium
for exploitation. In Russia, Sergei Karaganov, President Boris
Yeltsin's top foreign policy advisor, presumably had the *Bolshaya
Igra* (the Great Game) in mind when he called the contract part of
a "century-old game." Several months earlier, on July 21, 1994,
Yeltsin had signed secret directive number 396, for the "protection of the interests of the Russian Federation on the Caspian Sea,"
which clearly stated that Russia should uphold its sphere of influence in the Caucasian and Central Asian republics.[7] Moscow's
political elites despised the idea of their former colony Azerbaijan
hitting the oil jackpot while Russia would be left empty-handed.

Right away, Western investors in Baku were faced with the
problem of how to get the oil and gas from the landlocked Caspian Sea to the markets of the industrialized world. Determined
to keep precious raw materials out of Russia's reach, the United
States equally rejected a southern route through Iran. Zbigniew
Brzezinski, President Jimmy Carter's national security adviser,

has described what was—and still is—at stake: "Azerbaijan's vulnerability has wider regional implications because the country's location makes it a geopolitical pivot. It can be described as the vitally important 'cork' controlling access to the 'bottle' that contains the riches of the Caspian Sea basin and Central Asia. An independent, Turkic-speaking Azerbaijan, with pipelines running from it to the ethnically related and politically supportive Turkey, would prevent Russia from exercising a monopoly on access to the region and would thus also deprive Russia of decisive political leverage over the policies of the new Central Asian states."[8]

The U.S. government has lobbied since the mid-1990s for a third option: a gigantic westbound pipeline, covering a distance of 1,090 miles, from Azerbaijan's capital Baku, across the neighbouring country of Georgia, to the Turkish Mediterranean port of Ceyhan. Unlike Novorossiisk, Ceyhan is a deep-water port that can accommodate tankers of up to 300,000 tons capacity. Fearing an increasing number of tankers from the Black Sea that could conceivably lead to accidents in the narrow Bosporus Straits (with catastrophic consequences for Istanbul), the Turkish government first proposed the Ceyhan project. It would also enhance Turkey's geopolitical significance to the West, on the wane since the end of the Cold War. For its part, the United States was keen to prop up the moderately Islamic Turkey as a regional power. With President Bill Clinton as moderator, the heads of state of Azerbaijan, Georgia, and Turkey met in Istanbul on November 18, 1999 and signed a treaty authorizing the construction of the Mediterranean pipeline from Baku to Ceyhan.

In order to meet U.S. Ambassador Ross Wilson, Washington's most important diplomat in the Caspian, in Baku, I have to pass several times through a metal detector that keeps beeping until I have fished every pen from my pockets. The security guards then completely dissemble each pen and confiscate all electronic gadgets, even a PDA planner.

"As you can imagine, this region has become even more important to Washington," Ambassador Wilson, a Minnesota native, offers after we sit down on a sofa, underneath the portraits of President George W. Bush and Secretary of State Colin Powell. "We do not see ourselves as part of a Great Game with Russia, least of all in a zero-sum game. We have our interests, the Russians have theirs—but they don't necessarily need to collide." In his mind, the Mediterranean pipeline is not an American attempt to counter Russian influence in the region but to "make sure that the Caspian oil gets to the markets." Then Ambassador Wilson clarifies himself. "Of course, the Azeris try and play off America and Russia against each other. But they understand that the United States alone is the guarantor of their independence." It sounds like a decision when Wilson announces in a firm voice, "The oil will never go through Russia."

In order to deter investors from the Ceyhan pipeline and thus thwart the project, Russia has in the past destabilized the southern Caucasus, Georgia in particular. "Then Moscow got a little problem called Chechnya. Now the Russians have become more cautious." Wilson argues that overall, however, there is good cooperation with Moscow on many Caucasus issues.

As for Iran, Azerbaijan's southern neighbor, Ambassador Wilson's comments are less tempered. "Iran is a competitor for Azerbaijan and is trying to control the Caspian Sea. On a regular basis, Iranian ships penetrate Azerbaijan's territorial waters, and Iranian fighter jets enter Azeri airspace." The United States has responded by giving two new patrol boats to the Azeri border police.

Despite the slight rapprochement with Tehran during the war against the Afghan Taliban, it remains out of the question for the State Department that Caspian oil be pumped through a pipeline running across a country ruled by Shiite mullahs. "Iran supports terrorism and is determined to acquire weapons of mass destruction," Wilson explains. "Therefore we must curtail all its means of generating revenue which would help the government fund those activities." The U.S. Congress imposed economic sanctions against Iran in 1996 as part of the Iran-Libya Sanctions Act, prohibiting

American companies from doing business with that country. The law was renewed in 2001, against the opposition of several business-friendly Republicans. A few weeks after my talk with Ambassador Wilson, President Bush would name Iran, along with Iraq and North Korea, as part of an international "axis of evil."

The great Mediterranean pipeline is supposed to be built by a consortium led by Socar and BP Amoco. However, Washington's geopolitical pet project encountered initial skepticism in corporate headquarters. The oil executives considered the pipeline too long and, at construction costs of $2.9 billion, too expensive. Additionally, it would run across politically unstable territories—the southern Caucasus and Kurdish-populated eastern Turkey—which make any investment appear very risky.

The first leg of the route through Azerbaijan and Georgia worried the planners the most. Since the fall of the Soviet Union, several ethnic conflicts and political power struggles have broken out in the region. In the early 1990s, Armenian troops wrestled the predominantly Armenian-populated enclave Nagorno-Karabakh from neighboring Azerbaijan. Tens of thousands died and almost a million Azeris were expelled from their homes. After numerous ethnic pogroms hundreds of thousands of Armenians fled from the hitherto multiethnic and cosmopolitan city of Baku. Many Russians likewise moved away. At the same time, Georgia sank into chaos when its provinces of Abkhazia and South Ossetia seceded, leaving thousands of people dead. None of these conflicts has yet been resolved. They keep smoldering below a deceptive surface of diplomatic negotiations and UN peace troops. Add to this volatile mix the Chechen war, along with the fact that the proposed Mediterranean pipeline is only a day's march away from any of these war zones, and the likelihood of even a drop of Caspian oil reaching Ceyhan seems remote.

No one in Baku knows how dangerous a place the Caucasus can be better than Vahid Mustafayev. The thirty-five-year-old TV journalist reported from the theaters of war in the Caucasus, ranging from Nagorno-Karabakh via Abkhazia and South Ossetia to Chechnya. Often, he was the only person to have pictures of the most perilous frontline situations. When Mustafayev came to realize how badly foreign TV stations pay local freelancers for their risky work, he founded the Azerbaijan News Service (ANS). Today he is the CEO of the only television and radio network in the country to be both commercially successful and independent from the government.

We meet in the studio in the southern hills of the city. The midday news has just been produced, and the cameras are being turned off. Mustafayev, wearing an immaculate dark suit matched with a thick yellow tie and fine Italian leather shoes, proudly shows me around the studio, filled with modern and Western-made broadcasting equipment. "We set all this up on our own in the past couple of years, without a single dollar but instead much opposition from the government," Mustafayev says. "And now these microphones are the only ones in the country that the government does not control. And we have more viewers and listeners that any other station." Mustafayev no longer has the time to roam with a camera but is all too familiar with the motivating forces behind the conflicts he was covering. "All the Caucasian wars are, at least partly, about oil. The Russians are trying to prevent the big pipeline from Baku to Ceyhan from being built." In the 1990s, Russia tried to destabilize the southern Caucasus by ensuring that crises and conflicts would percolate indefinitely. "Russia still views Azerbaijan as part of its empire. Once it loses this country, the entire Caucasus is lost." To keep the Americans out, Mustafayev continues, Russia had even aligned itself in the south with its old rival, Iran. Together, the two countries were trying to pinch Azerbaijan from both sides to restrict its dealings with the West. "In Baku, there are more agents and spies than businessmen—most of them are Russians and Iranians."

Mustafayev asks his secretary to fetch a map of the Caucasus. With a red pen, he draws the planned route for the pipeline to Ceyhan. "Russians are good people until they see a map and start drinking vodka. Then they go berserk. They incited the Armenians to fight against us and they supported them." From 1994 to 1997,

Moscow delivered $1 billion worth of weapons to the Christian country of Armenia, Russia's only ally in the Caucasus. MiG-29 jet fighters and S-300 missiles were part of the generous military aid. "No peace—no oil," Armenia's President Robert Kocharian often said. The direct route of the planned pipeline would have run across Karabakh and Armenia. Instead it now makes a big northern detour around those territories.

Suddenly, Mustafayev's face darkens. He is thinking of the day in 1991 when his brother, also a cameraman, died while filming in Karabakh, torn to pieces by a grenade. We walk into the studio's hallway, where a blurred picture is exhibited in a showcase. It shows nothing but a swatch of grass and sky. "That was my brother's last camera shot after he had been hit and fallen to the ground." His voice turns very soft, but is still determined. "It is about time that our army win Karabakh back. We must take revenge for our dead, and the Armenians will have to pay for their crimes." But would that not lead to further bloodshed? Are negotiations not a better solution? Mustafayev shakes his head. "For ten years our governments have negotiated and the Armenians have not moved one bit. That leads to nothing. Our refugees live in abject poverty, not one of them has yet been able to return to his home."

Mustafayev turns out to be a proud Azeri nationalist. Every day, his station ANS put pressure on the Aliyev regime to solve the Karabakh issue by way of a consistent war policy. "Of course, it is disagreeable to the powerful that, amid their enthusiasm about the oil boom, we remind them of their patriotic duty. With the help of the oil money our armed forces need to be modernized and made strong again." Would he himself go to the Karabakh front to fight? "Of course! The sooner, the better. We must fight this war against the Armenians now. We cannot leave this job to our children." Then Mustafayev sends for his own limousine, an oversized, armored Range Rover, to take me back to the hotel. The car radio plays a warlike-sounding song by a well-known Azeri rap band: "Karabakh or Death!" The lyrics tell of massacres perpetrated by Armenians, and of the blood revenge the Azeris will soon take. The band's singer shouts over and over "Jihad! Jihad!"

I ask the driver, what radio station we are listening to. "This is ANS, what else?"

The next day, I board the train from Baku to Tbilisi in Georgia, the pivot for the Mediterranean pipeline plan. "Lock the door to your cabin," the train conductor advises me after checking my ticket. "The Georgians are all bandits."

Stalin's Legacy: Georgia

"We need the big oil pipeline so that we will continue to have the United States on our side against Russia. You see, Georgia has got nothing else to offer to the world, we have to sell our geographical position," says Alexander Rondeli, a senior diplomat in the Georgian foreign ministry, after a drink from our third bottle of wine. We have met at a café on Rustaveli Square in the capital, Tbilisi, long viewed as the most beautiful and multicultural city in all of the Caucasus. "We are beggars, but we would rather be beggars than live under Moscow's yoke again!" It is a cloudy evening, and the first autumn leaves fall onto the square.

During the nineteenth century, Tbilisi was an ethnic stew of Georgians, Persians, Armenians, Tatars, Jews, Chechens, Cherkessians, Ossetians, Swans, Awaras, Kurds, Abkhazians, not to mention Russian overlords. Today, the city appears old and tired, miles away from the hectic atmosphere of Baku. The streets exude a moribund charm at best, as only a few new shops have opened up since the end of communism. In other words, Tbilisi is a city ripe for a substantial infusion of oil money, should the Caspian pipeline ever be built.

Rondeli, a tall man with white hair, sips from his glass. "The oil per se does not matter. Sure, it will generate customs and transit fees but that money will once again end up in the pockets of the wrong people anyway." He laughs bitterly, as it is common knowledge that Georgia has rampant levels of corruption unmatched by

31

any other former Soviet republic. Foreign truckers accept detours of several thousand miles around Georgian territory rather than risk harassment from policemen seeking bribes. "But the pipeline attracts international investors," Rondeli adds finally. "Then the Americans can no longer afford to abandon us."

More than for any other country on the Caspian Sea, the Mediterranean pipeline is a matter of national security for Georgia. Eduard Shevardnadze, former Soviet foreign minister under Mikhail Gorbachev and, since 1993, the president of Georgia, has concentrated all his efforts into making the pipeline a reality. His aim is nothing less than Georgia's reestablishment as the center of a new Great Silk Road, linking Europe with Asia, as it did in the Middle Ages. Shevardnadze, who was party to the signing of the Ceyhan pipeline treaty in 1999, assured observers at the time that the agreement was not intended as a rebuke to Russia. The former top communist would have hardly believed that himself, however, thinks Rondeli, who is also a professor of international relations at Tbilisi University.

"The Russians have always been our enemies, and that is what they still are today. For us Georgians, an independent policy invariably is an anti-Russian policy." He remembers the Soviet times when most Russians saw Georgians as little more than a minstrel troupe, performing dances for foreign visitors. "Since we have become independent, Moscow has done everything to destabilize and fragment our country."

He points to the Iveria, a high-rise hotel only steps away from Rustaveli Square. Once the best place to stay in Tbilisi, its balconies are now enclosed with chipboard to create more living space for the more than one thousand Georgian refugees from the secessionist Black Sea province of Abkhazia who have filled its rooms to overflowing since the bloody civil war in 1992–93. They are only a fraction of an estimated three hundred thousand who fled the fighting and ethnic cleansing in Abkhazia, which was at one time Georgia's most idyllic and fashionable Riviera. Close to eight thousand people lost their lives there. The Iveria now serves as a constant reminder to Tbilisi's residents of unfinished business.

The first ten years of Georgia's independence have been marked by civil wars, political anarchy, and economic chaos. In 1990, the small nation of five million was the first Soviet republic to elect a noncommunist government, led by the romantic ultranationalist Zviad Gamsakhurdia. After he was violently overthrown in December 1991, the country drifted deeper into crisis until Shevardnadze, who had been the head of the Communist Party in Georgia from 1972 to 1985, returned home from Moscow and was elected president. His first months in power saw the virtual disintegration of the country, as Abkhazia and the pro-Russian South Ossetia province, whose border runs only a few kilometers north of Tbilisi, practically seceded from the rest of the country. To make matters worse, the president of the Ajaria province along Turkey's border has for years ignored any instructions from the central government in Tbilisi. Teetering on the brink of collapse, Georgia is a classical case of a "failed nation."

"Moscow fomented and fanned the civil wars in order to bring back its troops to Georgia, as so-called peacekeepers," Rondeli says, a belief that many people in Tbilisi share. In return for a cease-fire in Abkhazia in 1994, Russia forced Georgia into joining the Soviet successor organization, the Community of Independent States (CIS), and accepting its troops on Georgian territory. "Today Moscow keeps sixteen thousand troops in our country. This is how the Russians keep fanning the conflicts in the South Caucasus which are useful to them," Rondeli complains. Russia maintains three Soviet-era military bases and large arsenals in Georgia, without a legal basis despite Tbilisi's repeated protests. The Organization for Security and Cooperation in Europe (OSCE) mandated at its 1999 summit that Russia negotiate a shutdown of the bases with Georgia, but Moscow has yet to respond. In Rondeli's view, Russia still relies on military might and direct control, rather than negotiation and partnership. For Russia, Georgia is the key state in the South Caucasus. "The fact that we want to be independent is seen in Moscow as sheer ingratitude."

President Shevardnadze, detested by many in Moscow as a traitor for his role as Gorbachev's foreign minister during the breakup of the Soviet Union, has survived several assassination attempts. In August 1995 a car bomb exploded in the parliament's courtyard. In February 1998 grenades were fired on his limousine, killing his chauffeur and his bodyguard. The then-minister of state security, Igor Giorgadze, suspected of organizing the 1995 attack, fled into a safe and comfortable exile in Russia. Georgian demands for his immediate extradition are ignored.

"Sooner or later the Russians are going to attack us directly, with military means," Rondeli says. "And the question is: Are the Americans going to stand on our side, or look away? The pipeline could decide that question." More than anything else, the war in Chechnya has strained relations between the two countries. Since 1999, Moscow has accused Tbilisi of giving shelter in the Georgian mountains to Chechen rebels. They are said to be among some five thousand Chechen refugees who fled from the Russian forces to the Pankisi Gorge. The area in northeast Georgia, two hours northeast of Tbilisi, has long been a haven for criminals involved in kidnapping, extortion, and violence. Ragged and demoralized Georgian security forces did not dare enter the Pankisi for fear of attacks, and most international aid organizations suspended work there after four Red Cross nurses were kidnapped in August 2000.

After the September 11 attacks, high-ranking Russian politicians invoked the same right to self-defense against Chechen "terrorists" in Georgia as Washington did against Al Qaeda. Russian fighter jets had already bombed Georgian villages on the border to Chechnya twice since 1999. President Shevardnadze, supported by Washington, strongly protested the military action, while conceding that injured Chechen rebels were indeed recuperating in Pankisi.

"Why should we let the Chechens die?" asks Rondeli. "After all, they are our neighbors and we always strive to get on well with them. We respect them, they are great warriors." The diplomat smiles derisively. It was only ten years ago when, during the Georgian civil war, many Chechen warlords such as Shamil Basaev and Ruslan Gelaev fought with the Abkhaz, killing Georgian civilians by the hundreds. Far from being labeled terrorists then, they were armed and trained by the Russian military. "It is all a big game between the Russians and us Caucasians," Rondeli continues. "But if the fighting in Chechnya spins out of control, we in the Caucasus will get Thomas Hobbes' *bellum omnia contra omnes*—a war of all against all."

Washington takes Russian threats of military strikes against Chechen militants in Pankisi very seriously. In May 2002, the Pentagon stationed five hundred elite U.S. Special Forces soldiers in Georgia to train the country's ragtag army in antiterrorist warfare. It was the first substantial deployment of American troops in the Caucasus since the collapse of the Soviet Union. The Green Beret trainers included specialists in mountain fighting and urban combat. The Georgian recruits in the new antiterrorist battalions are paid $190 a month, compared with just $20 for conscripts in the regular army. The Pentagon's $64 million program also includes supplying the Georgian military with new small weapons and ammunition, uniforms, and communications equipment. The seventeen–thousand-strong Georgian armed forces also receive military aid from the United States, including new combat helicopters. While the U.S. government justified its involvement by claiming a number of Al Qaeda fighters from Afghanistan are suspected to be hiding in the Pankisi Gorge, a relieved President Shevardnadze hailed the U.S. military presence as "a very important factor for strengthening and developing Georgian statehood."[1]

At first, the Russian government maintained an attitude of "grin and bear it." American troops in the Caucasus would not be a "tragedy," President Vladimir Putin commented in early March 2002 and assured Washington of Russia's cooperation in the struggle against terrorists in the Pankisi Gorge. However, in Moscow's higher echelons of power, especially the military, the American advance into this century-old Russian sphere of interest evoked opposition. The presence of U.S. troops in Georgia "should worry every Russian soldier," Deputy Defense Minister Alexander Kosovan said in April 2002.[2]

Only a few months later, renewed tensions over the Pankisi Gorge flared up into a major international crisis. It started when, in late July, Chechen fighters killed eight Russian border guards, in an attack that Russian officials claimed was launched from inside Georgia. In the fierce fighting that ensued, fourteen armed rebels, half of them wounded, fled across the border into Georgia, where they were detained by local authorities. President Putin immediately demanded their extradition but Shevardnadze refused, asking Moscow to produce solid evidence that the detained rebels had been directly involved in terrorist activities. The Kremlin reacted with fury, ordering its military to get ready for a mop-up operation in Pankisi. "The international community has just crushed the nest of international terrorism in Afghanistan," Defence Minister Sergei Ivanov fumed. "We must not forget about Georgia nearby, where a similar nest has recently begun to emerge."[3]

In late August 2002, Russian fighter jets reportedly bombed Pankisi villages, killing at least one civilian. The rattled Georgian parliament convened for an emergency session, calling on the government unilaterally to set a deadline for the shutdown of Russian military bases in Georgia and to put an immediate end to the Russian peacekeeping mandate in breakaway Abkhazia. In New York, Georgia's ambassador to the United Nations accused Russia of aggression, and asked the Security Council to assess Moscow's "flagrant violation" of international law. Despite the raids' being confirmed by OSCE monitors on the ground, the Kremlin officially denied them, drawing an unusually sharp rebuke from Washington. The White House deplored what its spokesman Ari Fleischer called a "violation of Georgia's sovereignty." He added that the raid belied Moscow's assurances of its support for Georgian "independence and territorial integrity."

To preempt further Russian actions in the Pankisi, Shevardnadze ordered his own Interior Ministry troops to move into the valley to search for Chechen militants. They came up empty-handed because the operation had been announced days earlier, thus giving the guerrillas plenty of time to abandon the area. Far from satisfied, the Russian government further stepped up its saber-rattling and megaphone diplomacy. "We have proof that international terrorists are hiding in Georgia," said Nikolai Patrushev, director of Russia's Federal Security Service, FSB (formerly the

KGB), in mid-September. "We will apply force to neutralize them so they don't reach Russian territory."[4]

In early October, Putin and Shevardnadze ended their angry standoff in an eleventh-hour meeting in Moscow. Seemingly tired of thumbing his nose at the Kremlin, the Georgian president agreed to hand over all the rebels detained in the summer. However, regardless of how long the truce will last this time, Russian military action in Pankisi demonstrated that Moscow's forces are still to be reckoned with in the South Caucasus. Using the Pankisi as a pretext, the Kremlin still itches to reel Georgia, the linchpin country for the export of Caspian oil and gas to Western markets, back into its orbit. Although presence of American troops in Georgia will give investors in the Mediterranean pipeline project a sense of security, they continue to be concerned about the extent of Georgia's domestic chaos, corruption, and banditry.

I get a firsthand impression of this on a weekend excursion to Ajaria, the province comprising the entire southwestern quarter of Georgia, where the planned pipeline is to run straight through on its way to Turkey.

As I have missed the last bus back to Tbilisi, a friendly Georgian, also on his way to the capital, gives me a lift. Giorgi, a thirty-five-year-old electrician, has just crossed the border from Turkey, and is driving a dark blue Volkswagen Golf that he bought secondhand in Germany. "Even if I take off the money for petrol on the long journey home, three thousand kilometers, this Golf still costs me less than to buy a comparable car in Georgia."

Only a few miles into our journey, we are stopped at a police checkpoint. "They have seen the German export license plate," Giorgi whispers with a sense of foreboding. "This will be expensive." Inside a one-room building are four men. Their fat bellies cause their unbuttoned uniforms to stick out and look like wings. The fee for using the roads in Ajaria is fifty dollars, they say. After Giorgi squirms and pleads for a while, the fee is decreased to thirty dollars.

Nailed to the wall is a framed portrait of Ajaria's President Aslan Abashidze, who rules the autonomous province as if it were his private fiefdom. Abashidze tolerates no interference from Tbilisi, pays no tax revenue to the federal finance minister, and regularly (and publicly) insults President Shevardnadze. The Ajarian's belligerence stems from his close friendship with the commander of the Russian troops stationed near Batumi. In the eyes of many Georgians, Abashidze is little more than Moscow's puppet, who would give the Russians direct access to the Mediterranean pipeline.

Giorgi fishes out a twenty-dollar bill, almost half the average monthly income in Georgia. The police are satisfied and allow us to drive on, over a pockmarked road along beautiful and empty Black Sea beaches. Old peasant women sit by the side of the road, selling melons, raspberries, and dried peppers. When we reach the provincial capital, Batumi, another group of official bandits are waiting for us. A policeman pulls out a white cane and signals Giorgi to pull over.

Batumi was once one of the world's most important oil ports, connected to Baku with a Rothschild-built railway line in 1883. It was also the first port to give Western markets access to Baku oil. In August 1892, the world's first modern oil tanker, the *Murex,* was loaded in Batumi and sailed via the Suez Canal to Singapore and Bangkok. Today, Batumi's port is far too small for modern oil tankers, which instead sail further north to the port of Poti.

The town's biggest money-maker now appears to be collecting bribes from travelers—we need to pay up if we intend to drive through Batumi. Another road toll, just as in the Middle Ages. "But I cannot give you people money every two kilometers!" Giorgi protests. A valid point, so the policemen make us a special offer. For thirty dollars, we would get an official escort to Ajaria's provincial border, allowing us to bypass all additional checkpoints. Giorgi agrees and a young policeman sits, rather like a hijacker, behind the steering wheel of Giorgi's Golf.

We soon realize the "escort" is a bargain. Every three hundred yards there are policemen who attempt to stop us. When they see our driver they step aside and let us pass. Some of them look disappointed, others delighted. Giorgi, who does not speak a word to the policeman, explains, "There seem to be several different police gangs who compete for bribes. Those we see grinning belong to the same unit as our protector, and they know that tonight they will get their share of the money."

Batumi's ugly concrete buildings fly past the car windows, along with many old Volga cars and horse-drawn carts. At a railway crossing near the oil refinery, two Russian army officers greet our driver, laughing. He drives at an insane speed, while Giorgi's face betrays concern for his car.

"From a business point of view this makes sense," Giorgi reasons. "The faster the policemen race along, the more escorts they can provide per day." Twenty minutes later, we reach the border between Ajaria and its neighboring province. Our driver stops the car at a police checkpoint and, without a word, gets out and walks over to his smiling colleagues. Back behind the wheel, Giorgi sighs, "On my entire journey from Germany via the Balkans and Turkey, all policemen treated me correctly. Only in Georgia, my home, they rob me straight away."

Back in Tbilisi, the rampant corruption plaguing Georgia also infuriates Nia Lomadze, an economic analyst who works at the American embassy. We decide to go for a walk from the Kura River through the old town of Tbilisi. Traces of its former ethnic diversity remain to this day. Armenian churches, a synagogue, and a Sunni mosque all stand side by side. Most of the houses we pass are dilapidated; their once splendid wooden staircases and balconies dangle above the cobblestone streets, damaged beyond repair. Some buildings have already collapsed, as if after an earthquake. On a small acacia-lined square we discover a 1960s model Volga with its tires removed and a small tree growing from the driver's seat through the shattered side windows.

As an economist, Lomadze has little appreciation for the romance of decay. "At the end of the 1980s we said that we would prefer to eat grass if only we could be independent from Russia— now this is more or less what is happening." At the U.S. embassy, the thirty-eight-year-old analyzes the Georgian economy, and occasionally advises Western companies that consider investing into the country. "The picture that I have to present to them is very gloomy," she says. "Our economy is totally rotten. The big pipeline, if it comes, won't change much of that." Foreign

investment is a paltry $30 million a year. The nation's largest for-
eign investor, the U.S.–based utility corporation AES, is likely to
pull out because of rampant theft. Corruption and nepotism have
reached catastrophic levels, destroying the country and society
at almost every level. "The top brass is playing along with this,
as is the common man in the street."

Lomadze cites the Georgian power supply as a typical example. In most parts of the country, electricity is available for
about four hours a day. On my journey with Giorgi, I noticed that
the villages and small towns along our route were almost entirely
dark. Only very few private diesel-run generators provided energy,
so people lit kerosene lamps for light. "Only one-third of all electricity bills are paid at all," Lomadze observes. "The people rather
pay bribes to the inspector who, in turn, hands on part of the
money to his superiors. That man does the same, in turn, and so
on, and so on. And yet at the end of the day, the people spend more
money on kerosene for their lamps than they would have to pay
for electricity." Reforms in the industry are unlikely, as Nugzar
Shevardnadze, the president's nephew, controls the country's
kerosene business. "But at that people merely shrug their shoulders: everybody knows that honest work leads to nothing. We
respect the wealth of the rich but nobody asks where all their
money comes from." Traditionally, relations and connections always carry more weight than the rule of law. "This is a clan-based
society," Lomadze says.

We stroll down Rustaveli Boulevard, Tbilisi's beautiful, tree-
lined promenade. To our left, the parliament buildings appear,
constructed by German prisoners of war after Berlin's surrender.
On its stairs, on April 9, 1989, special troops from the Soviet interior ministry attacked peaceful demonstrators who had gone on
a hunger strike to protest Moscow's support for Abkhaz separatists. Lomadze was one of the protestors. "The Russians arrived
in tanks," she recalls. "And then they attacked us with sharpened
spades. With spades! At first, we could not believe our eyes that
the Russians under Gorbachev would still do this to us." Twenty-
one demonstrators were killed, martyrs to a people with only one
goal: liberation from Russian rule.

Western countries were initially very supportive of Georgia's path to independence. In Germany in particular, Shevardnadze's popularity remains high because the former Soviet foreign minister is seen, alongside Gorbachev, as one of the architects of German reunification in 1990. Georgia's principal ally, the United States, has grown increasingly frustrated with his inability to clean up his country. "The Americans, like so many Western diplomats, are thoroughly fed up with the corruption in our country," Lomadze believes. "They are losing patience with us."

Two parliament guards chase off one of Tbilisi's countless beggars, most of whom are elderly living off pensions of less than twenty lari (ten dollars) per month. The bullet holes in the parliament's façade, results of the violent putsch against the Gamzakhurdia regime in December 1991, when almost two hundred people lost their lives in street fighting, have long since been painted over. "We Georgians have wasted the time and the international sympathy we had," Lomadze concludes. "We still have not learned to deal with our freedom. We have yet to understand that freedom must go hand in hand with responsibility."

A few days later, I take the bus to Gori, an industrial town on the Kura River about an hour's drive west of Tbilisi. On December 21, 1879, Joseph Vissarionovich Dzhugashvili, later known as Stalin, the "man of steel," was born here. The Soviet dictator's ruthless policies in the Caspian region, especially the wholesale deportation of entire ethnic groups and the arbitrary drawing of borders, still bear consequences in the region's many bloody conflicts. Perhaps more than any other historical figure, Stalin set the stage for the new Great Game, the current struggle for Eurasia.

Born to an alcoholic father, and a mother who worked as a laundress, Stalin spent his most formative years growing up in Gori. Nicknaming her son "Soso," Stalin's mother wanted him to become a priest. Young Joseph excelled at the church school in Gori and at the age of fifteen was sent to the Theological Seminary in Tbilisi, where he first encountered Marxist writings.

Stalin's Gori chapter is a brief one, but in the town square, named Stalin Square, is an imposing steel statue of the man himself, more than fifty feet tall. Wearing a gray coat, the Soviet leader greets the proletarian masses. This statue is one of the last of thousands of monuments that at one time, during the 1950s, graced every small town in the Soviet empire, from Wismar to Vladivostok.

Not far from the statue, along Stalin Avenue, is the Stalin Museum, built in 1957, a year after Nikita Khrushchev had denounced his predecessor's crimes at the Twentieth Party Congress. It displays countless photographs, numerous presents from state visitors, and the dictator's cabinet that had been shipped from the Kremlin to Gori. One picture of Stalin, taken in the early twentieth century, shows a surprisingly handsome man whose features and long hair exude romance. While thorough, the museum's exhibits omit any reference to the Great Purges of the 1930s, the countless gulags, or Stalin's pact with Hitler.

Stalin's museum is only a brief side trip before I board a 1972 Russian MI-8 helicopter to the secessionist province of Abkhazia, an important battlefield in the new Great Game. The helicopter's long, crooked rotor blades dangle off the top, resembling a giant, broken umbrella. The cockpit door opens, and one of the two Ukrainian pilots greets me with a heavy accent and a strong whiff of vodka: "Come in! Welcome! No problem, don't worry, no problem!" In his mouth, a row of gold teeth shines in the morning sun.

We are flying in a UN helicopter, which offers little comfort or protection. Anyone who has witnessed the United Nations in action in crisis zones knows that the UN logo and the blue flag are worth only as much as local conditions and decision-makers allow.

In this case, the transport budget of the Military Observer Group of the United Nations in Georgia (UNOMIG) was obviously too small to pay for more than a few old Russian helicopters. The UN's policy that a mission in the former Soviet Union rely on local products is understandable, but as I noticed on an earlier visit in the West African country of Sierra Leone, even the UN's largest peacekeeping mission uses the same decrepit Russian MI-8 helicopters. They routinely crash, killing on average half a dozen UN employees each time.

However, there is no other way into Abkhazia. No airline offers flights there, and since the province's secession ten years ago, Tbilisi has imposed a total blockade. All roads and railway lines are cut off, and the border along the Inguri River is densely mined. Abkhazia is essentially controlled by some seventeen hundred Russian troops stationed in the province. They marched into northwestern Georgia in late 1993, allegedly to keep the peace between two opposing armies, and have stayed ever since.

Only a day's march separates the Russian soldiers from the planned Mediterranean pipeline, and a smaller existing pipeline that links BP Amoco's Baku oilfields and the port of Poti. The Russian troops could quickly join their colleagues stationed in the Ajaria province south of Poti. More importantly, the three hundred thousand Georgian refugees will not be able to return to their Abkhaz homes without Russian support, forcing Tbilisi not to get too friendly with the West. Abkhazia has therefore become the former colonial power's main trump card in the game over oil pipelines in the South Caucasus.

I once got a firsthand impression of Russia's role in Abkhazia when I tried to enter Abkhazia from the Russian Black Sea resort of Sochi. At the border crossing, Russian soldiers blocked my way: "Foreigners are not permitted to pass. Abkhazia is a prohibited military area." I showed them the Georgian visa in my passport but they barked: "That is not valid on the other side. If you show that to the Abkhaz you will never reach Georgia alive. Now get lost!" In 2002, Moscow conferred Russian citizenship on the residents of Abkhazia, most of whom accepted it. To Tbilisi's fury, the Russian Duma also passed legislation allowing other states or parts of other states to join the Russian Federation.

The Russians had their hands in the Georgian civil war from its very beginning: When Shevardnadze sent the National Guard to Abkhazia's capital, Sukhumi, in August 1992 to quell the uprising, the rebels fled to a Russian army base north of the town. A bitter partisan war began, but soon the loosely organized militia groups drove the army into retreat. They were helped by the Russian military, whose fighter jets attacked Georgian positions. They also gave arms to the Abkhaz and sent mercenaries into battle. In September 1993 the Georgian troops were forced to withdraw from Abkhazia. A cornered Shevardnadze was left with no choice but to ask Moscow to negotiate a truce. In return, the Kremlin curtailed Georgia's new independence: the country was forced to join the CIS organization, hand over three military bases to the Russian army, and accept Moscow's peace troops in Abkhazia.

I sit down in the narrow, hard seat behind the cockpit. The shredded safety belt is useless. On the steel wall in front of me hangs an old fire extinguisher equipped with a funnel. Along for the ride are five UN employees in civilian clothes and a uniformed Southeast Asian soldier.

The UN mission in Georgia is supposed merely to monitor the shaky truce in Abkhazia, not to enforce it. This distinguishes it from other peacekeeping missions in Kosovo or Sierra Leone. Only about one hundred or so UN soldiers from twenty-three countries patrol the former war zone, looking for cease-fire violations, in addition to an equal number of civilian bureaucrats. As a policy, the UN mission demands that Georgia's territorial integrity be restored and all refugees be allowed to return to their homes.

Flying above Abkhaz territory, it is impossible to miss the traces of fighting. Not a single building has been left unscathed. One-time villages lie in black, roofless ruins. The rubble reminds me of the burned-down villages in Bosnia, the result not of regular combat but of systematic ethnic cleansing. Georgian and Abkhaz militia gangs marched on village after village of the opposing ethnic groups, burning, pillaging, raping, and killing. Nothing moves beneath us, save for some cattle grazing in overgrown fields.

After a twenty-minute flight, we reach the Black Sea coast and turn north, starting our descent. In the distance lie the snow-capped peaks of the Caucasus mountains. The barren landscape of Georgia's interior has given way to a lush and luxuriant green coastline from which many tall palm trees stand out. It is this wet and mild maritime climate that once made this part of Georgia the most popular holiday destination within the Soviet Union.

The Sukhumi airport looks fairly abandoned. Near the end of the landing strip, four old Russian combat helicopters sit rusting

on the tarmac. Next to them is a Tupolev-134 with an Aeroflot logo
that looks equally unlikely ever to get airborne again. Further down
the runway I notice Shevardnadze's presidential jet, a white Jak-40.
He used it to visit Sukhumi in 1993 in an effort to boost the morale
of his beleaguered troops. This trip to the frontlines almost cost
him his life. That same day, Abkhaz units encircled Sukhumi and
took aim at Shevardnadze and his entourage. At the eleventh hour,
the Russian president Boris Yeltsin ordered the Abkhaz leader via
satellite phone to let Shevardnadze go. During a two-hour break
in the attack, Russian troops liberated the Georgian president and
flew him out, leaving behind his white jet along with the most
beautiful part of his country.

I meet Jorosé, political advisor of the UN mission in Sukhumi,
in front of the freshly painted terminal. Originally from Ghana and
dressed in an elegant gray suit, he seems oddly out of place in this
forgotten corner of the former Soviet empire. "This is a unique
place," he says as we get into the white UN four-wheel-drive Toyota
FrontRunner, and drive into town. "Right now the situation is calm
but tense. As early as tonight, the shooting could start again. These
people are unpredictable."

On both sides of the long cypress avenue, parallel to the
beach, are gutted buildings, many of which have burned down to
the ground. The sight is reminiscent of the ruins along Sarajevo's
infamous "sniper alley." Old Ladas, still bearing Soviet license
plates, slowly maneuver across the road's potholes. It is a ghost
town, with only a few elderly people in the streets. Fewer than
150,000 inhabitants are believed to live in Abkhazia today, compared to half a million, two-thirds of them Georgians, ten years
ago. We stop in front of an ugly concrete building whose walls are
punctured with artillery hits. Burned-out houses line the block
around us. "This is the Foreign Ministry where you need to regis-
ter and apply for a visa," Jorosé explains. What if the visa is denied? The Ghanaian smiles: "It won't be. The Abkhazians need
every dollar they can get. Ask for Mr. Shamba's office on second
floor."

Inside the dark, empty building, the air smells musty. I climb
up several flights of stairs. An old man, tightly holding on to the

banisters, moves down the stairwell at a painfully slow speed. He wears a felt hat, and his brown jacket is studded with numerous Soviet medals. Finally, at the end of a long corridor covered with green linoleum floor is the visa office. Four elderly ladies sit behind typewriters. The prospect of issuing a visa causes them considerable excitement. Two of them rush off together to look for the right form, while a third searches for a pen.

For a modest twenty dollars, I receive a green slip of paper with the heading "Republic of Abkhazia." One of the women asks, "Would you like to speak to a representative of the Abkhaz government?" Sure, I reply, if that can be arranged. She takes me to an office where a man in a white shirt and tie is just leaving. In a hushed voice, the lady speaks to the man, who then turns to me. "Would you like to speak to the Foreign Minister of Abkhazia?" he asks. To the minister himself? I nod, slightly confused. Only if that were possible, of course. "Sure. Come into my office, please. I am the foreign minister."

On the wall behind Foreign Minister Sergei Shamba's desk is a life-size embroidered picture of a naked woman with remarkable breasts. She is not alone. Shamba has a total of seven framed nudes, all of them buxom and posed invitingly. "The artist is a friend of mine, from Sukhumi and, well, you know, I thought why not?" Shamba mumbles, slightly embarrassed. Once a respected archaeologist, Shamba does not have to worry about many state visitors he may receive in his office, because the Republic of Abkhazia is not recognized by any government in the world, not even by its own protector, Russia. Occasionally, a UN representative or a Russian peace troop commander might drop by, but in more than ten years of its existence, not a single embassy or consulate has been opened in Abkhazia.

So how is life as the foreign minister of a state that nobody recognizes? "Well, there are not too many receptions. But that is not important anyway, for official recognition will come on its own one day." For the time being, Shamba emphasizes, it is more important to build schools and hospitals, and to provide for national security by protecting the homeland against a Georgian revenge attack. Surely, I suggest, Russia is helping out with that? "Moscow is an important ally for us, that is correct." Does Abkhazia receive arms from Russia? "So what? Georgia is getting arms from America, is it not?" In fact, Shamba continues, Russia helps enforce the international blockade of Abkhazia, and would not even allow foreign ships to enter Sukhumi port. "The Russians are trying to control us. They have not yet really understood, either, that we want to be truly independent. Last year a big Turkish investor came to Sukhumi on his private yacht and wanted to start a company here—until the Russians kicked him out!"

Anger rises in Shamba's voice. He prefers to speak Russian rather than Abkhaz. "We know full well that Russia is using us for their own ends. That is the game of the Russians. But in the Caucasus it has always been like that. In the same way, the Americans abuse the Georgians to pursue their own interests. With the help of this oil pipeline and the new Silk Road they are trying to drive the Russians out of the Caucasus."

Shamba adds, in typical post–September 11 rhetoric: "The Georgian government gives sanctuary to international terrorists, especially Chechens. Together they will try to reconquer Abkhazia."

Yet was it not Chechen militias who in the early 1990s fought side by side with the Abkhaz against the Georgians? In 1993, the notorious Chechen warlord Shamil Basaev, who is number one on the Russian army's most wanted list, single-handedly beheaded dozens of Georgian civilians in Sukhumi's sports stadium. "True, but now they seemingly want to show gratitude to Shevardnadze for his help in their struggle against Moscow by opening a new theatre against the Russians. In the Caucasus, alliances change swiftly, you know," Shamba grins. "But Shevardnadze needs to be careful. Very soon the Russians could launch a direct attack on his own country. According to my information from Moscow, this is very likely." Such an attack would suit Abkhazia's foreign minister just fine. "Then the Georgians can forget all about their oil pipeline, too."

On my way out, I overtake the old man with the felt hat and Soviet medals, who has still not reached the bottom of the stairs. He has five steps ahead of him. With any luck, he will reach home just before Abkhazia opens its first foreign embassy.

*   *   *

The path to the UN headquarters leads past a seaside promenade that only ten years ago was considered one of the most exclusive resorts of the entire Soviet empire. It is a sorry sight: where grand luxury hotels, built in a Russian imperial style, once stood only bombed-out ruins are left, with small trees growing over them. A balcony hanging precariously off a black façade is all that remains of the Hotel Riza's royal suite, where a century ago Russian aristocrats marveled at the endless blue vista before them. The promenade, lined with rhododendron and oleander bushes, is almost totally deserted. A few old men have gathered in the shadow of a eucalyptus tree to play backgammon, using bottle tops for checkers. In the distance, cows graze in front of the ruins.

The barracks of the Russian peacekeeping troops lie directly on the beach. Next door is a former sanatorium where Russian tourists can spend their holiday. They come here because they likely cannot afford the more elegant resort town of Sochi further north, or perhaps the Abkhaz mineral water, which they are served regularly, is so refreshing that they can forget about the chaos around them. The sight of obese women waddling to the beach in tight bikinis, escorted by Kalashnikov-toting soldiers in combat fatigues, is one of the more surreal scenes that the former Soviet Union has to offer. Despite an 8 P.M. curfew, the beachgoers seem to feel at home in Sukhumi. Abkhazia's currency is the still the Russian ruble, the clocks run on Moscow time, and Baltika beer direct from St. Petersburg is available everywhere, even at the infamous brew strength No. 9 (16.5 percent alcohol). However, a Russian commander willing to chat about his peace mission—and perhaps even a bit about tourism—is nowhere to be found. At the gate of the barracks, guarded by two bored sentinels, a larger-than-life Comrade Lenin is immortalized in a stone mosaic, wearing a tasteless bright blue tie.

Already waiting for me at the UN headquarters is the patrol squad who will take me straight through the Abkhaz hinterland to the cease-fire line. The squad leader is Captain Zsolt Romvari, a Hungarian with a large, shaved head, and arms as big as Canadian timber. "Before I came to Abkhazia, I jobbed weekends as a bouncer in a nightclub at Lake Balaton," the thirty-six-year-old says with a menacing look. That job served to supplement his meager salary as a pilot in the Hungarian air force.

As if he felt the need to prove his strength, Romvari grabs a nearby Pakistani lieutenant and lifts the man up like a small child. A passing Turkish captain briefly stops and chuckles at the bizarre scene. After the Magyar giant sets him down, the Pakistani salutes and hurries off. Captain Romvari puts on his Top Gun–style aviator shades, and we race off in the ubiquitous white Toyota FrontRunners. In the squalor and misery through which UN officials routinely travel, the shiny off-roaders always look a bit like flashy suburban toys. It is no wonder that FrontRunners get stolen all the time—almost a hundred of them in a single night in Kosovo.

"We patrol this road every day, both on the Abkhaz and the Georgian side," Romvari explains. "We ascertain whether the cease-fire is being observed or whether the opposing armies surreptitiously try to sneak soldiers or heavy weapons into the demilitarized zone, which they are not allowed to." Near a conspicuous, burned-out building Romvari reports our position via radio to headquarters, adding that all was well. "Actually, we are obliged to wear bulletproof vests but they are so terribly uncomfortable," says the Hungarian who, like all UN employees, is unarmed. The only immediate danger here seems to come from cows that, as everywhere in the Caucasus, stand or lie in the middle of the road, stubbornly refusing to budge for approaching vehicles.

But Romvari is more cautious. "Again and again Georgian partisans from the Kodori Valley cross the cease-fire line and enter this territory. Only last month they killed almost all men in an Abkhaz village. There is still a lot of hatred between them."

The government in Tbilisi tolerates such paramilitary activity from groups who call themselves "white legion," "forest brothers," and "Cobra." UN employees are especially at risk for attacks or kidnappings, a lucrative business for local bandits. "Last year many of us were kidnapped but were released a few days later." The UN never pays ransoms, forcing the Georgian government to intervene. And what are the Russian troops up to? "Without the Russians the Georgian army would long have been back in Sukhumi," Romvari says. "And we could all go home."

By the side of the road, signs warn of mines buried in the fields. A team from Halo Trust, one of the largest mine-clearance organizations active in war zones worldwide, is working the field, using sticks to poke carefully into the soil. This highly dangerous occupation provides jobs for nearly two hundred locals, making Halo Trust the biggest international employer in the province.

We arrive at the UN base in Gali, the last village before the cease-fire line. Heavy fighting broke out in this buffer zone in May 1998, when Abkhaz militias burned down about two thousand buildings, killed more than a hundred Georgians who had stayed behind, and drove out another thirty thousand—all in the presence of Russian peacekeepers who did nothing to intervene.

I bid Captain Romvari farewell and join a UN patrol about to cross over to the Georgian side. The convoy is led by an old acquaintance, Captain Stefan R., an Austrian who after the war in Yugoslavia served as public affairs officer in the UN mission in Kosovo. "Actually, when I left Pristina I meant to join a mission somewhere in Africa but now they sent me here." We drive up to the bridge that crosses the Inguri River, in a South African–made Scout, strong enough to take a direct mine blast. On the other side of the bridge we see a Russian armored vehicle with a group of young recruits in olive green uniforms sitting atop it. They look at us with resentment. "The Russians," says Captain R., "have got their very own agenda here."

A few days later, Georgian guerrillas shoot down a UN helicopter en route to Sukhumi. All passengers and crew members lose their lives. During intense fighting in the following days, almost fifty Abkhaz and Georgians are killed. Among the dead on the Georgian side are also a few Chechen mercenaries, which is yet another reminder that the greatest threat to stability, and Western oil interests, in the Caucasus stems from the war in Chechnya, where I am headed next.

Bandits and Oil Barons: Chechnya

In January 1999, when the second Russian campaign against Chechnya began, Beslan Albukarov boarded his small grocery shop in the capital of Grozny, already looted and wrecked by Russian soldiers during the first war from 1994 to 1996. Together with his wife and his two small daughters, Albukarov escaped to Ingushetia, Chechnya's tiny neighbor in the North Caucasus. Near the city of Nazran, they found refuge in the former kolkhoz MTF Altieno. During the Soviet era, a thousand pigs and five hundred sheep were kept on this farm. Today, two thousand human beings, Chechen refugees, eke out a living in the stables.

"We are approaching the third winter in this camp, we are desperate," the short, wiry Chechen says as we walk across the sandy courtyard. The wind scatters rubbish around, and the air is thick with the stench of feces. In the center of the courtyard is a communist-era steel statue of a farmer, wearing a traditional high Caucasian felt hat, shaking hands with a Russian agrarian planner. "Socialist friendship between the peoples, but Russian-style," the forty-three-year-old Albukarov comments, trying to laugh. The total number of refugees now in Ingushetia is estimated at two hundred thousand, civilians who fled the brutality of both the Russian army and the separatist rebels. Some live in tent cities, but most have merely found squalid places like the kolkhoz. The United Nations High Commissioner for Refugees (UNHCR) euphemistically calls these camps "spontaneous settlements."

Below the communist monument, a large olive green tent houses a makeshift school. Wooden tables and benches are assembled in front of a board. "This was set up by an aid organization from Poland," Albukarov says. "Our children are supposed to be taught here but at the moment there isn't any money for teachers. At least that is what they tell us." The camp's children, left to their own devices, play hide-and-seek amid dilapidated concrete buildings. Albukarov motions for his daughter, a pretty ten-year-old named Milona. She is more familiar with the camp than her father, as she and her mother had already spent the first war there. She has only faint memories of her old home in Grozny. "All my friends are now from the camp," she says.

We walk into one of the long stables where Albukarov and his family now live. The concrete center aisle is lined on both sides with former pigpens, separated by iron bars. Makeshift chipboard and wooden planks have been fixed as walls to ensure a modicum of privacy in these cramped conditions. Before Albukarov enters his own "flat" in the middle of the stable, he takes his shoes off. Amid all this misery this simple gesture, common in most Muslim countries, has a particular dignity, so I do the same. The concrete floor of the pen has been covered with rugs, and a curtain separates the parents' plank bed from that of the children. Albukarov's wife is not in. "She is probably out fetching water," her husband says.

There is a kerosene lamp on a table, and a gas cooker with a teapot underneath. "There is electricity, but only very rarely. At least we have a roof above our heads." The room has no shower or sink. All refugees share a few primitive outdoor toilets behind the stables. "In winter it is very tough to wait out there in the cold, and sometimes arguments break out over who gets in first," Albukarov says. How long does he believe he and his family will have to stay here? After a brief pause he replies, "Until there is peace." When will that be? This time the answer is immediate. "When the last Russian has left our country." What is this war really about? For almost a minute, Albukarov mulls over the question in silence. He shrugs his shoulders and shakes his head. "I do not know. But everybody says it is about money."

*   *   *

In the autumn of 1991, Dzhokhar Dudaev, a general of the Soviet Air Force, declared the small Caucasus republic of Chechnya an independent country. At the time, Moscow was not overly concerned. The Soviet leadership had more pressing issues. Secretary General Mikhail Gorbachev had barely survived a putsch by reactionary communist hardliners, with the help of Russian President Boris Yeltsin, who then challenged Gorbachev in a fierce power struggle. Yeltsin insisted that the Soviet Union dissolve itself, and give independence to Russia. "Take as much independence as you can swallow," Yeltsin proclaimed on his travels through Russia in 1991. Many took him at his word, including Russian provinces such as Chechnya, which in an attempt to emulate the Soviet republics' example, demanded independent statehood.

After the collapse of the Soviet Union, Chechen leaders negotiated a withdrawal of all Russian troops from the republic. By the summer of 1992, not a single Russian soldier was left on Chechen soil. No other part of the former Soviet empire, not even East Germany, had seen Russian troops leave this quickly. It was a decision Moscow would almost immediately try to recant. Tolerating Chechen independence would have set a dangerous precedent that other predominantly Muslim mountain republics in the North Caucasus—Cherkessia, Kabardino-Balkaria, Ingushetia, and Dagestan—could have tried to follow. The powerful people close to President Yeltsin, whose swearing into office had been publicly condoned by the patriarch of the Orthodox Church, loathed the prospect of Islam spreading on the country's southern flank. After all, Chechen President Dudaev had taken his oath of office on a copy of the Koran.

All this only partially explains Russia's motives for attacking Chechnya in November 1994. Equally important is Chechnya's position in the new Great Game. Only a few weeks prior to the invasion, Azerbaijan and transnational energy corporations had signed the "Contract of the Century." But if plans for a westbound pipeline somehow failed to materialize, the oil from Azerbaijan would, out of necessity, continue to be pumped through the only existing pipeline to the Russian Black Sea port of Novorossiisk. This pipeline runs straight across Chechnya, and the rest of the North Caucasus. If Russia wanted to profit from the oil boom in Baku through transit fees, while trying to hold on to the only export route as a powerful lever vis-à-vis Azerbaijan, then it had to regain control over the secessionist republic.

Along with its geographic significance, Chechnya sits on considerable oil reserves, discovered and developed in the late nineteenth century. Grozny was second only to Baku as the biggest oil town in the Russian empire. In 1980, some 7.4 million barrels of crude were extracted from more than 1,500 Chechen oil wells. Grozny became even more important as a processing center, employing some eighteen thousand people working across three giant oil refineries, with a combined capacity of seventeen million tons by 1991.[1] Grozny was the center of a major network of pipelines linking Siberia, Kazakhstan, and Novorossiisk, with the flow of the Caspian pipeline traveling in reverse, from Grozny to Baku. The Soviet leadership decreased production at Azerbaijan's oil fields to such an extent that Baku was receiving oil via Grozny from West Siberian reserves.

Despite an official blockade after Dudaev seized power in late 1991, the Russians kept delivering millions of tons of crude to the Grozny refineries. Oil accounted for two-thirds of all revenues in Chechnya, an estimated $800 million to $900 million in 1993 alone. Corruption and the black market flourished in the lawless republic, allowing the Russian mafia to infiltrate the oil business. Towards the end of Dudaev's anarchic rule, the Chechen oil system collapsed. Anyone with access to the pipelines stole crude oil while the refineries' managers sold enormous amounts out the back door. By this point, Moscow had completely lost patience with Chechnya, making the 1994 invasion an all but foregone conclusion.

Russian general Alexander Lebed, then a member of the National Security Council, repeatedly hinted at the government's reasons for attacking Chechnya in 1994. In his capacity as the Kremlin's special envoy to the region who negotiated the withdrawal of Russian troops with Chechen leaders after the first war, Lebed accused powerful financial circles in Russia of having coerced President

Yeltsin into invading Chechnya. Unfortunately, Lebed died in a mysterious helicopter crash in Siberia in April 2002.

The "small victorious war" that Yeltsin publicly envisioned in 1994 ended in a bloodbath, costing the lives of sixty thousand people. Among the dead were fifty thousand Chechen civilians and more than six thousand Russian soldiers, including President Dudaev, who was ripped to pieces by a Russian missile that homed in on signals from his satellite phone. With Dudaev a martyr, and the war's increasing unpopularity in Russia, the Kremlin asked the rebels for a cease-fire. However, despite the troops' withdrawal from Chechnya, the military elites never accepted defeat and sought revenge.

Their chance came in the autumn of 1999 when Chechen rebels attacked villages in the neighboring republic of Dagestan, and Moscow was rocked by horrific bomb blasts, leaving hundreds dead. Though the circumstances of the Moscow attacks remain unclear to this day, the Russian government quickly singled out Chechen terrorists as prime suspects. President Yeltsin, encouraged on by his prime minister and successor Vladimir Putin, decided on a second Caucasus campaign. The Russian military bombed Grozny, founded in 1818 as a Russian fort, to pieces, killing tens of thousands of civilians. The Chechen leadership, now headed by the relatively moderate President Aslan Maskhadov, fled into the mountains to fight a guerrilla war. In early 2001, the Kremlin officially declared the secessionist republic "pacified," and has since called upon refugees to return to their homes, but to no avail.

"Peace?" Ruslan breaks into laughter. "The peace that exists in Chechnya is a Russian peace," says the Chechen, combing back his thick, dark hair with his hands. Were it not for his clean-shaven face, the strong thirty-one-year-old with piercing brown-green eyes would be indistinguishable from mug shots on wanted persons lists at every Russian police checkpoint in the north Caucasus.

Ruslan is not a rebel, nor is he a refugee. Having never lived in a camp, he moved in with his relatives in Nazran in 1994. Many

Ingush took in Chechens at the time. Both peoples speak similar languages, though the Ingush tend to view their eastern cousins as romantic hotheads. After he got a good job as a driver for an international aid organization, Ruslan, together with his wife and son, moved into a reasonably priced flat in town. "Nazran is now my home," the Grozny native says.

We drive through the town in Ruslan's battered black Volga 3100. In the back seat sits his friend Amerhan, a rather taciturn Ingush who has pulled the collar of his black leather jacket up to his ears. The two men want to show me a monument outside town. It is late afternoon, and the traffic on Nazran's squalid streets is chaotic. Small Ladas are competing with horse-drawn carts for every inch of space. Old men drag wheelbarrows laden with potatoes or kindling wood for the coming winter. There are also some brand-new BMW and Audi limousines with darkened windows negotiating traffic in a region that is officially one of the poorest in the former Soviet Union. "There is a lot of money around in this town," Ruslan explains. "A war is being fought not far from here, you see, and that always makes for good business."

"Both sides make enormous profits from arms sales, looting and kidnappings, but in this war everybody wants to win in order to control the refineries and the pipeline that runs through Chechnya," Ruslan says. "They would all like to put their hands on that pipeline. Now that is worth fighting for, is it not?"

It is an open secret that the Russian military is directly involved in the theft of oil in Chechnya. Local residents have reported troops collecting bribes at checkpoints to allow trucks carrying oil to pass, and demanding protection money from operators of makeshift refineries. In May 2002, the top military commander in Chechnya, General Vladimir Moltenskoi, publicly admitted that his troops were cooperating with oil bandits and siphoning off a major share of the thirty-two thousand barrels produced per day.[2]

Throughout the first war, the Baku-Novorossiisk pipeline was completely shut down. After the defeat and withdrawal of Russian troops in 1996, Moscow tried to buy off the Chechens with a lump-sum payment of $1 million as transit fees on future oil. The separatists countered by demanding $265 million to be paid as reparations.

Both sides compromised on a hefty fee of $2.20 per ton of crude, and agreed on a joint effort to repair the pipeline for future use. In the meantime, a new bypass of the Baku-Novorossiisk pipeline has been built through Dagestan and around northern Chechnya—closer to Russian army positions. The brand-new CPC pipeline runs just north of Chechnya, linking the giant Tenghiz oil field in Kazakhstan with a modern terminal in Novorossiisk. About 560,000 barrels per day can flow through the 1,030-mile pipeline, which cost $2.8 billion to build and is operated by an international consortium led by the merged American oil giants Chevron and Texaco. The first crude flowed to Novorossiisk in mid-October, despite the U.S. government's preference for Kazakh oil to wait for the Baku-Ceyhan pipeline's completion.

Ruslan steers the car onto a quiet side street to avoid the many police checkpoints in Nazran. Newly constructed red-brick villas appear on both sides of the street, each boasting countless oriels, arches, and balconies. The roof ridges and garden walls are richly decorated with tinwork, like Gypsy castles in Romania. "This part of town is called West Berlin," Amerhan says from the back seat. "It was created in the late 1980s. We Ingush, we chose that name in order to vex the communists in Moscow."

Following the main road out of town, we reach a replica of an old defensive tower, which for centuries provided refuge for inhabitants of Caucasian mountain villages when they were faced with a stronger enemy. The tower is wrapped from top to base in barbed wire. "With this monument we commemorate the deportation of our people and the many men, women, and children who did not survive it," Amerhan says.

The wholesale deportation of ethnic groups, one of Stalinism's darkest chapters, began after Hitler's attack on the Soviet Union in June 1941. On Stalin's orders, one million Volga Germans were forcibly relocated to Siberia and Central Asia. In the early hours of February 23, 1944, some 100,000 troops, along with special forces of the NKVD secret police, cordoned off all villages in the republic of Chechnya and Ingushetia. Falsely accused of collaborating with the German troops (who actually never made it to Grozny), Chechens and Ingush alike were loaded onto American Studebaker trucks, which the Russians had leased from the United States, and taken to the Grozny railway station. The people were packed into more than twelve thousand carriages and, like cattle, shipped to Kazakhstan. The few who managed to stay behind in inaccessible mountain villages died in bombing raids. A week after the operation began, its organizer, secret police chief Lavrenty Beria, reported to Stalin in a telegram, "By 29 February 1944, 478,479 people, including 91,250 Ingush and 387,229 Chechens, have been deported and loaded into troop trains." Chechnya-Ingushetia ceased to exist as a republic.[3]

In the Kazakh steppe, where the deportees were left without protection in the unbearable cold, more than 150,000 did not survive during the first four years. The shared exile united the two peoples in their hatred of Russians and goes far to explain the Chechens' bitter resistance against the Russians today. Only in 1957 did Stalin's successor, Nikita Khrushchev, allow the Chechens and Ingush to return to their homeland. However, by then Moscow had given the Ingush region of Prigorodny on the Terek River to the Christian-populated Northern Ossetia, Russia's only historical ally in the north Caucasus. Years of festering tension led to bloody clashes between Ossetians and Ingush in late 1992. With the Russian army's support, nearly seventy thousand Ingush were driven out of North Ossetia.

"We do not want people to forget what was done to us," Ruslan whispers as we walk back to the car. Above our heads, coming from the east, flies a Russian Air Force helicopter, a large troop transporter. "We call them 'the flying hearses,'" Amerhan says.

From Nazran it is an hour's drive to the border with Chechnya, across a flat and brownish landscape. In Sernovodsk, the last town on the Ingush side, expensive and presumably stolen BMW and

Mercedes cars with darkened windows and no license plates roam the streets. Some of the Chechen refugees here carry barely concealed guns while police are nowhere to be seen. My attempts to strike up a conversation with some men at a kiosk meet with hostile suspicion, and a scar-faced man wearing a cowboy hat shouts at me to get lost as long as I was still able to.

Driving on to the border through a barren no-man's-land, I am stopped at a Russian army checkpoint. Half a dozen bored-looking soldiers stand by the side of the road, and two more sit in the grass. "*Dokumenti!*" demands a private in a patchy olive green uniform, clutching his Kalashnikov. His face unshaven and his breath reeking of vodka, he leaves through my passport uncomprehendingly, while his comrades form a circle around my car. Then the squad leader squeezes himself into the passenger's seat, rifle between his legs, and announces he will take me to a nearby army base.

After a ten-minute drive, we arrive at a crossroads where several Russian tanks, draped with camouflage nets, have taken position. The dozen or so young recruits sitting atop the vehicles and staring at us indifferently are no older than nineteen, their simple faces betraying provincial origins. For years now the Russian military have conscripted hardly any young men from the big cities where the level of education tends to be higher, and where many people oppose the war in Chechnya. After the squad leader trudges over to a tent to report our arrival, a lanky young officer strides out toward me. His clean, dashing uniform distinguishing him from the regular soldiers, he introduces himself as Lieutenant Mikhail M. from the city of Rostov-on-Don. In surprisingly good English, he asks me what the hell I think I am doing in Chechnya. When I reply that I would like to visit "pacified" Grozny, Mikhail looks at me aghast. That would not be possible, he states, and I would have to turn around immediately. Why? "For your own security, I am afraid. Chechen bandits are still active in this area and you could be kidnapped."

Could he not provide a military escort? Mikhail shakes his head. "Then you would run an even greater risk of being attacked." But surely, I insist, the war against the separatists is long over and

won, as Moscow claims? "Moscow is far away," Mikhail says laconi-
cally, casting a nervous glance to the commanders' tent. "Listen to
me, you don't seem to get it. The problem is not the Chechens but
certain Russian units. If I let you carry on to Grozny, do you believe
that you will ever get there in one piece? On the way, they will stop
you twenty times, and that will be very unpleasant for you." Fixing
me with his eyes, Mikhail lowers his voice. "Not every Russian soldier is as nice as I am, you understand? Now get the hell out of here!"
Thanking Mikhail for this clear piece of advice, I turn around.

A few weeks later, Chechen mujahideen would attack this
border post, killing nearly a dozen Russian soldiers.

Human Rights Watch and Amnesty International regularly
document the atrocities committed particularly by the Russian
army and their mercenaries, but the Chechen rebels have proved
equally merciless fighters. Until recently, they even had their own
Internet website (*www.kavkaz.org*), which, alongside current
frontline reports and political pamphlets on Chechen liberation,
offered an endless selection of gory photographs and snuff videos
of armed engagements with Russians.

A typical short film showed a group of mujahideen, sinister-
looking men with long beards, lying in wait in a ditch for a Russian convoy. Three military vehicles approach the ambush.
Suddenly a mine explodes beneath a truck, and the rebels start
shooting. Too surprised to raise any effective defence, Russian
soldiers fall to the ground. In the final gruesome sequence, Chechens, laughing triumphantly, cut the wounded Russians' throats
with daggers. The Russian secret service suspects that the authors
of the website, whose content was renewed every day, worked
underground from Georgia or Turkey, where many of their sympathizers live. It is estimated that the home page was visited by
tens of thousands of people every day. In the Internet cafés in the
Caucasus hardly a computer can be found where *www.kavkaz.org*
is not listed among the browser's bookmarks.

The Russian military deal with the rebels—and with many
Chechen civilians—with similar cruelty. Human rights activists
denounce in particular the Russian tactic, known as *zachistki* or
besprediel, of surrounding Chechen villages at dawn to comb them

in search of rebels and other suspicious men. During such cleansing operations, innocent civilians have often been tortured or killed. Adolescents have been routinely abducted, purportedly for questioning, only to be tortured until their relatives scraped together one thousand dollars to buy their freedom. Similar amounts are also paid to get corpses back.

Back in Nazran, the Ingush capital, the International Red Cross has set up its headquarters in the city center. Surrounded by high tin-studded walls, dozens of people are employed here, most of them locals or Chechen expatriates. Alongside refugees in Ingushetia, the Red Cross also supplies medication and food to the suffering inhabitants of Grozny and other Chechen settlements.

The mission's Swiss administrator is courteous, but categorically refuses to talk about the human rights situation in the embattled republic. "It has traditionally been the policy of the Red Cross to remain neutral in conflicts and not to comment in a one-sided manner on any such crimes that may have been perpetrated," he tells me. Does that mean that comments on human rights abuses would in this case necessarily turn out to be one-sided? "You may very well think so but I am not going to answer your question. I would otherwise endanger the continuation of our humanitarian activities," he responds. I ask why he chooses to remain quiet about what he sees in Chechnya. "I have to. In our work, we are dependent on the cooperation of the Russian authorities."

Next, I visit the United Nations mission in Nazran, which is situated in a new part of town where dozens of Western-style villas have been built around an artificial lake. They are rented out to foreign organizations for thousands of dollars a month. Almost the entire international community of nongovernmental organizations (NGOs) and official institutions have settled within these well-tended and strictly guarded premises. Even the republic's former president has moved into one of the houses, right by the lake, where on weekends he occasionally plays football with the villas' other occupants.

Ben, a young Canadian and one of the UN mission's heads, is slightly more forthcoming than the Red Cross. "Well, in Chechnya things are not pretty," he says. "What the Russians are doing is dodgy, very dodgy." What are they doing, exactly? I ask. "Why, that is well-known, is it not? But at the UN, we really cannot comment on that, the Russians are very sensitive about this. You see, officially the UN does not even have permission to sustain a mission in Ingushetia. Actually, we are accredited in Moscow." Still, what does the UN do when atrocities are being committed in Chechnya? "We talk to the Russian authorities about it but not officially. That would look as if the UN were taking sides."

Markus, the administrator of a small German aid organization, is the most direct. His is one of the last groups that still transport food directly into Chechnya for distribution to starving civilians. Most of the larger international organizations have strictly limited their involvement, partly because of the high risks, and partly because the donations they receive for the region are getting smaller and smaller.

I meet Markus in the bar of a Nazran hotel. "Let's go up to my room, there we can speak more freely than around here," he says wryly. Once behind closed doors, Markus talks about his daily two-hour trip from Nazran to the ruins of Grozny, with a local driver as his only company. "The government in Moscow can claim whatever they like; it is no wonder that the refugees are not returning to their homes. They are scared. In Chechnya, anarchy and violence are worse than ever," he says. Order and hierarchy in Russian combat units are repeatedly breaking down, and many soldiers are corrupt, undisciplined, and addicted to alcohol. "The other day, at an army checkpoint near Grozny, I was discussing some matter with a Russian colonel when a regular soldier, drunk off his head, walked up to my driver and demanded money—under the eyes of the officer who did not step in!"

Worst of all, Markus continues, are the mercenaries hired by the Russian Defense Ministry. They receive meager salaries with the understanding that they can earn extra money from robbery and kidnappings. "One of my Chechen employees had a little brother who was perhaps fourteen or fifteen years old. Last month, mercenaries raided the village where his family lives. They just dragged the boy away, for questioning, as they claimed," Markus says. "Immediately, the family started collecting money to ransom the boy but they were unable to get the thousand dollars together on time. A few days later, the boy was found dead in a field." Before he died his tormentors had pulled out all his fingernails. "On every journey to Grozny I am seized with horror," Markus says after a long silence. "But in the West no one gives a damn about what is going on here."

A few days after my stay in Ingushetia, I am arrested by Russian police in the North Ossetian town of Vladikavkaz, thirty miles down the road from Nazran. After being interrogated for several days, I am accused of espionage. After the police have taken away my car, my videotapes, and a considerable sum of American currency, I am expelled from Russia and put on a plane to Istanbul. The following day is September 11, 2001. Vladimir Putin is the first head of state to officially express his condolences to President Bush. Reminding him that Russia has suffered from Chechen terror for years, he assures Bush of his solidarity and cooperation in the war against terror. In return, the Kremlin basically obtains carte blanche in Chechnya. During the following months, with the world's attention focused on the war in Afghanistan, Russian forces intensify their operations against the Chechens, whom Moscow now labels as "Islamic terrorists" without fear of contradiction by the West.

Throughout 2002, on an almost daily basis, Russian servicemen and members of the Chechen administration installed by Moscow were killed in bomb attacks and assassinations. In the summer, the fighting for the first time spilled into Ingushetia, with troops and rebels clashing in several villages. Local Ingush supported the rebel incursion by giving Chechens shelter. In August 2002, rebels shot down a Russian helicopter outside the military headquarters at Khankala, near Grozny, killing 114 people. It was the country's worst military air disaster. Most shockingly to the Russian military, the helicopter was brought down by a surface-to-air missile similar to the Stinger missiles used by the Afghan mujahideen in their victory against the Soviets in the 1980s.

In late October 2002, Chechen rebels finally took the war to Moscow itself. A group of about forty militants, almost half of them war widows, stormed a theater during a performance, taking some

750 people hostage. The attackers, led by the relatively low-level commander Movsar Baraev, threatened to kill all the hostages unless the Russian government meets their one demand: an end to the war in Chechnya. Refusing to negotiate, Putin ordered his Special Forces to storm the theater, using a mysterious poison gas for cover. The Chechens who offered no resistance were executed on the spot, shot in the back of their heads. The poisonous gas also killed some 120 hostages because authorities refused to inform the hospitals what kind of gas was used or how to treat its effects on the body.

Western criticism of the disastrous rescue operation was muted, as the Putin regime once again managed to argue that Chechen rebels are in fact no different from Al Qaeda terrorists. Putin repeatedly compared the hostage crisis with the September 11 attacks, presenting the Chechen cause as part of a global Islamic terrorist conspiracy. However, while some ties to radical Islamists do exist, the Chechens are essentially waging a struggle of national liberation. Since the beginning of the second war, the comparatively secular rebel leader Maskhadov has specifically ordered his fighters not to attack civilian targets within Russia. However, the hostage crisis, combined with Putin's propagandistic spin, has discredited Maskhadov as Russia's only viable negotiating partner for a settlement in Chechnya. Now there are no rebels left with whom to talk peace.

In November 2002, Russian security forces began to shut down refugee camps in Ingushetia. Despite the freezing cold, the authorities also cut off the gas supply to the tents, telling the Chechens to return to their homes. Instead, thousands of refugees signed and sent an open letter to the government of Kazakhstan, asking for asylum in the country where Stalin once exiled the entire nation. In their despair, the Chechens seem to be prepared to return to the bleak Kazakh steppes rather than the Hobbesian hell their homeland has become.

Meanwhile, a couple of hundred miles to the south, in Azerbaijan's capital of Baku, the Western oil corporation BP Amoco takes a momentous decision, which could soon affect the Chechen conflict.

The Big Pipeline:

Decision in the Villa Petrolea

It is still early morning when I arrive at the Villa Petrolea, BP Amoco's corporate headquarters in Baku, to meet the company's president, David Woodward. Waiting for his assistant in the lobby, I start counting the little red dots with which the high stucco ceiling is studded. They are small hammers and sickles, each painted a scarlet red. It is one of the more subtle ironies of history that this villa, from which one of the world's richest capitalist corporations manages its Caspian operations, was a government building of the Communist Party only ten years ago. On the walls behind the security barrier, official Soviet five-year-plan announcements have been replaced by BP advertisement posters.

Along with President Aliyev and his son Ilham, David Woodward is arguably the most powerful man in the "BP country" of Azerbaijan, administering a budget of about $15 billion that is ready to be invested off the Azeri coast over the coming years. BP Amoco's position in Azerbaijan is so dominant that hardly any important government decision concerning oil is made without Woodward's (albeit unofficial) consent. The company, by far the biggest enterprise in the republic, owns more than one-third of all shares in the Azerbaijan International Operating Company (AIOC) consortium that develops the Azeri energy resources. "If we pull out of Baku," a former BP spokesman once told me, "the country would collapse overnight."

Woodward is a BP veteran whose résumé contains job postings from Alaska to Aberdeen. "We have made a decision. We will build the pipeline to Ceyhan, and we'll fill it with oil. It will be profitable. Construction will start this summer." Despite years of pressure from Washington to build the pipeline as quickly as possible, BP Amoco's decision, Woodward stresses, was motivated solely by economic considerations. "This is not a political project. We are not a welfare organization. If the whole thing did not make economic sense we would have said to the Azeris and the Americans: 'Sorry, but it is not working!'" Woodward concedes that this had been BP's fear for years, but now management is certain that the oil resources lying off the coast are sufficient.

Woodward does not mention that BP Amoco conducted very tough negotiations with all the governments involved, ensuring extraordinarily low transit fees and profit taxes. The Turkish government agreed to as little as $1.50 in transit fees per barrel, while Georgia gets a paltry forty-three cents. By the time Azeri crude reaches Rotterdam via Ceyhan, though, it will have devoured $10 for production and transport per barrel.

The construction of the 1,090-mile-long, 42-inch-wide pipeline will take about three years. The cost is astronomical: $3.2 billion. If the price tag climbs, the Turkish government has declared its willingness to pay for the additional costs. The projected daily load of the pipeline by 2008 is one million barrels of crude from the Azeri Chirag oil field. With the die being cast, Woodward is in no mood to discuss the alternative routes, though he does concede that a north-south corridor through Iran would be shorter, cheaper, and probably safer than the planned pipeline through a Georgia continuously threatened by an ongoing civil war. "But we comply with the American sanctions against Iran. As the biggest oil company in the United States, we have to act as if we were an American company. On top of that, our Azeri hosts do not want to be dependent on Iran—and we have to respect that." Needless to say, pipeline security is an important issue in the wild Caucasus. "We will bury it several meters underground and build walls and fences around all installations such as pumping stations. We will guard the pipeline and strictly control access to it," he says, adding that

BP has successfully operated the small pipeline to the Georgian port of Supsa.

Woodward believes that even the Russian government's opposition to the project is decreasing. In October 2001, at the peak of an antiterrorist Russian-American détente, Woodward travelled to Moscow to give the first ever presentation of the Baku-Ceyhan project in the Russian energy ministry. Only a year earlier this would have been unthinkable. "The deputy minister was present and he seemed to be very interested in the project. He asked intelligent questions and showed no resistance to the project." The minister assured Woodward that Russian companies wanting to participate in the pipeline would not face any political obstacles.

Still, after the experiences of south Caucasian countries with Russia's erratic policies, Woodward remains cautious. "The pragmatic Putin may be the driving force at the moment but there are still many different positions within the Russian government. Some powerful people, such as the Russian pipeline operator TransNefteGaz, for example, will continue to be against our project." Woodward pauses. "It is good to have American support for the project," he says finally, and I wonder if he is referring to American special forces units currently stationed in Georgia.

Leaving the Villa Petrolea, I take a taxi to the headquarters of Socar, the state oil concern, to see Valeh Aleskerov. The strongly built man known in town for his expensive suits occupies a key position at Socar. For almost ten years, the fifty-year-old has negotiated contracts for drilling concessions with foreign oil companies. The "Contract of the Century" in 1994 was largely the brainchild of this former oil engineer who studied business at the prestigious Soviet government academy. Naturally, Aleskerov is already in the picture on BP's step across the Rubicon. "The pipeline will be built!" he calls out as I enter his office. The triumph on his face is impossible to overlook. "All those years people have talked the project down. You cannot pay for it, they said, you won't find enough oil and so on—and now we are doing it anyway!" The night before, Socar's chief negotiator returned to Baku from talks in Moscow and Washington. "Very interesting negotiations, but more I cannot say," he comments cryptically, brushing some imaginary fluff off his dark striped suit's sleeve. Suddenly, one of the six telephones on Aleskerov's desk starts ringing. "Silence, please! This is the line to the President Heydar Aliyev's office." He picks up the red phone's receiver, and after a brief exchange, excuses himself, agreeing to meet with me again later in the day.

In the evening, I meet a nervous Aleskerov, who is hastily smoking a Marlboro cigarette. "Exxon is causing trouble," he says curtly. A company spokesman had announced that ExxonMobil was about to cease all operations off the Azeri coast. Exxon engineers had drilled into a suspected offshore oil field, to a record depth of 6,700 meters, and found nothing. The oil well was dry, the disappointed geologists concluded. Exxon had dropped nearly $100 million in the mud of the seabed, and management decided to cut its losses, seal the well, and pull out all its workers. "But Exxon cannot simply walk out of this now. They are bound by contract to dig a second hole," Aleskerov grumbles, clearly annoyed. "Statistics worldwide show that for every oil discovery you need about ten test drills. It is a hit-and-miss. For heaven's sake, in the North Sea they found 123 dry wells before they made the first hit!" In Azerbaijan, only six test drills have come up with nothing, with a full three-fourths of all oil reserves awaiting discovery. "It does not matter, they are just playing the usual games," Aleskerov concludes. "If need be, we'll take Exxon to the international court in Stockholm, then we shall see what happens."

Stubbing out his cigarette, he returns to the day's good news. Sketching a map of the region on a sheet of paper, he draws a red line from Baku to the Turkish port town Ceyhan. "This route—not Iran, not Russia—is the best option for us to get maximum cash to Baku. Maximum cash!" he says slowly, savoring every syllable. The Azeri derives great satisfaction from knowing that Russia, a vocal pipeline opponent, is powerless to prevent it. "Azerbaijan is an independent country, and I don't run to Moscow to ask for permission for anything. Those times are over." He clearly looks forward to terminating Socar's oil transports to the Russian port of Novorossiisk, currently totaling fifty thousand barrels a day. For years, Socar has complained about exorbitant transit fees and the Russian practice of mixing Azeri crude with low-quality crude from Siberia. If Aleshkerov knows Russia has no say in Azeri oil, he also knows to whom Azerbaijan owes its independence. "Only the United States," he says. "The Americans are helping us. Not, of course, because they like us, we know that. But because they want our oil."

At Finnegan's, word has already spread that the pipeline will be built. The pub is a local watering hole for oil rig men, mostly Scots, looking for the comforts of home. At Finnegan's the loud-speakers above the zinc bar play rock music, you can pay in American dollars, and the TV set on the wall shows Manchester United playing Chelsea.

"The pipeline is a great thing," says Thomas, an oil engineer from Germany, who came a few months earlier from Libya to the Caspian Sea, the new Wild East of the oil industry. "If they really went ahead and built it, that would be reason to celebrate." That afternoon, a BP Amoco helicopter had taken him from the oil field of Chirag, eighty kilometers offshore on the open sea, back into town. "A shaky flight. Makes you wonder when the next chopper is going to crash into the sea," Thomas says. A Scot listening to him explains that he had just made a bet with a few colleagues on whose helicopter would be the first to go down. "Everybody has placed his bet on his own flight—that way, at least you have won the bet when you plunge down."

Thomas works as a production engineer at Chirag, one of the biggest Caspian oil fields, which holds an estimated seven billion barrels, or roughly one billion tons. A shift on the rig lasts seven weeks, after which Thomas recuperates for five weeks on terra firma. His monthly salary of $7,000 affords him an easy life in Baku, with the company also paying for his large flat in the center of town. "It is of Western standard, with parquet floor, a mixer tap in the shower, all mod cons."

"Digging for oil is the greatest adventure I can think of. My job on the rig is to make sure there are no blowouts." In the oil business, a blowout is the worst kind of accident imaginable. Crude is sucked from the soil by osmosis, created by negative pressure in the drill nozzle. If the pressure differential suddenly becomes too great, loads of hot crude and gas rush into the pipe in seconds, racing to the top. Then the valves burst, shooting oil up into the air to rain down on the rig. In old black-and-white films about the first oil discoveries, a blowout is a moment of joy, with pioneers and investors dancing and partying arm in arm in the dirty rain. In fact, it is every oil worker's nightmare: due to the high gas content in a blowout, a single spark is enough for the whole rig to explode. Those who cannot reach the rescue boats fast enough after a blowout are burned alive. "Today, of course, modern technology helps me notice if deep down there is something nasty brewing," Thomas says. "But still you always have to be alert at all times—things can go wrong very quickly."

On a chilly September day, the construction of the Mediterranean oil pipeline, long derided as a white elephant by skeptics, finally begins. At the Sangachal terminal, twenty-five miles south of the capital Baku, President Aliyev is joined by his Georgian counterpart President Shevardnadze and Turkish President Ahmet Necdet Sezer for the groundbreaking ceremony. While the strong wind covers their faces with layers of dust, the three heads of state each shovel dirt onto the symbolic first section of pipe lowered into place by a crane. Next to the pipe is buried a time capsule, containing a joint message to future generations.

Also present at the groundbreaking, shovel in hand, is U.S. Secretary of Energy Spencer Abraham. "This project is one of the most important energy undertakings from America's point of view, as well as for this region," he said at an earlier meeting with President Aliyev. During the ceremony Abraham stresses that the pipeline would give Western nations "greater energy security with a diversified supply" of oil, thus decreasing their dependency on the Middle East. Abraham then reads a personal letter from President George W. Bush. "Although it will be some time before the first barrel of oil flows through this pipeline," Bush writes, "it has already made a significant contribution to the future of this region."[1]

The Russian government has sent neither a letter nor a representative but has instead made several frosty statements. "We are ready for cooperation but will not put up with attempts to crowd

Russia out of regions in which we have historic interests," Foreign Minister Igor Ivanov comments,[2] while Deputy Prime Minister Viktor Khristenko claims not to be concerned about the pipeline project: "It is a long way between the project launching ceremony and completion."[3] Both politicians' statements sound ominous in the light of the escalating crisis over Georgia's Pankisi Gorge in the weeks leading up to the groundbreaking ceremony. On the same day of the Khristenko statement, Russian Defense Minister Sergei Ivanov threatens Georgia—the transit country for the pipeline—with military strikes on suspected rebels in the Pankisi.

The Russian oil giant Lukoil, long considered a powerful extension of Russian foreign policy, refuses to join the pipeline project. Soon after, Lukoil's CEO Vagit Alekperov, an ethnic Azeri, announces it will sell its 10 percent stake in Azerbaijan's Azeri-Chirag-Guneshli oil field to a Japanese company for $1.375 billion. The sale is as much a political retreat as a commercial one.

In the days following the groundbreaking ceremony, Azeri television replays President Aliyev's triumphant speech. "I can tell you that for Azerbaijan, today's event is a dream come true." Yet outside the boom capital Baku, the country's provinces have been slipping into destitution, and nowhere has the slide been more precipitous than in Sumgait, once the Soviet capital of chemical manufacturing and only twenty minutes north of Baku. Until about ten years ago, the petrochemical complex of fourteen factories provided jobs for some 150,000 people. There were two chemical plants, a steel mill, and an aluminium factory, all of which led to Sumgait's water and soil being more poisoned than those of any other Soviet city. Today, pollution levels have improved slightly, thanks only to the fact that all fourteen state companies have since been shut down. Not one of them was profitable.

The giant factory halls on the outskirts of town are falling apart. The windows are broken, and some of the roofs have already collapsed. Weeds grow through the tarmac of the yards, once busy with thousands of men and women on their way to work. Dozens of goods cars rust on crooked railway tracks. Parts of the tracks themselves have been torn up and taken away for scrap metal. In this apocalyptic postindustrial desert, men and women poke through the rubbish in search of some aluminium scrap that they might be able sell for a few cents on the black market in Baku.

Many of them are Karabakh refugees. They fled here ten years ago when Armenian troops overran the enclave. Some fifty thousand dispossessed men, women, and children have squatted in Sumgait's half-empty gray concrete buildings. Others live in sheds built from wood and corrugated iron. Nearly every adult is unemployed, drug abuse and crime are rampant, and many children do not attend school. Most of the one million Karabakh refugees in the country still live in squalid tent cities. They are part of the dark side of the Azerbaijan oil boom, and a great threat to the peace in the Caucasus. Whipped up by nationalist politicians, the refugee groups demand that their homeland be retaken from Armenia. The funds required for a powerful rebel army are ostensibly to come from the projected windfall of oil revenues.

In front of a decrepit concrete building, a few men sit on their haunches in the sand and talk, muffled up in ragged dark clothes and thick felt hats drawn low into their weather-beaten faces. One of them, Jamil Agaev, a farmer from Karabakh, invites me to have a tea in his flat. To get there, we walk up a dank staircase, reeking of urine. The entrance is a rectangular hole in the wall, with a curtain for a door. "Please come in!" says the seventy-two-year-old Agaev, breathing heavily. Inside a room of eighty square feet, the old man lives with his wife, two sisters-in-law, and three other members of the family. Two narrow bunk beds are placed against the walls. The women, wrapped in colorful woolen garments, sit on a floor covered with old rugs and attempt to warm a loaf of Turkish bread in an electric stove. They cook quickly because electricity, like running water, rarely works in this building.

Several black-and-white portraits of two young men hang on the wall, with plastic flowers sticking out from behind their frames. "They are our two sons, they died in the war," Agaev says. Nine years ago, the remaining members of the Agaev family fled the war to Sumgait. "One night the Armenian troops attacked our village, and we had to run away," the farmer recalls, adding almost as an afterthought that he dug his sons' two bodies from the village cemetery and took them along in a box on a cart. "I could not leave them behind. For weeks we carried them around. Luckily, winter arrived and the corpses froze and did not stink that much anymore. I reburied them here."

The commander of the Azeri unit guarding their village had, for no apparent reason, ordered his men to withdraw the night before. "He sold the village to the Armenians, for dollars," Agaev believes. During the war, corrupt Azeri commanders routinely took bribes from the enemy.

Agaev's son-in-law Heydar, who lives with his family a few blocks down the road, enters the room and joins the conversation. "None of the powerful men in this country is really interested in our plight and our homeland, Karabakh," the twenty-nine-year-old says, speaking as a former infantryman both in the regular forces and in militia groups. "We have hardly received any help from the government. For years they have been talking about the enormous wealth the oil will bestow on all of us—and all we get is 15,000 manat a month for bread," a sum equal to three American dollars. "The oil money should also be invested in our army so that we can win back our land—something has to happen. We cannot carry on like this." Looking at the photographs of his two brothers-in-law, Heydar says emphatically: "I am prepared to fight again to wash off the blood of my relatives." He pauses. "But this time I will only go to the front if everybody joins the fight, including the president's son."

While for the Agaevs the Baku oil boom may one day mean war, people living on the Kazakh shore of the Caspian Sea several hundred miles to the north struggle with different but no less dangerous risks.

The New Oil Dorado: Kazakhstan

From a distance, it looks like a church on an island in Venice's lagoon, were it not surrounded by frozen water. Shimmering blue ice floes cover the northern Caspian Sea to the horizon. As we move closer, the offshore duomo becomes a drilling tower, the church an oil platform, as wide as a football field. We are about thirty miles off the coast of Kazakhstan, on our way to visit the oil platform named Sunkar, which is Kazakh for "eagle." In fact, it is a cumbersome raft, which plowed the Nigerian swamps until just a few years ago. Then it was towed over thousands of miles up along the West African coast, then across the Mediterranean and the Black Sea, up the Don River and down the Volga, and finally into the Caspian Sea.

"This is where we found it, and it was big," says Neil Booth, a manager of the Italian oil corporation Agip. Headquartered in Atyrau, a small Kazakh town on the northern shore of the Caspian, Agip is part of an international consortium overseeing the Kashagan field, which is most likely the largest oil find on earth in decades. In July 2000, geologists discovered a giant oil bubble at a depth of about fourteen thousand feet, below an ancient coral atoll. In whatever direction they moved the drill, the valves aboard the Sunkar nearly burst with highly concentrated brown crude. It took only a few days to realize that not since the sensational oil find in Alaska's Prudhoe Bay in 1970 had so much crude been discovered in one place.

74

"We were all totally perplexed," remembers Booth. The fifty-year-old Englishman had already experienced the oil bonanzas at Prudhoe Bay and Aberdeen in the 1970s when he was a manager for BP. He pours some coffee from one of the espresso machines that are placed on every floor of the company's headquarters in Atyrau. "At first, nobody wanted to believe the results that were coming in. After all, it had been a 'wildcat,'" an industry term for searching for oil in a place where no one has ever drilled before. As the northern Caspian Sea had been a nature reserve under Soviet rule, there were no previous experiences with offshore drilling with which to compare it. "A wildcat is a gamble. The odds for a hit are one in twenty, not more." Encouraged by their findings, the geologists set out to measure the oil field's size. The drill went down a second time, at a place some twenty-five miles from the first hit. It was a bold move, but again crude bubbled forth. "The chemical composition of the oil from both finds is very similar," Booth acknowledges. "This indicates that we are indeed looking at a single oil field." With a twenty-five-mile-wide oil bubble, experts believe that Kashagan holds an astronomical thirty billion barrels of crude. The Kazakh government, though not entirely objective, optimistically estimates the content at fifty billion barrels, which would make Kashagan the second largest oil field on earth. (Only the Ghawar field in Saudi Arabia, at eighty billion barrels, is larger, while the combined oil fields in the North Sea still hold about seventeen billion barrels.) Booth is careful not to confirm any estimates. "At this point we cannot make public how much is down there. That would anger our shareholders. But we are looking at a fair amount."

The discovery of the Kashagan field promises massive profits, which in turn has shaken up the geopolitical balance in the Caspian region, ushering in a new and dangerous round in the great world power scramble for raw materials and pipelines. Kazakhstan, only a few years ago a backward Soviet republic, is now poised to become the one of the world's largest oil exporters. By 2020, the country could sell up to ten million barrels of crude per day to the world, as much as Saudi Arabia. This prospect is a potential

nightmare for the international oil cartel OPEC, as it is highly unlikely that nonmember states will respect production limits and
price agreements. Along with Russia, also not an OPEC member,
Kazakhstan could break the Saudi monopoly and be a major strategic force in the twenty-first century.

The Kashagan find has kicked off a crucial stage in the New
Great Game because one question remains to be answered: How
will the crude get from Kazakhstan to a deep-water port? The
Kazakh government, loath to make its potential wealth dependent
on Moscow, has rejected the idea of a pipeline routed through
Russia, much to Washington's delight. There is already talk of a
second pipe along the Baku-Ceyhan pipeline through the southern Caucasus. To achieve this, however, tankers would first have
to ship the Kashagan oil across the Caspian Sea, which is both
expensive and complicated. This leaves a final option, a south-
bound route to the Persian Gulf. Such a pipeline could run through
either Iran or Afghanistan.

Pipeline politics already came into play in early 2001, when
the group of oil corporations exploiting Kashagan faced the task
of choosing an operator from their midst. Initially, ExxonMobil and
the French company TotalFinaElf were the most likely candidates.
However, as an American company subject to U.S. economic sanctions against Iran, ExxonMobil was unable to embrace the lucrative Iran option. For the reverse reason, Total was unacceptable
to the Americans, for the French—in the best Gallic tradition—
pay no heed to American sanctions in their dealings with Iran. At
an all-night emergency session at Heathrow Airport in February
2001, the Kashagan partners reached a compromise and elected
the politically neutral Agip.

With production in Kashagan scheduled to start in 2005,
project leader Booth feels like a pioneer. "This is an extremely
difficult and expensive operation: the oil field lies far out in the
open sea, which is frozen all winter." Additionally, the northern
Caspian is very shallow, only six to thirty feet deep in some parts.
When a strong north wind drives the water south, the depth
decreases even further, changing the coastline overnight. "Then
the whole place is one big puddle and our icebreakers hit the

bottom of the sea." Operations are made even more difficult by a peculiarity of the Caspian Sea, which has mystified scientists for decades. Sea levels periodically rise and fall by several feet. In 1977, the water level was about ten feet under the level of the 1930s. For the past twenty-five years, however, the water level has once again risen dramatically. Scientists blame underwater springs or tectonic shifts for the sea level changes. Unfortunately, Soviet planners ignored this natural phenomenon and located settlements and industrial sites near the Caspian shores. Today, the sea has reclaimed most of them, causing millions of dollars' worth of damages.

Atyrau is a town in transition. The old town is a desolate place, consisting of row after row of crumbling Soviet apartment blocks, with but a handful of trees in the center. A neglected park boasts a bust of Lenin. The wide and meandering Ural River, which marks the geographical boundary between Europe and Asia, cuts through town, eventually flowing into the Caspian Sea. Most of the 150,000 inhabitants eke out a living in the stagnant fishing and shipbuilding industries, where those not in the majority of unemployed or alcoholic residents can make thirty dollars a month. Illegally catching the few remaining sturgeons in the Caspian Sea for caviar earns a greater return.

Then there is the new Atyrau, already christened by the *Wall Street Journal* as the "new Houston." Tupolev airplanes from Moscow are filled with smart-looking businessmen who tap away at their notebook computers during the flight. Large billboards along the newly asphalted main road in Atyrau announce the construction of new bank and office buildings. On the shores of the Ural River, an Italian company has erected a black glass office complex that will include a luxury hotel. Oilmen from the Kashagan rig still stay at the hastily constructed Chagalla hotel, where a whopping $149 is the going rate for a single room with all the charm of an economy class ferry cabin. Tall barbed-wire fences cordon off the expatriate residence from the rest of the city, and armed guards at the gate allow locals in only after a thorough check of their documents and clothes. In the lobby, Italian oilmen cluster around espresso machines after work before retreating to their rooms. Their British colleagues prefer to meet up for drinks at O'Neill's, the brand-new Irish pub on the hotel premises. With a heady mix of alcohol and testosterone, tough guys compete with stories of the Wild East, of women and other pleasures. As there is no official closing time for pubs in Kazakhstan, nights at O'Neill's often end in debauchery.

With such a firm line between the old industrial Atyrau and the new oil-rich Atyrau, residents are taking sides. Galina Chernova leads the struggle of those in Atyrau—and there are many—who do not trust the oil boom. Five years ago, the ecologist founded a movement to stop offshore oil drilling. In a country like Kazakhstan, environmentalism is not for the faint-hearted and Chernova, who weighs nearly two hundred pounds and has large, burning green eyes in an intelligent face, looks like a difficult person to intimidate.

"The oil companies must pull out of Kashagan because the entire northern Caspian Sea has been a nature reserve since 1971," says Chernova on our walk along the frozen Ural River, where dozens of old men are busy hacking holes into the ice to catch some fish. "The big corporations have persuaded our government to suspend the protective status—just like that. Even under the Soviets it was strictly forbidden to drill off our coast. Up here in the north, the sea is a unique habitat, there are 308 different birds and 209 other species."

The best-known among them is the Caspian seal, with a population of about four hundred thousand animals. Many fish migrate up the Ural and Volga rivers to spawn, among them the sturgeon, caught for its delicious caviar eggs. About 90 percent of all caviar sold in the world comes from the Caspian Sea. The earth's largest freshwater fish, which can live up to a hundred years, is now threatened with extinction. Due to illegal overfishing and water pollution, the official catch per year dropped from 30,000 tons in the late 1970s to a paltry 550 tons in 2000. To avoid a collapse of the caviar market, the Caspian states have imposed a temporary ban on sturgeon fishing. As a further protective environmental measure against water pollution, Chernova demands that oil drilling be stopped at once. "The oil companies tell us that their work causes no harm to the environment but nothing could be further from the truth," Chernova complains. "The sea up here is so shallow. Even if there never was a major spill, small quantities of heavy metals are enough to totally contaminate the water."

"The people here are worried about what the whole oil boom means for them," Chernova continues. "We do not want to see the big corporations run away with the money, leaving us behind in a dead environment." Along with thirty fellow volunteer activists, among them biologists, geologists, and lawyers, she has submitted to the Kazakh parliament petitions and proposals for new laws. "But the government does not care about us. It stands 100 percent on the side of the oil companies, and together they want to steal our wealth." However, most people in Atyrau are more concerned with unemployment and money than with the survival of the Caspian seal. "But the jobs which the oil corporations keep talking of do not exist, either. They hardly hire any local labor." Chernova remembers a public hearing about environmental protection organized by the oil companies. "The room was packed. Hundreds of people showed up. I was delighted. Then it turned out that most of those chaps had come to recommend themselves to the companies for jobs."

At Agip, spokeswoman Penny Esson is eager to demonstrate the oil company's concern about the environment, and suggests a talk with the company's environmental officer, David Preston. With no company car available for the three-minute drive, we are left with no choice but to walk the short distance. Esson's high-heeled shoes repeatedly get stuck in the gray mud of the road, while passing Ladas threaten to spray dirt on her long white mink coat that the spokeswoman has put on for our walk. Some amazed Kazakhs even stop in the street to stare at her. "It is such a lovely coat, is it not?" Esson asks. "It is so wonderfully warm. Now I know why these animals are never cold in winter."

Preston greets me warmly. "The people out here are very, very concerned about the environment," he says. "This is because the Soviets never did anything against pollution. There is a deep-seated anger in the population that the government has permitted us to drill inside the natural reserve." He enumerates every precautionary measure Agip has taken to ensure against the threat of an oil spill, including rapid reaction containment forces. "Of course, it is impossible to exclude categorically the possibility of an oil spill. Still, we are doing everything we can to avoid it. After all, we have the most to lose: money to pay for fines as well as our reputation." In the normal run of operations at Kashagan, Preston claims that a zero-discharge policy ensures that not a single drop of oil gets spilled into the sea. When I ask if I can personally visit the rig to confirm this, Preston and Esson flinch, telling me that in principle such a visit would be possible. But unfortunately, they add, there would be no room on any helicopter in the coming days.

Kashagan is not the only oil field people in Atyrau are worried about. Some thirty miles east of the town lies Tengiz, the sixth largest oil bubble in the world containing up to twenty-five billion barrels of oil. Following its discovery in 1979, Soviet engineers never managed to cope with the oil field's enormous depth of 13,000 feet and the unheard-of pressure of 800 bar at which the crude shot to the surface. A fatal blowout occurred in 1985, killing and injuring many oil workers. The well was ablaze for more than a year, with 700-foot flames shooting up into the sky.

When the firefighters finally managed to put out the fire, the communist leadership uncharacteristically decided to obtain Western know-how and contacted the U.S. corporation Chevron for help. After the Soviet Union's collapse, Chevron bought a drilling concession for Tengiz from newly independent Kazakhstan in 1993, becoming the first Western oil company to massively invest on post–Soviet territory. Forming the joint venture Tengizchevroil with the state-owned Kazakh oil company, Chevron has invested more than $2 billion into what is its largest international project. With the help of a further $2 billion, the company hopes to increase the daily output to 700,000 barrels by 2010, to be pumped through a recently completed $2.2 billion oil pipeline across the northern Caucasus to the Russian Black Sea port of Novorissiisk.

Unfortunately, the Tengiz oil field is not just a success story but also the center of a huge corruption scandal, involving shady business deals and hundreds of millions of dollars paid in bribes. It began in the autumn of 1995 when Lucio Noto, CEO of Chevron's American competitor Mobil, decided to buy his way into the Tengiz joint venture. Noto had a company jet pick up Kazakhstan's President Nursultan Nazarbaev, and flew him to the Bahamas for negotiations. Nazarbaev, a former steel mill blast furnace operator, was a longtime head of the Communist Party in Kazakhstan and member of the Politburo in Moscow, acting as the primary mediator in the power struggle between Mikhail Gorbachev and Boris Yeltsin prior to the Soviet Union's disintegration. After the sixty-three-year-old had himself elected as Kazakhstan's president, he received universal praise for voluntarily handing back all the country's nuclear warheads to Russia.

In the Bahamas, Noto asked Nazarbaev how much half of the state-owned Tengiz shares would cost. According to journalist Seymour Hersh, the Kazakh leader made a series of extravagant demands. Apart from an undisclosed sum of money, he asked for a new Gulfstream jet aircraft, four trucks equipped with satellite dishes for his daughter's television network, and new tennis courts at Nazarbaev's home in Kazakhstan.[1] Mobil has since denied it met any of these demands. However, an internal investigation has revealed that in the mid-1990s, Mobil paid hundreds of millions of dollars to bogus companies in both Russia and Kazakhstan. Mobil investigators also discovered questionable accounting practices and multimillion-dollar transfers without, as they put it in their report, "any apparent valid business purpose." Recently, Mobil and other American oil companies active in Kazakhstan have been questioned by federal grand juries in Washington and New York. The U.S. Department of Justice is investigating possible violations of the Foreign Corrupt Practices Act. Passed in 1977, this law makes it illegal for any American to bribe foreign officials, either directly or through an agent, during the course of a business transaction.

In May 1996, Mobil bought a quarter of all Tengiz shares for the "official" price tag of $1 billion, and was instructed by the Kazakhs to transfer the money to Swiss bank accounts. A year later reports surfaced that half the money, $500 million, did not appear in the Kazakh budget but had vanished without a trace. Under intense pressure, President Nazarbaev shifted the blame to his prime minister, who fled into exile in London and began to set up an opposition movement. Nazarbaev immediately orchestrated a police crackdown on any internal opposition. However, he could not avoid an investigation from the U.S. Department of Justice, which in 1999 convinced the Swiss government to freeze more than $120 million in a number of bank accounts registered under the names of Nazarbaev's children and relatives. Outraged, the potentate dispatched special Kazakh emissaries to Washington to demand an end to the investigation. In October 2001, two of Nazarbaev's top aides raised the issue of the frozen accounts and the legal inquiry in a talk with U.S. Vice President Dick Cheney, all to no avail.[2]

In March 2002, Nazarbaev finally admitted to the public that he had stashed the $1 billion from Mobil in a secret Swiss bank account. He explained that he acted out of concern that such a large infusion of cash into the Kazakh economy would throw the currency into a tailspin but just to be on the safe side, Nazarbaev had his puppet parliament rubber-stamp a new law granting him lifelong immunity from prosecution for misdeeds committed in office. Since independence, up to one-fifth of the country's wealth is believed to have ended up in Swiss bank accounts, so for good measure, Kazakh parliamentarians also voted for an official legalization of money laundering. Kazakhs are now free from having to account for funds brought back to the country, much less pay taxes on them. Who stands to benefit the most from this new law is not difficult to figure out.

Not only Kazakhs have lined their pockets with the enormous sums paid for Tengiz deals. Acting as a middleman between Western companies and the Kazakh government, the Californian James Giffen also made millions. Born in 1931, the lawyer started developing business relationships in the Eastern bloc during the Cold War. Representing an American steel producer, he spent years selling oil drilling technology in the Soviet Union. In the mid-1980s Giffen, whose physical appearance resembles that of billionaire Donald Trump, set up a bank called Mercator in New

York, continuing to cultivate contacts with Soviet leaders. When Nazarbaev won the presidential elections of 1991, he hired Giffen as his personal adviser. The modern-day Rasputin soon became a flamboyant key figure in the country's booming oil scene. Provided with a Kazakh diplomatic passport, bodyguards, and several Mercedes limousines, the courtier initiated numerous deals with foreign companies.

When Chevron bought the drilling rights for the Tengiz oil field, it was no surprise that Giffen acted as middleman. For his services, he charged a "success fee" of seven cents for every barrel of oil extracted from the soil by Chevron. At current levels of production, he makes more than $15,000 a day, approximately $5 million a year. Giffen also accompanied Nazarbaev to the Bahamas in the Mobil deal, for which Giffen received an official commission of $41 million. He first caught the authorities' attention in late 1997 when a Jordanian business partner filed a lawsuit in London against Giffen, the Kazakh oil minister, and a Mobil subcontractor. The plaintiff accused the three men of cheating him out of millions of dollars in commissions for various oil deals. The trial disclosed enough of Giffen's shady activities for the U.S. government to also begin investigating him for corruption, fraud, and money laundering.

At Tengizchevroil (TCO) headquarters near Atyrau airport, company executives turned down repeated requests for interviews. Paying an unannounced visit, I finally meet with the director general of TCO, Tom Winterton. He refuses to discuss the issue of corruption, saying that he had been instructed by TCO's bosses not to respond to my requests for an interview. "We are a conservative lot, you see," Winterton says.

After some discussion, the Tengiz director agrees to reply in writing to a few questions. While most of his answers are empty and dismissive, Winterton's written statement about Chevron's commitment in Kazakhstan seems ironic in light of the Giffen affair and the corruption charges against President Nazarbaev: "Obviously, making that kind of investment in a newly independent country in the early stages of developing its legal and regulatory framework initially posed significant political risks. The strong leadership and strategic vision provided by President Nazarbaev and the ROK [Republic of Kazakhstan] government efforts to create a stable and positive investment climate have effectively mitigated those risks."

I get far more unscripted answers about oil corruption a few days later when, through a contact, I obtain a seat on the TCO company aircraft, scheduled to fly in the evening from Atyrau to Astana, the new capital of Kazakhstan. "Cherdabaev is going to be on board, too, the president of TCO," my contact, a young Kazakh woman, whispered while she surreptitiously passed the special ticket to me. Three hours later, I am in the airport's VIP lounge. A small, newer model white Tupolev has been moved into position on the tarmac. The other fifteen or so passengers waiting to board are mostly Kazakh oil engineers and middle-ranking managers. Suddenly, Boris Cherdabaev strides into the lounge, clad in a dark cashmere coat and accompanied by two bodyguards. A stocky man with a distinctly Asiatic yet slightly bloated face, the former vice president of Kazakhstan's state oil concern is one of the elite "oiligarchs," men who have gained enormous wealth and power through post–Soviet petro-dollar deals.

In a clan-based country like Kazakhstan, the Cherdabaevs are the most powerful family in Atyrau. Appointed by President Nazarbaev in 2000, the forty-eight-year-old Cherdabaev succeeded as the head of TCO his own older brother, who served for many years as oil minister and governor of Atyrau. Today, Cherdabaev's brother controls the state oil concern's operations in Ukraine, while a nephew holds a high post in the energy ministry.

On the plane, Cherdabaev unwittingly takes the seat next to mine, right behind the cockpit. "Who are you?" he asks me in fluent English. "And what are you doing aboard my plane?" The bodyguards, standing in the aisle next to us, seem also very much interested in my answer. I introduce myself as the plane rises to about ten thousand feet. After a long silence, Cherdabaev asks me, in a slow, hushed voice: "My boy, how do you like our Kazakh girls then?"

Cherdabaev grew up in a village near Tengiz, then studied at the prestigious Soviet Institute for Oil and Gas in Ufa, Siberia. "When the Tengiz field was discovered in 1979, I was working there as an engineer," he recalls while a steward serves us salmon and champagne. "But we just did not manage to drill down to 4,000 meters and cope with this incredible pressure. We needed Chevron's technology and money," he observes, still disappointed in Kazakhstan's dependence on Western assistance. In the past decade, the country has attracted close to $10 billion in foreign investments, far more than its neighbor Russia. More recently, however, the government has toughened regulations, now allowing foreign companies to invest only in Kazakh-controlled joint ventures. Many of the oiligarchs, who have since become rich with foreign partnerships, support this new policy, holding the view that the Kashagan contract should be annulled and renegotiated. Does Cherdabaev believe that foreigners acquired the Tengiz and Kashagan oil fields for under value? His face frozen in Central Asian inscrutability, the Kazakh falls silent, refusing to answer a still taboo question.

In the dusk below us lie the blurred contours of the Caspian coastline. Tiny islands seem to float in a sea of ice floes, while on shore, pipes from the Tengiz oil field spew cloud-sized orange flames, excess gas that has escaped during production. In the light of the flares, enormous yellow slabs lie in the steppe like giant gold ingots, composed of 4.5 million tons of solidified sulfur, spewed from the ground with the crude since day one of drilling. Every day adds another 4,500 tons of sulfur, sprayed onto the yellow piles where it solidifies into a porous mass. In an effort to dispose of the acidic material, TCO has begun to process it into fertilizer granulate, which is then sold in Europe.

"Which is the best university in Great Britain?" Cherdabaev suddenly asks. "I want to send my son there. He is fourteen years old and no school in Kazakhstan is good enough for him." Cherdabaev has already sent his two daughters to a college in Boston, Massachusetts. He wonders what people there, and in the West in general, thought of Kazakhstan as a country. Only good things,

I reply, though corruption is seen as a big problem. Cherdabaev laughs. "Yes, corruption is a problem but not only here—in Europe and America, too."

It is rumored, I add, that foreign oil companies in Kazakhstan have had to pay bribes in order to get drilling concessions. "Oh, yeah? That is what people are saying, are they? And who are the Americans to accuse us of such things? A woman who sleeps with two men should not call another woman a whore just because that woman sleeps with five men!" One of Cherdabaev's bodyguards glances at us as his boss works himself up. "For so long, we suffered under Soviet rule down here! As a young man, I was so fed up with the stagnation. And then, all of a sudden, we were left to our own devices and had to solve our problems on our own. The past ten years have been exciting, yes, but they were not easy. Everybody had to look after himself. And take care of his family, too."

The steward refills our glasses with more champagne. "Corruption! They are talking! How did George W. Bush become president of America, tell me," he protests, angrily sticking a fork into the salmon on his plate. "It is okay that the Americans are coming here to help us. Fine! But they must not think that they can teach us any lessons," he concludes just as the pilot announces our landing in Astana. The pilot recommends warm clothes, as temperatures have dropped way below zero.

In front of the terminal, a dark four-wheel-drive limousine is waiting for Cherdabaev, who offers to drive me into town. We stop in front of a hotel in the center of town, where he accompanies me inside and persuades the receptionist to give me one of the nice rooms. "I would pay for your room, my boy," he says, walking back to his limousine, "but that would smell a bit of corruption, wouldn't it?"

"Of the oil profits, nothing seeps down to the people," says Elena Karaban of the World Bank office in Kazakhstan. "The gap between the few rich and the impoverished masses is unbelievably wide." Karaban supports nongovernmental organizations, which scrutinize how the government spends its petrodollars. She relates how corruption and injustice cause social tensions, potentially leading to violent political crises in the country. "In large segments of the population there is enormous anger about how the wealth is being distributed. There is a feeling that the government and foreign corporations are plundering the country's assets."

With the overwhelming majority of the sixteen million Kazakhs living in poverty, nowhere is there more ample evidence of squandered wealth than in Astana. Once a provincial town, President Nazarbaev declared in 1995 that the government would move from the attractive city of Almaty to a new capital. Located in the northern steppe, the town was still called Akmola, which is Kazakh for "white grave." This being a somewhat inappropriate name for a capital, Nazarbaev renamed Akmola "Astana," which sensibly means "capital," and set out to spend more than a billion dollars in construction projects, including $50 million on a new presidential palace and a parliament building.

Historically, Almaty was the country's cultural center, but political observers suspect that Nazarbaev wanted to send a deliberate message to Moscow. Barely half the country's inhabitants are ethnic Kazakhs, while more than a third are Russians who live predominantly in the north. After the ex-Soviet republic's independence, Russian nationalists demanded that the northern parts of the country be added to the Russian Federation. By moving the capital up north, Nazarbaev sought to nip this irredentism in the bud.

The vast square between the government buildings in Astana is decorated with frozen water fountains and odd lampposts made in China that look like palm trees. Their tops consist of a bouquet of fluorescent tubes in which blinking neon lights wander up and down, hinting at a serious drug habit the designer appears to have had. Also nearby is a shopping center. Done in light marble, the mall's three floors (linked by escalators) boast an array of luxury boutiques. As the prices are far beyond what the average Kazakh can pay the mall is completely empty, save for the sales assistants. A magazine shop sells Russian newspapers under a sign that reads "International Press."

On the shore of the Ishim River, sumptuous twenty-floor buildings, filled with mostly unoccupied flats, rise up to the sky. In the high-rises' shadows are decrepit residential units. In a bid to impress state visitors, the government had these houses' shabby gray walls covered with Potemkinesque plastic façades meant to look like marble. Unfortunately, most of the "marble" has already begun to peel off at the edges.

"In dealing with its sudden oil wealth," says Andrew Rearick, director of a think tank in Almaty that counsels foreign companies investing in Central Asia, "Kazakhstan has not yet done as badly as Nigeria but, God knows, it is not Norway, either." The Scandinavian country is seen as the one model for how a country manages to absorb the shock of an oil jackpot without serious political or social crises, while at the same time distributing the wealth on a relatively equal basis. In almost every oil state across the globe, the sudden windfall of petrodollars has proved more of a curse than a blessing, leading to corruption, social tensions, coup d'états, and civil wars.

After the oil crisis of 1973, most governments of oil exporting countries spent their new massive revenues on enormous investments in social programs, infrastructures, the military, and subsidized state companies. However, the economies were unable to absorb such a massive cash infusion and in the 1980s, when the oil prices dropped, these luxuries were no longer affordable and the boom ended. The modern skyscrapers of Lagos and Caracas sat empty while unemployment and poverty skyrocketed. In most oil countries, economic growth in the two decades following 1973 was lower than before the oil rush, and per-capita incomes dropped.[3]

Many countries experienced deep social and political crises. In Iran, the shah's modernizing program of the "Great Civilization" led to the Islamic revolution, while in Nigeria one general's putsch was followed by another. Algeria and Sudan drifted into bloody civil wars, while Venezuela has been plagued by constant riots and military overthrows, bringing the country (and its oil industry) to a virtual standstill under the present rule of President Hugo Chavez.

To stave off economic collapse, OPEC countries obtained billions of dollars in loans. Today, Saudi Arabia and many other

states suffer from double-digit inflation rates and immense foreign debt. Economists have blamed this on a phenomenon called
"Dutch disease," striking countries that rely too much on one
particular branch of industry while neglecting all others. Often,
governments that collect high revenues from the export of raw
materials no longer deem it necessary to sustain manufacturing
and agriculture. Companies in those sectors go bankrupt, causing people to lose their jobs and sending well-trained workers
abroad. A sudden oil wealth also keeps national currencies artificially overvalued, harming the country's exports. Rearick's
assessment of the situation in the new Wild East is sobering: "In
all of the Caspian countries, the Dutch disease is beginning to
be rampant."

However, it is corruption that is the main scourge of countries with sudden oil wealth. "Oil increases the stakes in political
power struggles," Rearick explains. Norway prevented this danger by channeling North Sea revenues into a special oil fund that,
among its various uses, can help finance hospitals and universities. This policy is seen as a model for other developing oil states
and, encouraged by Western governments, Caspian countries such
as Azerbaijan and Kazakhstan have also established such national
oil funds. "In 2001 alone, President Nazarbaev poured one billion
dollars into the Kazakh fund," Rearick says. "The only problem
is that he simply skimmed the money off the national budget."
The oil fund is managed, unsurprisingly, by friends of President
Nazarbaev. Expenditures are not clearly earmarked, nor are there
any guidelines as to where the money should be spent. "Nobody
knows what they are doing with the money. They are telling the
people, 'trust us, we are doing the right thing for you.' But in
Kazakhstan nepotism is not seen as corruption but as responsibility for the clan."

No other problem poses a greater threat of engulfing the Caspian
region—and with it the rivaling external powers—in conflict than
the ultimate fate of the oil pipelines. Kazakhstan's northern neighbor

Russia continues to lobby for Kashagan oil to be pumped through its existing pipeline network to the Russian Black Sea port of Novorossiisk. However, with one new 1,065-mile pipeline already transporting Tengiz oil across Russian territory, Kazakhstan will be cautious not to make its entire oil exports dependent on Moscow's goodwill. The Kashagan consortium also fears Russia's exorbitant fees, shutdowns, and acts of bureaucratic sabotage, which the operators of the Tengiz pipeline have struggled with in the past.

The United States wants the oil to be shipped by tankers across the Caspian Sea to Baku, where it would be fed into the planned pipeline to the Turkish Mediterranean port of Ceyhan. Iran has suggested a route along the eastern shore of the Caspian in Turkmenistan, and onward through Iran to the Persian Gulf, offering a financial contribution toward the pipeline's $1.6 billion price tag. Another possibility, mentioned by President Nazarbaev during a state visit to India in early 2001, would be a southeastern route through post-Taliban Afghanistan.

The game for Kazakh oil has attracted yet another regional power. In 1997, China's communist leadership, whose foreign policy is increasingly driven by oil, ordered the Chinese National Petroleum Company (CNPC) to buy 60 percent of all shares in Kazakhstan's third largest oil field of Aktubinsk. Paying far above market price, the Chinese soon afterward bought two additional oil fields, while simultaneously reaching an agreement with the Kazakh government to build a 1,250-mile pipeline from the Caspian Sea through the Kazakh steppe to Urumqi, capital of the western province of Xinjiang.

Ultimately, the Kazakhs will have the final say on which pipeline will be built for Kashagan oil. Sabr Yessimbekov is the official chief planner for all oil pipelines in Kazakhstan. Once the Kazakh ambassador to Japan and now a young rising star within the Kazmunaigaz corporation, Yessimbekov belongs to a new, Western-educated generation of Kazakhs whose English is nearly as good as their Russian. He has just returned from an inspection tour of a construction site where Chinese and Kazakhs work on a medium-sized pipeline that could later be extended to

Xinjiang. "It is a good project," he says. "In general, we do not want to pump our oil to the West but to the East, where the hungry markets are."

As soon as the Chinese have found enough oil in Kazakhstan, Yessimbekov believes the enormous construction costs will no longer be an issue. However, rolling his eyes, he recalls his last visit to the site. "It is very difficult to work in a team with the Chinese. Their style is still very Soviet: They have their five-year plan, and they will see it through, no matter what. Bureaucratic and inflexible, that is what they are." Yessimbekov's resentment at the massive Chinese commitment in Kazakhstan is common among many Kazakhs. Soviet propaganda against the "yellow plague," after Khrushchev and Mao Zedong had fallen out in the late 1950s, has ensured that racial prejudice is deeply ingrained, fed by an old fear of China's desire for living space in the West.

"Historically, China, together with Russia, has always acted at the expense of the Kazakhs," Yessimbekov says. "And now the Chinese have once again become very aggressive. They are trying at all costs to get into Kazakhstan. And that is why it is good that the United States have stationed their troops in Central Asia—they keep the Chinese out. The soldiers give us security and make it clear to the Chinese and the Russians that the world has changed. America has now encircled China militarily. Who believes anyway that for the Americans this so-called war on terror is about Osama bin Laden? This war is about us—it is our oil they want."

However, the U.S.-backed Mediterranean pipeline to Ceyhan is not Yessimbekov's favorite solution to export the Kashagan oil. "Georgia remains the problem. The country is too unstable. It would just take one crazy man to blow up the pipeline." For Yessimbekov, the pipeline choice is an obvious one. "We believe that the route through Iran is the most cost-effective and economically sensible. And we will opt for the solution which is best for Kazakhstan." President Nazarbaev has repeatedly urged the Bush administration to end its opposition to the Persian project. In their talks, the Kazakhs have tried to refresh the memory of U.S. Vice President Dick Cheney, who as the CEO of the petrologistics Halliburton Corporation, which has major business interests in Iran, vehemently lobbied for a suspension of American sanctions.

However, even after September 11, 2001, when there were signs of thawing relations between the United States and the anti-Taliban regime in Iran, Washington stuck to its hard line. During a visit to Astana in December 2001, U.S. Secretary of State Colin Powell emphasized, "I see nothing in the post–September 11 environment that leads me to think we should change the U.S. policy on the routing of pipelines from Central Asia." No sooner had Powell finished than Nazarbaev grabbed the microphone and said the Iranian pipeline route "would be the most profitable and efficient" for Kazakhstan and all oil companies active in the country. With Powell looking on stone-faced, Nazarbaev stressed his intention to build the Persian pipeline.

A month later, President Bush identified Iran during his State of the Union address as part of an "axis of evil," which some observers also interpreted as a warning shot for Kazakhstan.

On a state visit to Kazakhstan in April 2002, Iranian President Mohammed Khatami spoke before an audience of international businessmen and Almaty's entire diplomatic corps, including the U.S. ambassador. Dressed in his typical brown mullah robe and a black turban, Khatami began his speech with the Islamic formula *"Bismillah-ir-Rahman-ir-Rahim!"* ("in the name of Allah, the kind and merciful") only to castigate the United States' policy in the Near East and to warn of a unipolar world. Sitting next to his guest, Nazarbaev nodded enthusiastically. Khatami then called the presence of American troops in Central Asia a "humiliation" of the region. A high-ranking Kazakh government official commented on Khatami's speech by saying that "the Americans do not understand that for us they are neither neighbors nor relatives, just rich and powerful people who live very far away. We seek their friendship only because it is always useful to be on the side of the winners."

The Bush administration has pressured the Nazarbaev regime to stop schmoozing with Iran. "They are threatening us with the imposition of sanctions against Kazakh companies, with support for the opposition in London, and more talk about human rights," said Maulen Ashimbaev, the director of the Kazakh Institute for Strategic Studies and a close aide to President Nazarbaev. "And the U.S. Department of Justice could push ahead with the investigation against our president. That would be very annoying."

In November 2002, relations between the United States and Kazakhstan hit a new low when ChevronTexaco unilaterally decided to indefinitely postpone a long-planned $3 billion expansion of production at the Tengiz oil field. The move came after an intense dispute with the Kazakh government over how to finance the project, which would have increased output to up to 430,000 barrels of crude a day by 2005. "We had no option but to suspend all activity," a frustrated Peter Robertson, vice chairman of Chevron, said. The company has insisted that the new investment be paid for from current production profits, resulting in a massive reduction in the amount of taxes paid to the Kazakh state. The government feared that reinvesting profits would cost the state up to $200 million per year in unpaid taxes until 2006, and demanded that the terms of the Tengiz contract be reviewed. This sprang from the widely held view that many agreements signed with Western oil corporations in the early 1990s were unfair and took advantage of the Caspian states' inexperience and need for foreign cash. ChevronTexaco, tired of posturing, called the government's bluff and the next day about a thousand oil workers found pink slips in the mail. Soon afterward, the Kazakh government caved in, asking the company to return to the negotiation table.

"Kazakhstan gets a lesson in oil politics," read the *New York Times* headline that day, but does this standoff really constitute yet another one of the fierce power struggles between a Western transnational corporation and a Third World national government characterizing the globalized economy these days?[4] Or does it mark a turning point in the new Great Game at the Caspian Sea, dealing a heavy blow to U.S. interests? To answer these questions I ask Ambassador Steven Mann, senior advisor to President Bush for Caspian energy diplomacy. The career diplomat is Washington's top official regarding all energy issues in the region. A former envoy to Turkmenistan, Mann acquired notoriety in Central Asian diplomatic circles when the eccentric Turkmen dictator Saparmurat Niyazov, discontented with U.S. foreign policy, once forced Mann at a state banquet to drink a jugful of vodka in one go. Undaunted, Mann is rumored to have risen to the task.

Receiving me in his office at the State Department, the affable diplomat, who in his white-collared blue shirt looks more like an investment banker, is clearly disappointed by the developments in Kazakhstan. "The Kazakh government really bullies Chevron," the fifty-two-year-old Mann says, reclining in a plush armchair with a cup of coffee. "The Kazakhs want to see how far they can push on investment climate issues." His job is now to engage in what he calls "commercial advocacy," helping to solve the dispute. "Of course, we try to get a fair deal for U.S. companies. So we sit down with the Kazakhs and discuss." The point is not, Mann stresses, to pressure the Kazakhs but merely to persuade them that their stance is unwise. The U.S. government would ideally leave it to private companies to use their own commercial leverage. "I like to say in the region that I represent the most powerful forces in the world," Mann grins. "Market forces!" As for the Bush administration, he adds, its interest is to bring the Caspian oil onto the market at a competitive price. "As non-OPEC oil it can help set the marginal price. After all, in the Caspian we are looking at the largest non-OPEC production growth worldwide."

A few hours earlier, Mann was informed that a Kazakh court, in apparent retaliation, fined Chevron $70 million for environmental violations, penalty for storing the by-product sulfur on company premises. "They are a sovereign nation, they can do what they want—at least they can try," Mann says, though he warns that the Nazarbaev regime should be aware of the effects of their actions on future investors. "They have to understand that they are in global competition. Their competitors are not the other Caspian states, but Angola, Brazil, and Mexico. These days it is all about who offers the best investment climate." Mann brushes aside Kazakh claims that the oil production agreements of the early 1990s were overly advantageous to the Western transnationals. "They were not inexperienced. They knew that for companies taking the risk of going into the former Soviet Union, there had to be a first-entry premium." And yet, I ask, is it not legitimate for a national government to secure as much tax revenue as possible for the benefit of the local population? "That is not our problem," he replies dismissively. "That is an internal matter."

The diplomat looks at his watch. In a few hours, he is scheduled to fly to London to chair negotiations between Kazakh government officials and the BP-led operators of the Baku-Ceyhan oil pipeline. "This is our first meeting to set a timeline for Kazakh participation in the pipeline. We want the Kazakh oil to be fed into Baku-Ceyhan." I ask Mann if recent developments with Chevron would not push the Nazarbaev regime further toward an Iranian pipeline route. "Look," Mann retorts, "that Iranian pipeline has been talked about for ten years but it is our pipelines that are being built." The Iranian option is based on an "idealized belief," he adds, that U.S. opposition would go away. "But it won't," Mann insists. "It represents the American popular will and it is firm. That means the World Bank won't pay for any Iranian pipeline."

On the wall behind Mann hangs a propaganda poster exclaiming "retribution" in Russian. Printed in 1919, it shows Tsarist cavalry, on splendid white stallions, forcing a wretched-looking Lenin and his Bolshevik comrades into an abyss. At its bottom, fire-spitting dragons torture the communists to death in fairly graphic detail. "I like to look at the poster, it appeals to me aesthetically and ideologically," Mann, who speaks fluent Russian, says with a laugh. "I am an anticommunist. The revolution was clearly the worst thing that ever happened to Russia. The Whites should have won the civil war."

His ideological firmness may soon help Mann in dealing with what is likely to be the United States' most formidable Great Game rival in Central Asia: communist China.

The Waking Giant: China

To get from Almaty to China, I travel on to Kazakhstan's southern neighbor Kyrgyzstan, and cross the border halfway up the Irkeshtam Pass, about 180 miles southeast of the Kyrgyz city of Osh. From there I take off at dawn in an old Russian UAS off-roader for the city of Kashgar in the western Chinese province of Xinjiang, which is fast becoming another important Great Game playing-field. Sergei, my Russian driver, looks hung over as he tells me his story. He worked in a factory that produced water pumps for the entire Soviet empire, but like the steel mill and the textile factory, the plant has long been shut down. Now almost everybody in Osh is unemployed, with the only prosperous company in town being the vodka distillery. "And for that to remain this way, I do like a drink every now and then," he says with irrefutable logic. Five hours later the car struggles up the last hundred yards of the pass, where the road has long degenerated into a muddy track. We are at an altitude of 9,000 feet, with a thin layer of snow covering the slopes of the Pamir Mountains. We have already passed several army checkpoints, and are now at the last border post.

The post consists of several derelict portacabins lining a muddy square. At its far end, a barbed-wire gate blocks the way for a number of Kamaz trucks loaded with scrap metal. The Kyrgyz border guards, unshaven and dressed in poorly tailored, almost threadbare uniforms, appear somewhat confused. "The Chinese border is closed," one of them says to my driver. "There has been an accident." A truck has overturned right in the half-mile of no-man's-land between the two countries. The road is blocked. Two officers approach our car and sheepishly ask Sergei if he could perhaps take them to the site of the accident, as their official car is out of petrol. Sergei agrees, and the three men take off. Meanwhile, the other border guards invite me into a portacabin to join them for a drink of vodka.

A wood-burning stove inside keeps things warm. We sit down on sacks of potatoes, apparently left behind as a customs fee by a truck driver. The men throw their hats, still emblazoned with the red Soviet star, onto a table and produce three bottles of vodka and a can of oily sardines. Two or three hours and several rounds pass. One of the border guards, an Afghanistan veteran, pulls out a fluffy toy elephant from under his jacket. Its soft belly contains a battery that produces a trumpet-like sound whenever the soldier jerks the trunk. "Made in China!" he grins. Three pretty young women enter the room, one of whom introduces herself as Ludmira. They down a few glasses with us with a good deal of laughter. Ludmira then asks me across the table if I did not fancy going to another cabin with her for one hundred sum, or about two American dollars.

Sergei and the two officers return. The Chinese have removed the crashed truck from the road, reopening the border. With one last drink for the road, Ludmira wishes me "Good luck in China!" One of the Kyrgyz truck drivers drives me through no-man's-land to the Chinese border post. His Russian Kamaz truck and the trailer are loaded, like all the other trucks on this road, with huge chunks of scrap metal, the remnants of factories shut down and dismantled in Kyrgyzstan and the other ex-Soviet republics. Chinese businessmen buy the metal in order to melt and reuse it for the construction of new factories, a rising empire robbing the corpse of a fallen one.

In first gear, the Kamaz convoy creeps past a red flag, and behind a turn in the road the Chinese border post appears. It is an incredible contrast to the state border that I have just crossed. In front of us is a sparkling white complex of buildings made of steel and blue-tinted glass resembling a modern airport terminal.

Red Chinese characters proclaim "People's Republic of China." A big clock shows Beijing time, which is the same time for the entire country. The roof has been festooned with hundreds of colorful miniature flags. Technical equipment is state-of-the-art, including electronic barriers, X-ray machines, and video cameras surveying the entire premises. In lieu of the ramshackle military vehicles driven by the Kyrgyz, the Chinese border guards have a fleet of brand new Mitsubishi Pajeros at their disposal. Fuel does not appear to be a problem.

The dirt track gives way to a neatly asphalted road and a large parking lot, complete with curbs and flower beds. The truck drivers park and switch off their engines. Two Chinese border guards in dashing uniforms stride from one truck to the next and collect our passports. Though barely five feet tall, the Chinese treat the Turkic drivers with condescending arrogance. "They think that we are just barbarians," says one of the men, an Uzbek. Grabbing his overnight bag, he gets out and locks the cab. "Let's call it a day. They won't let us cross before tomorrow morning anyway."

There is no sign of anyone returning with our passports, and though the sun is still high in the sky, Beijing time means closing time. The gates are locked and, as military music blares from loudspeakers across the premises, the border guards form a column and march in step to their living quarters. The drill is impeccable, all boots moving at exactly the same speed and height, which looks slightly absurd in the mountainous solitude around us. With no hope of reaching the oasis town of Kashgar by evening, I spend the night with the truck drivers in one of the cheap hostels that Chinese entrepreneurs have set up in sheds next to the parking lot. It is bitterly cold, but plenty of vodka and a Chinese noodle soup keep us warm.

The next morning, loudspeakers awaken us with the now familiar sound of marching songs. The sun is still hidden behind the gray mountains, but the Beijing clock shows nine o'clock. In front of the terminal building, the border guards assemble for the morning roll call. After an officer barked orders at them, the guards once again march over to their workplaces. During the passport inspection, I strike up a conversation with Wan. "We opened this border crossing three years ago," the officer from Beijing tells me in reasonably good English. "But the job is very difficult because smuggling is a big problem." He looks over at the scrap-laden Kamaz trucks. "Underneath that bulky stuff you can hide all kinds of things, like drugs for example." International law enforcement agencies have discovered that Afghan opium and heroin are increasingly being trafficked to Russia via Xinjiang. "A much greater problem," Wan continues, "are weapons taken by smugglers across the border to be given to the separatist terrorists."

This is why I have traveled to Xinjiang in the first place. I want to find out how strong the Uighur independence movement is that tries to reverse the province's colonization by Han Chinese. The separatists have been blamed for several terrorist attacks on state-owned facilities in Xinjiang in the 1990s. Since the nine million Muslim Uighurs are closely related to the Turkic peoples of Central Asia, their struggle has inevitably drawn China into the new Great Game.

Officer Wan returns my passport and wishes me a good stay in China. Exactly twenty-four hours after I reached the surreal Kyrgyz-Chinese border crossing, I hitch a ride with a Chinese van driver to Kashgar. The perfectly asphalted road winds past spectacular sandy ridges, interspersed with Uighur villages of mud houses. The air gets palpably drier, the temperature milder, as wild camels cross the road, their double humps covered by thick long fur. In the south, the snow-capped Pamirs rise on the horizon, and to the east ahead of us stretch the sandy wastes of the Taklamakan Desert. I get a sense of how the British diplomat and writer Fitzroy Maclean must have felt when his "eastern approaches" first led him to this part of the world: "Few inhabited areas of the world are more remote and, to the ordinary traveller, more inaccessible, than Sinkiang, or, as it is also called, Chinese Turkestan. On the maps Sinkiang is simply shown as an ordinary province of China, but, though much can be learned from maps, they do not always tell the whole story. Geographically Sinkiang is separated from China by the formidable expanse of the Gobi Desert while its inhabitants are for the most part not Chinese but Turkis, akin in race and language and religion to the inhabitants of Russian Turkestan."[1]

For centuries, various khans ruled over the region until Chinese troops of the Qing dynasty conquered it in the mid-eighteenth century. Later, China's legendary General Zuo Zongtang, also known as General Tso, consolidated Chinese control over what he renamed as Xinjiang, or the New Territory. It remained inaccessible to Westerners until well into the nineteenth century. Then Chinese Turkestan became a Great Game hotspot after a Tajik military adventurer and one-time dancing boy named Yakub Beg conquered Kashgaria in the mid-1860s. The Muslim, who claimed to be a direct descendant from the medieval emir Tamerlane, expelled the Chinese rulers and installed himself as king. The wily despot began to look for allies against a revenge-thirsty Manchu dynasty, offering commercial concessions to both the Russians and the British. A cunning man, he sought to work one Great Game player against the other. However, the Tsarist regime was at first reluctant to deal with Beg, lest it offend China. The Russian explorer Nikolai Przhevalsky undertook an expedition to Kashgar in the mid-1870s only to note: "Yakub Beg is the same shit as all feckless Asiatics. The Kashgarian Empire isn't worth a kopek."[2]

The British had no such qualms and eagerly seized the opportunity to expand their influence within the region. In the autumn of 1868, trader and adventurer Robert Shaw was the first Englishman to reach the mysterious city of Kashgar. Beg received him in his palace and the two immediately hit it off. "The Queen of England is like the sun, warming everything she shines upon," Yakub Beg declared to Shaw. "I am in the cold, and desire that some of its rays should fall upon me."[3]

To the annoyance of both Russia and China, the British in subsequent years sent several missions from India across the Karakoram Mountains to Kashgar, giving up their policy of "masterly inactivity" in favor of a more aggressive forward strategy in Central Asia. However, in 1877 Yakub Beg died and the Chinese soon reconquered their western province and held it under tight rein. It was only in 1933 that Uighur separatist rebels succeeded in declaring a short-lived Eastern Turkestan Islamic Republic in Kashgar. They also governed other parts of the province as semiautonomous areas under the Kuomintang, until Mao's communists seized power in 1949. A final Uighur uprising in Hotan failed in 1954.

When the Soviet Union collapsed in the early 1990s, the Chinese suddenly found themselves confronted with a geopolitical power void on its western border. At first, the communist rulers saw the newly independent neighboring states as a threat to China's territorial integrity. In Xinjiang, the example set by the ex–Soviet republics encouraged the Uighurs to resist Beijing's control. Islamic extremism, spilling across the Chinese border from ex–Soviet Central Asia, made the problem appear even more serious. Hundreds of Uighurs began to study at Pakistani *madrassas* while honing their battle skills with the Taliban in Afghanistan. The Chinese government has urged its Central Asian neighbors, where several tens of thousands Uighurs live, to keep a tight lid on Uighur political activities.

Just why is Xinjiang so important to Beijing, and to the new Great Game? It is the biggest region in China, comprising one-sixth of the country's overall territory. It is home to only one-sixtieth of its population, but it has three-quarters of its mineral wealth. Huge reserves of oil and gas are buried mainly in the Tarim Basin in northern Xinjiang. The area is also important as a potential pipeline conduit for crude oil from Kazakhstan.

China's rulers have also realized the potential opportunities to be gained by cooperating with its new neighbors. Trade across the two-thousand-mile long border with the former Soviet republics has flourished for some time, reaching a volume of about $950 million in 1998. Free trade zones have been established, along with frequent mutual state visits. In June 2001, Beijing and Moscow formed an economy and security pact with all Central Asian states, with the exception of Turkmenistan. The Shanghai Cooperation Organization has become the most important geostrategic alliance in the region. Although it was created to combat terrorism, for Beijing it is also directed against an American intrusion in Central Asia. Its objective, in the words of China's then President Jiang Zemin, is to "support multipolarity in the world." In October 2002, China even held joint military exercises with Kyrgyzstan, marking the first time Chinese soldiers ever participated in maneuvers abroad.

*   *   *

After a four-hour drive, we reach ancient Kashgar, the fabled Muslim oasis on the Silk Road once traveled by countless medieval traders between Europe and China. We are stuck in traffic, in a sea of motorcycles, horses, donkey carts, buses, trucks, and exhaust-belching tuk-tuks. It is Sunday, market day, and the bazaar streets bustle and heave with tens of thousands of people. Shouts of "*boish-boish!*"—Uighur for "watch out!"—fill the air.

There are faces from all the Central Asian ethnic groups in Kashgar: Kazakhs, Kyrgyz, Uzbeks, Tajiks, and even some Turkmens. The Uighurs have very similar, slightly Mongolian features. Many men have long, yet thin, beards and wear *doppa* skullcaps. The elderly are mostly dressed in traditional boots and *hitay,* long black coats, with some carrying precious daggers in their belts. The women's outfits vary widely, from orthodox to secular. Some wear long skirts and a *hijab,* while others prefer nylon trousers and have their hair falling freely onto their shoulders. A large number of women, young as well as old, are covered from head to toe in a strict adherence to the Islamic code that I have otherwise seen only in Afghanistan. In lieu of the colorful silken *burqa* robes used there, an ugly brown knitted cloth is draped over the head and shoulders of Kashgar women. The cloth does not even have slits for the eyes like the *burqas,* although the rough-meshed fabric allows for some visibility.

Occasionally, Han Chinese appear in the crowd, including a few as policewomen on motorcycles. Most people are farmers from the neighboring villages who have come to town to sell produce and meat. Giant heaps of melons lie stacked up by the side of the road; the vendors cut them into juicy slices and hand to passersby. Traders offer hand-woven carpets, rugs, boots and hats, metal pottery, and tools. At the food stalls, one can choose between *naan,* the bagel-like bread of the region, *laghman* egg pasta, and the ubiquitous *plov* of rice and mutton. A local specialty is singed and cooked sheep's heads. Uighurs gnaw with pleasure at what little meat there is on the bones, with only the broken eyes in the sockets left behind.

The livestock market, on an open field outside the town, is where hundreds, if not thousands, of sheep, cows, and camels change hands. The air is filled with bleating and the stench of fresh excrement. Herds wander about, their hooves kicking up thick clouds of dust. One farmer inspects the strength of a camel's teeth, another test-rides a donkey. He lashes the poor animal madly with a whip even though it shows no sign of stubbornness. Only when the sun sinks over the vast expanse of the Taklamakan Desert, with the yellow poplars casting long shadows, does the bazaar finally dissolve.

After the long journey, I treat myself to a hotel suite in a building in the city center that once housed the Russian consulate in Kashgar. It is still furnished with distinctive European furniture of the late nineteenth century when it was the residence of the formidable Russian consul Nikolai Petrovsky. Turning the consulate into a major listening post of the Great Game, the Anglophobe used his great influence with the Chinese rulers to keep British traders and political agents out of Xinjiang. However, the British viceroy in Calcutta was determined to break Petrovsky's monopoly, and in 1890 dispatched the famous English explorer Francis Younghusband, accompanied by George Macartney, on a mission to Kashgar. Welcomed by the *taotai,* the Chinese governor, they set up the first British consulate, known as Chini-Bagh, or "Chinese Garden." Today, it has been turned into a luxury hotel, also named the Chini-Bagh. Petrovsky viewed the arrival of the Britons with suspicion and schemed to thwart their plans. "He was agreeable enough company in a place where there was no other," noted Younghusband. "But he was the type of Russian diplomatic agent that we had to fight hard against."[4] While the explorer took off to the Pamir mountains again after nearly a year, the twenty-four-year-old Macartney stayed on as British consul for the next twenty-eight years, playing cat-and-mouse with Petrovsky. Both became legends of the Great Game. The consulates were closed down in 1949 when the Chinese communists won the Civil War.

The next day, I meet Mamtimyn, an Uighur who works as a teacher in Kashgar. "Simply the fact that I talk to a foreigner could be a great risk for me," whispers the medium-built man, nervously scratching his dark mustache, and I assure him that I will not use his real name. "At the moment, the Chinese authorities are very, very sensitive about this." Mounting his Suzuki motorcycle, the thirty-six-year-old suggests a tour of his home town. With the engine roaring, Mamtimyn laughs, "Now we can talk freely."

We start with a monument of Mao Zedong. At a height of more than seventy feet, the 1971 steel statue of the communist leader on People's Square is one of the tallest in all of China. With his coat flowing and a classical hat with a red star on his head, Comrade Chairman holds his right arm straight up, leading the way into a better future. This is markedly different from the Soviet statues of Comrade Lenin, who always appears to be pointing down.

We reach Kashgar's business quarter. In stark contrast to the bazaar romance, both sides of the six-lane, freshly paved main road, filled with an amazing number of top-notch luxury cars, are lined with sparkling high-rise office complexes of steel and blue-tinted glass. On new wide sidewalks, separated from the road by neatly tended flower beds, fashionably dressed Chinese ladies saunter past luxury boutiques. Shop windows are filled with all kinds of Western products, from jeans to perfume. The shop names and advertisements are all written in Chinese, followed by an Uighur version in small Arabic letters underneath. On one billboard, the government announces the imminent opening of a giant business center outside of town where products from across Central Asia are to be traded virtually duty-free. It has officially been given the English name Yield Fast, which complements with the "Get rich!" dictum of Mao's successor Deng Xiaoping, whose radical economic reforms in the late 1980s paved the way for China's ongoing vigorous growth. "Almost all people living and working here are Han Chinese," explains Mamtimyn over his shoulder, the anger in his voice clear even over the noise of the engine. "We Uighurs do not feel very comfortable around here." He points ahead of us to a white concrete block dominating the city's skyline. Its sides constructed in perfect symmetry, it has a giant antenna on the roof. Armed guards are posted outside the gate. "This is the state security building," hisses Mamtimyn and accelerates.

The Chinese juggernaut of modernization has not stopped outside the fabled medieval city quarters. Large parts have been torn down to create space for new roads and high-rise office blocks. Tens of thousands of residents, all of them Uighurs, have been forcibly moved to modern settlements on the city's outskirts. "For the government, this is all about destroying our culture and shattering all Uighur communities," Mamtimyn believes. In Urumqi, the region's capital, there are now more Han Chinese than Uighurs, due to a decades-long conscious policy by the Communist leadership of settling Xinjiang with Han Chinese. Multibillion-dollar investments in the economy, along with juicy tax benefits, lure more and more workers and business people from the southeast to western China. In 1949, there were only about three hundred thousand Chinese among the five million inhabitants of Xinjiang. Now they make up close to ten million. "Many of those Chinese act toward us like colonial lords," says Mamtimyn.

Driving on, we reach a row of old buildings, or rather what is left of them. Following a straight line for a new road, demolition bulldozers have cut through them almost exactly in half. Brick wall projections and roofs come to a sudden end, as if cut by a razor. Where the walls have collapsed, gaping holes offer a view into living rooms that still contain pieces of furniture. In one room, three elderly Uighur women sit around and gaze down at the traffic raging below them. "Of course, some people are quite glad to be able to move out of their old and cramped houses and into modern apartments with electricity and water supply," Mamtimyn tells me. "But most are very sad." He adds that in the months to come 2,500 more buildings are to be razed, with an additional ten thousand people to be forcibly resettled.

Having parked the motorcycle, we go for a walk through the parts of the old town that have so far been left unscathed. Sand-colored adobe and clay buildings line the narrow alleyways where craftsmen such as ironsmiths, basketmakers, and wood carvers ply their archaic trades. Most people wear traditional Uighur costumes, while many women cover their faces with cloth. At one street corner, a group of boys step out of a Koran school. For Mamtimyn, discrimination against Uighurs in Kashgar is a part of daily life. "No

Chinese bank would give a good loan to an Uighur businessman.
And if an Uighur has been involved in an accident with a Chinese,
the police will regularly favor the Chinese," he says.

We hear children's voices coming from the courtyard of an
elementary school. About fifty Uighur girls and boys, dressed in
light red skirts and school uniforms, gather for the morning roll
call. A teacher leads the singing of a song, and all the children join
in. "It is a political song," says Mamtimyn and translates its lyrics.
"The Communist Party always serves the people/ That is their
calling. Without the Communist Party/ there will be no new China
in the world." Children and teacher alike sing the verses with the
same perfunctory indifference with which most American school
children recite the Pledge of Allegiance.

According to Mamtimyn, Uighur discrimination is worst when
it comes to education. For ten years the teacher has taught natural sciences at a middle school for 2,200 Uighur pupils, separated
from the Chinese children who attend a different school. "The
Chinese school has much more modern equipment," Mamtimyn
complains. "The authorities have installed computers and language labs, which we still lack. They already have central heat-
ing, while we still have stoves." However, Mamtimyn concedes, a
few months earlier, Deputy Prime Minister Li Lanqing came to
Kashgar and visited, of all places, the Uighur middle school. The
campus was crowded with Communist Party bigwigs, soldiers, and
bodyguards. Mamtimyn was asked to welcome the high-ranking
visitor. "As Chinese is also a foreign language for me, I addressed
him in English," he remembers. "Li was very surprised that Uighurs
can speak English. Then he promised us 500,000 yuan to set up a
new language laboratory." The politician made good on his promise and the money arrived.

Undeniably, Uighurs also benefit from the improving living
standards in the economic boom. Mamtimyn proudly tells me that
his monthly salary was raised from $200 to $250 in early 2002. At
the same time, the Uighurs, like all ethnic minorities in China, face
less strict rules of birth control. Unlike Chinese couples, who are
entitled to only one child, Uighurs are allowed to have two. For families living in the countryside, the official limit is set at three chil-

dren. Mamtimyn has fathered two daughters. "Exactly according to the government's plan," he comments sarcastically. Were his wife to become pregnant again, they would face a penalty of 10,000 yuan, about $1,250. "If we want a third child, I would have to submit a request to the authorities, and bribe the official in charge."

At a street corner we run into two former pupils of Mamtimyn who now run shops for spices and clothes. One of them invites Mamtimyn to his upcoming wedding, a huge feast in the old town. The bride is an Uighur girl from the capital, Urumqi. Could he have imagined marrying a Chinese, I ask the soon-to-be groom. He and Mamtimyn look at me aghast. "Never would I even touch a Chinese woman," the man answers angrily. "Chinese are impure. I do not want to see a single one of those pig-eaters at my wedding! They should just leave us alone." As we walk on, I notice a government-sponsored billboard at a crossroads showing a photo montage of the faces of Mao, Deng, and President Jiang Zemin. A slogan at the bottom reads, "For the unity of the nationalities!" Beneath the billboard stands a Chinese policeman.

We enter the Id Kah mosque, one of the largest in China. Built in 1442, the immense courtyard can hold up to twenty thousand worshipers. This afternoon, only a few old men have gathered in the shade of the tall plane trees. Since the Id Kah is too much like a museum for my tastes, I approach one of the smaller mosques, of which there are about ninety in the old town. Mamtimyn is obviously not comfortable with the idea but remains silent. As I walk up the stairs to the mosque, several Muslims from inside rush to the door and lock it in my face. "As a foreigner you cannot enter this mosque," Mamtimyn explains. "Otherwise, the community would get into serious trouble with the authorities." Since the Islam-inspired separatist movement in Xinjiang has regained strength, many mosques and illegal Koran schools have been shut down. All imams are controlled by the state. From March to December 2001 the eight thousand imams in the country were compelled to undergo a political re-education program. They were required to attend lectures on the government's religious policies and on the history of Xinjiang, as written by the Communist Party. "These lessons are essential to the long-term stability of Xinjiang," the official China

News Agency reported, "as they will guide our students away from ideological confusion and mistakes."[5]

Open political resistance against anti-Muslim discrimination in Xinjiang is virtually impossible. Han Chinese or Beijing-dependent Uighurs hold all important posts in the party and the administration, while the Uighurs lack a charismatic resistance figure such as the Tibetan Dalai Lama. One exiled opposition group, the East Turkestan National Congress, raises its feeble voice from its base in Munich, Germany, and occasionally, the masses vent their fury in open protests that are brutally suppressed by the government. In February 1997, hundreds of young Uighurs demonstrated for equal rights after the leaders of a religious youth club had been arrested. The police confronted them, and in the ensuing melee at least nine people died, according to eyewitness accounts. Scores of Uighurs were arrested and sentenced to long prison terms or to death. The unrest of the 1990s has led to a dramatic increase in official executions. Amnesty International has reported that between January 1997 and April 1999 at least 190 people in Xinjiang were executed. That is an average of nearly two a week. All were killed with pistol shots in the neck. The communist regime has conceded that some two thousand political prisoners are currently incarcerated in China, most of them accused of imperiling state security. This number does not include the countless people who languish in reform work camps without ever having had a fair trial.[6]

Since September 11, 2001, the government has massively stepped up persecutions, under the banner of the international struggle against terrorism. In January 2002, the Chinese State Council published a report called "Terrorist Forces in East Turkestan Will Not Get Away with Impunity," claiming that a number of groups perpetrated more than two hundred terrorist attacks between 1990 and 2001, killing 162 people. The report cites attacks on police stations and bus bombings, highlighting in particular the small and obscure East Turkestan Islamic Movement (ETIM). Allegedly affiliated with the Afghan Taliban and Osama bin Laden's terrorist network Al Qaeda, ETIM's leader, Hahsan Mahsum, has denied any such links in a phone interview with Radio Free Europe, defending at the same time the armed struggle against the Chinese "invaders" of Xinjiang.[7]

The U.S. special envoy on terrorism, General Frank Taylor, initially said after talks with Chinese authorities in early December 2001, "The United States does not designate or consider the East Turkestan organization as a terrorist organization." He added that legitimate issues "should be resolved politically rather than using counterterrorism methods."[8] One year later, however, Washington made an about-face. Following intense talks with Chinese officials on nonproliferation issues, Deputy Secretary of State Richard L. Armitage announced that the Bush administration had listed the ETIM as a terrorist organization. The Chinese government found warm words of praise for the move, which ensured that there will be no Kosovo in Asia anytime soon.

"Now the communists can portray their crackdown on us as part of a global war on terrorism," Mamtimyn comments as we sip green tea in a teahouse, our tour day at an end. "The truth is that nearly everybody here is opposed to terror, except perhaps a few disgruntled young men." Who finances their struggle, I ask. "Rich Uighur businessmen and, of course, many mullahs," Mamtimyn whispers in reply. Over the past couple of years, Islam in Xinjiang has gained momentum, as a political as well as a religious force. As early as the late 1980s, Uighurs were allowed, insofar as they could afford it, to go on a *haj,* the Islamic pilgrimage to Mecca. Many returned as "born again" Muslims, and some sent their sons to *madrassas,* or Koran schools, in Pakistan. There, radical Islamic Wahhabi preachers often brainwashed them. Several hundred Uighurs are known to have gone on to fight for the Taliban in Afghanistan. Since the war at Hindu Kush they have been returning to Xinjiang, which is where the Chinese authorities fear they could continue their jihad.

How many Uighurs want independence? "All of us, really," Mamtimyn replies. "But many are also worried about how things would go from there. I believe a civil war could easily break out between the mullahs and us normal people. They want *sharia* law, we want democracy." At the same time, with the government pumping so much money into the region, many Uighurs are content with their soaring standards of life. "The government in Beijing wants to demonstrate to us Uighurs that we are, as it were, in good hands in China. And of course our raw materials, too."

The next day is China's national independence day. In Kashgar, the Communist Party has organized an official flag-raising cere-mony on People's Square, where a military parade had taken place several days earlier. Before dawn the first buses arrive, bringing in Uighur farmers from the surrounding villages. Soon, the square fills up with thousands of people. Among them are the city's civil servants for whom attendance is mandatory. Mamtimyn cannot accompany me, as he is a member of the choir that will stand next to the Mao statue. On the VIP rostrum, party chiefs and other offi-cial dignitaries, all of whom arrived in Pajero limousines, take their seats. The farmers, oblivious to this disparity, spread out blan-kets on the ground and sit down for a good rustic breakfast con-sisting of *naan,* sausage, and tea.

A dozen soldiers march in a robotlike goose step and hoist the red Chinese flag. The choir sings the national anthem, with loudspeakers providing the melody. A party leader shouts a few slogans, the soldiers march off, and the ceremony is over. The farmers fold up their picnic blankets and board the buses. With hardly any wind blowing, the Chinese flag flaps limply in the sky.

I barely catch the eleven o'clock bus to Tashkurgan. The town lies in the southwest corner of Xinjiang where the borders of China, Pakistan, Afghanistan, and Tajikistan meet. The journey up to the Pamir mountains is tedious but breathtakingly beautiful. The sun in the pale blue sky casts the craggy slopes in ever-changing colors. Camels, yaks, and horses roam the high plateaus. As we reach the deep blue Karakul Lake, the first snow-capped 23,000-foot peaks rise up before us. The few villages up here are inhab-ited by Uighurs, Kyrgyz, and Tajiks.

By midafternoon, the bus arrives in Tashkurgan, a relatively ugly Tajik-populated small town. From there, a group of young

Chinese travelers agrees to give me a lift in their minibus. Following a long debate with soldiers at a checkpoint, we are allowed to continue for the remaining thirty miles to the Pakistani border. The road, through desolate and treeless terrain, ascends further and further until after an hour we reach the last post, a simple concrete building where three Chinese border guards stand shivering in the cold, thin air. At about sixteen thousand feet above sea level, the Chinese-Pakistani border crossing at the Khunjerab Pass is one of the highest on earth.

From here, the Karakoram Highway winds south into Pakistan. Called the ninth wonder of the world, the dazzling 750-mile-long mountain road was constructed between 1966 and 1980 by Chinese and Pakistani army units. It leads through the remote mountain kingdom of Hunza, a one-time hotspot in the nineteenth-century Great Game. Somewhere below where we stand, British and Russian troops came face to face for the first time in their Central Asian rivalry. Expeditions from both sides had been penetrating the area for some time, seeking to claim a fifty-mile-wide, uncharted "gap" between the borders of Russia and Afghanistan.

In late 1890, twenty-eight-year-old Francis Younghusband and his Russian counterpart, the formidable Captain Gromchevsky, met on a mountain trail. Once their armed escorts had pitched their camps, one next to the other, the two officers dined together. "The dinner was a very substantial meal," Younghusband wrote later, "and the Russian plied me generously with vodka."[9] With their tongues loosened by the alcohol, the men discussed their countries' rivalry in Central Asia. Gromchevsky admitted that the Russian army was keen to invade British India, which his Cossack soldiers confirmed with a loud cheer.

A subsequent British-Russian meeting was far less gentlemanly. Barely a year later, a Russian force of 400 Cossacks led by Colonel Yanov invaded the Pamir "Gap" and annexed it in the name of the Tsar. Inevitably, his path crossed that of Captain Younghusband, who was busy mapping the area. At first, the meeting, in a barren spot called Bozai Gumbaz, was friendly. Like Captain Gromchevsky before him, the affable Colonel Yanov treated Younghusband to a sumptuous dinner. Three nights later, however, Yanov appeared at the Briton's tent with thirty Cossacks, saying he had been ordered to escort him from what had since become Russian territory. Faced with an overwhelming force, Younghusband had no choice but to comply. The Russians' victory was short-lived, though, as diplomacy would eventually wrest the stretch of land back for the British.

Dusk is falling as I leave the windswept Khunjerab Pass, and I gladly accept the Chinese tourists' offer to take me back to Kashgar. The eight men and women are young professionals in their thirties from Shanghai, engineers, consultants, and public relations managers. Judging by their expensive Gore-Tex outdoor gear and photo equipment, the group members are indistinguishable from any Western tourists throughout the world. Far from being long-time friends, the group has just met for the first time, for the purpose of this journey, through the Internet.

We discuss politics in China. "There is no such thing as politics," says David, an engineer, in good English. "The Communist Party is going to stay in power for several decades more, and that is good. That way we'll have no civil war and the economic development can proceed." A lack of political rights, David feels, is the price the Chinese people have to pay for greater wealth. And what about the massacre on Tiananmen Square in June 1989, I ask. I am met with silence and averted looks. David is the only one to answer: "Well, what about it? We don't care. It is pointless to talk about it." The government made it clear back then that there could be no change through "emotional means," he stresses. He, too, had demonstrated, as a student in Shanghai. "Then we heard the news from Beijing and we knew that it was over. We went home and began to concentrate on our private lives and careers." Since then, life in China has changed radically. For David, what counts today is the economic boom. "This is what the students back then died for."

The young Han Chinese have come to Xinjiang for the first time to see the mountains. On the issue of the region's independence, they all share the same unequivocal view. "Xinjiang has belonged to China for two thousand years now, and we will not let it go, never," David declares; he reasons that without Xinjiang, China would disintegrate and descend into civil war like the former

Soviet Union. "And we also need the oil and gas from here for our economy," David adds, but hardly as an afterthought.

Today, coal still provides 70 percent of China's energy needs, choking all major cities under terrible air pollution. The government has begun to massively promote the use of cleaner gas, which so far accounts for only 3 percent of the overall energy production. Chinese companies are busy developing a giant gas field in the Tarim Basin in northern Xinjiang, having made an agreement with transnational companies to build a 2,350-mile-long pipeline from Xinjiang all the way to Shanghai, the country's commercial center. An international consortium, led by the Shell Corporation, is to pay for half of the $5.2 billion construction costs. From the year 2008 onward, the pipeline is supposed to pump $2 billion worth of gas every year to the country's most populous region in the southeast for four decades.[10]

Xinjiang also has large oil reserves, along with being in prime territory as a transport corridor for oil from Kazakhstan. China's economy has grown to such an extent that its own resources can no longer meet its energy needs. As a result, China has gone from being a net exporter of oil in 1993 to a large importer now. Already, the country consumes 250 million tons of crude per year, one-third of which has to be imported. Similar to the U.S. government, the Chinese leadership is worried about the country's dependence on the unstable Middle East, from where it receives three-fifths of all imports.

The U.S. Energy Information Administration estimates that China's oil consumption is likely to grow from 4.78 million barrels a day in 2000 to 10.5 million barrels a day by 2020, reason alone for the state-owned China National Petroleum Company (CNPC) to venture abroad. In a global shopping spree in 1998 and 1999, company executives spent more than $8 billion on concessions in Sudan, Venezuela, Iraq, and Kazakhstan. Recently, Beijing has held extensive talks with Moscow on the feasibility of pipelines that could supply oil and gas from Siberia. However, the Chinese leadership is wary of any energy dependence on Russia, a long-standing rival for hegemony in East Asia. The severe energy shortages after the Sino-Soviet rift in the 1960s, when Moscow pulled out its engineers from China's fledgling oil industry, are also very much a recent memory.

In Kazakhstan, CNPC has bought and is developing three large oil fields, with both countries agreeing to build a pipeline from the Caspian Sea, through the Kazakh steppe, to Xinjiang's capital Urumqui. To pay for the costs, estimated at $9.6 billion, the Chinese will have to bring Western investors on board. The 1,250-mile-long route also runs across very difficult terrain, including high mountain ranges near the border. Complicating the project further, planners in Beijing envisage a continuation of the pipeline for an additional 2,350 miles to Shanghai. Up to now, tanker cars have been taking Kazakh crude to the Middle Kingdom, which is inefficient and expensive.

On my return to Kazakhstan I visit the CNPC headquarters in Almaty to find out more. The Chinese have moved into a sumptuous white palace right in the center of town. Its front boasts a phalanx of massive pillars. By comparison, the U.S. embassy farther down the street looks like a garden shed. A high lattice fence and sinister-looking security guards surround the CNPC building. Above the main gate, a banner with Chinese lettering informs Kazakh passers-by: "We are doing big business in Kazakhstan!"

CNPC's director general in Kazakhstan is Zheng Chenghu, a courteous and intelligent man who wears small metal-rimmed glasses. "At the moment, we are producing about four million tons of oil in Kazakhstan, but that is not nearly enough for us. In the coming years, we want to acquire many more oil fields in Central Asia." If the Chinese economy keeps growing at current levels, the country will have to import more than a hundred million tons of crude from abroad in only a few years' time. That is why the CNPC, which employs about 1.5 million people, decided to buy its way into oil fields in Africa and South America. "I spent two years in a field in Sudan which we had purchased but now we focus on Kazakhstan," says Chenghu, a trained geophysicist. "In the near future, tenders will be invited for more than a hundred onshore concessions, and we want to win each and every one of them. That is how we will then fill our pipeline to Xinjiang." Yet for offshore drilling such as that in Kashagan, CNPC, by its own admission, still lacks experience.

For Chenghu, there is a much larger problem. "Our situation has much deteriorated recently. The Americans are driving us out of the region. Since September 11, the United States has become very aggressive in Central Asia. The fact that they have stationed their troops here is not good news, neither for the local people nor for us." Since the U.S.-led military campaign against the Taliban regime in Afghanistan in the autumn of 2001, thousands of American soldiers have been stationed at bases in Uzbekistan and Kyrgyzstan, only a few miles from the Kazakh border. In a sentiment echoed many times before, Chenghu says, "The U.S. troops are here in order to control the oil reserves in Central Asia."

American troops have not yet conquered and occupied any oil rigs, I say half-jokingly. "The control works indirectly," a resolute Chenghu continues. "Since U.S. troops have moved up to its gates, the Kazakh government prefers once again to sign contracts with Western corporations—and not with us." If current developments continued, Beijing could very well face having to write off the big pipeline to the East. "In Kyrgyzstan the American military is stationed very close to the Chinese border. The United States has bases in Japan, in the Philippines, in South Korea and Taiwan. And now here—China is going to be encircled!"

Although Chenghu seemed depressed when I left the CNPC headquarters, his mood likely improved in March 2003, when China's state-owned offshore oil company CNOOC surprisingly announced that it would buy a $615 million stake in the Kashagan oilfield in Kazakhstan. The deal, giving CNOOC control over nearly one-tenth of Kashagan, raises the prospect that oil could flow east instead of west, through pipelines across Kazakhstan to China. The Chinese counteroffensive against the increasing American influence in Central Asia has begun.

Yet China is by no means the only Great Game player Washington needs to keep an eye on. In the short term, a far greater threat to U.S. interests in the region is Iran.

Persian Trump Cards: Iran

After a seven-hour delay, I arrive in Tehran at night from Almaty, Kazakhstan. The Iran Air Tupolev-154's landing is so rough that several overhead compartments fly open and bags drop onto passengers. "Good-bye, we are sorry!" two flight attendants at the exit say to every traveler, but receive somewhat more aggressive replies. At the taxi stand outside the terminal, I bid farewell to the Iranian businessman I met hours earlier in the departure hall of Almaty airport. The handshake is strong and long. With a conspiratorial air, the tall man with the dark, tousled beard whispers, "Do not forget what I've told you. You will remember my words."

During the taxi drive to the hotel in southern Tehran, I cannot help but think about the wondrously coincidental encounter at the terminal in Almaty. Seated next to me was a Persian businessman, wearing a suit that was badly wrinkled after hours of waiting on hard chairs. After striking up a conversation, I asked him what he was doing in Almaty. He looked me over, unsure whether or not to trust me, but the solidarity with a fellow passenger stuck in Almaty prevailed over his suspicion. "I am an oilman," he said. "We have just had talks with the Kazakh government about an important business deal."

During the course of our conversation, I realized I was talking to one of the most cunning players in the new Great Game, Hamid Honarvar, Tehran's agent for risky oil deals in Central Asia.

Representing the world's fifth biggest oil exporter, Honarvar does not crave the limelight, instead choosing to pull the strings behind the Caspian scenes. Based in London, he uses the billion-dollar budget of the state-owned National Iranian Oil Company (NIOC) to a clearly defined end: thwarting America's plans for the Caspian Sea's energy resources.

Honarvar knows his opponents well. Like so many of the powerful Iranian elite, this son of a teacher studied in the United States in the 1970s, in the oil-rich state of Texas. At Southern Methodist University in Dallas, often called "Super Millionaire University," the young Honarvar enrolled in computer science. "There were hundreds of Iranian students at the university," he recalled. "As the United States was still aligned with the shah's regime, it was a piece of cake to get a visa back then." Honarvar soon joined a movement that demanded the abolition of the Pahlavi monarchy back home. "That was when I turned into an anti-American. I became conscious of how imperialistic the Americans were and how they controlled our country." Like so many exiled Iranians, Honarvar was unable to forgive the U.S. government its role in the takeover of 1953. Two years earlier, Mohammed Mossadeq, a seventy-year-old left-wing nationalist, had come to power in Iran and carried out far-reaching social and economic reforms. One of his first measures was to nationalize the Anglo-Iranian Oil Company, a daughter of British Petroleum, which as a monopolist had for decades exploited the country's oil wealth. In 1953, when the shah briefly fled the country, the CIA stage-managed a coup against the reformer Mossadeq. While the oil industry was not reprivatized, the American ambassador became one of the most powerful men in Tehran. The shah returned the favor by passing a law in 1964 that guaranteed all American soldiers in the country immunity from arrest and prosecution. Ayatollah Ruhollah Khomeini, the charismatic leader of the clerical opposition, protested bitterly, only to be forced into exile, first to Turkey and later to France.

The monarchy's demise began with the oil crisis of 1974. Within a year, the government's revenue from the oil business rose from $4 billion to $20 billion. The prodigal dictator passed the new wealth on to American arms dealers who sold him high-tech military equipment, which was then left to rust in the desert. Petro-dollars went into the pockets of a small elite, and any opposition was brutally suppressed. Deeming Iran an important crude supplier and capitalist ally in the Cold War, Washington looked the other way.

In November 1978, the shah imposed martial law and ordered his security forces to shoot hundreds of demonstrators in the streets. The regime gradually lost the support of the West. In Dallas, Honarvar neglected his studies and organized anti-shah demonstrations. "It was an exciting period. Tens of thousands came to our demonstrations all over Texas. I made manyspeeches condemning the exploitation of Iran by the Americans." In December 1978, with events in his home country turning revolutionary, Honarvar abandoned his doctoral thesis in order to support the struggle in Iran. "I took a plane to Tehran a few days before the shah's escape from the country. We had won." On February 1, 1979, aboard a plane from Paris, Ayatollah Khomeini returned to his country, greeted by millions of enthusiastic supporters. Two months later, Khomeini had himself appointed as supreme leader of the world's first Islamic republic.

For Honarvar, then twenty-seven years old, and his comrades-in-arms, the struggle was not yet over. True to Khomeini's battle cry of the "revolution after the revolution," he joined the four hundred "revolutionary guards" who in November 1979 stormed the American embassy and held fifty-two diplomats and employees hostage for 444 days. "Originally, we did not want to keep them for that long but there were many spies among them, and agents who were planning a counterstrike," Honarvar, said without trace of remorse. "We could not forget that for years the American ambassador had ordered our government around. It was our re-venge for the exploitation."

Was there anything at all that he liked about the United States, I asked. "Yes, everything!" The old revolutionary's face positively beamed. "I love America. It is a great country. For me it was the country of opportunities." When he noticed my amazement, he continued. "Our revolution back then was not directed against relations with the West and America per se—but against the un-just nature of those relations at the time." Like most Iranians,

Honarvar stressed, he has nothing against the American people, only against the government, which in his view has been hijacked by Zionists and imperialists. As a student, he had many American friends but lost touch with them over time. "Maybe one day I will search for them on the Internet."

It was prayer time. Honarvar fetched a small rug from his travel bag and strolled over to a quiet corner of the airport lounge. Unrolling the rug, he placed his black briefcase close by his side. Before kneeling, he asked two Kazakh men the direction of Mecca. Somewhat baffled by his question, the Kazakhs discussed this extensively, only to recommend that he move his rug slightly more to the right. Honarvar thanked them and in a quiet voice started to pray. People sitting nearby, almost all of them Kazakhs, watched him with curiosity, while others looked away, apparently embarrassed by such open piety, which, after seventy years of Soviet atheism, remains bewildering to most Central Asians. During his prayers, Honarvar did not once take his eyes off his black briefcase.

After twenty minutes he returned, still clutching the briefcase with both hands. I asked him about its contents. "No money, just documents," he replied. "It is not official yet but the talks here were very successful. We will do a big oil swap with the Kazakhs. A hundred thousand barrels per day, and that is just the beginning." If what Honarvar confided to me is true, the Kazakh government and possibly some Western oil companies have simply disregarded Washington's admonitions not to deal with Iran.

For years, Tehran has suggested oil swapping to Central Asian countries. The idea is very simple and practical: Although Iran sits on huge oil resources of its own, they all lie in the country's south. However, there is a great demand for refined oil five hundred miles farther north, in a part of the country where 80 percent of the seventy million inhabitants live. Every day, they consume about 1.4 million barrels of oil, which has to be pumped to the north through pipelines across the desert, a costly and complicated procedure. In an oil swap, tankers would ship crude from Kazakhstan across the Caspian Sea to the Iranian port of Neka. There, it would be processed in new refineries for consumption in the populous north, particularly by Tehran's fourteen million inhabitants. At the same time, Kazakh-chartered tankers would pick up an equivalent amount of crude from Iranian terminals at the Persian Gulf and take it to markets around the globe where the light and low-sulfur crude from the Iranian desert is much sought after. Iran's north would be supplied with energy, and Kazakhstan would not have to wait for expensive pipelines to cash in on its oil.

As early as May 1996, Nazarbaev had traveled to Tehran and agreed with then-President Ali Akbar Hashemi Rafsanjani on a series of oil swap deals. Within a year, a fleet of eighteen tankers took the first load of ninety thousand tons of crude from the Kazakh port of Aktau to Neka. It was the only such swap to date. In official statements, both governments justified the sudden stop of deliveries with the argument that the Iranian refineries needed technical refurbishments in order to cope with the high sulfur content of the Kazakh crude.

However, political reasons also played a role. The United States has repeatedly accused Iran of producing weapons of mass destruction, supporting international terrorism, and sabotaging the peace process in the Near East. In order to limit the mullah regime's means for funding such activities, American diplomats pressured the Kazakh government to call the oil swap off.

Washington's intervention was not only directed against the Kazakh government. Two years earlier, the U.S. Congress had imposed economic sanctions, making it illegal for American companies to do business with Iran. The sanctions explicitly forbade oil swaps. A controversial amendment, the so-called D'Amato Act, also threatened European companies investing in Iran with heavy fines. The crude that the Kazakhs offered to Iran for swapping originated from the Tengiz field, even though only a quarter of all shares were held by the state. The rest belonged to the American Chevron and Mobil corporations. The U.S. Department of Trade received evidence that Mobil, through intermediaries and subsidiary companies, was illegally participating in the oil swap with Iran. Sheila Heslin, a member of the National Security Council, summoned Mobil managers to her office and threatened them with legal action. Shortly thereafter, the deal with Iran collapsed.[1]

Now the Iran oil swap may get a second life. As early as 2005, the Kazakhs will supply up to five hundred thousand barrels per day. "The Kazakhs are very receptive to our proposals," Honarvar smiled. "They are disappointed in the Americans who have cheated them again and again. After all, just to get a bit of cash the Kazakhs have given away their best oil fields." After the United States got a bloody nose in Iran, he believed, it changed its methods for the domination of other countries. Direct political orders were now replaced with restrictive contracts that ensured that Americans were the sole beneficiaries. "The Kazakhs have realized that by now and they regret having put all their eggs in one basket. Now they are looking for new friends, and really nobody is closer to them than Iran."

Throughout the flight to Tehran, Honarvar talked endlessly about his successful negotiations in Almaty. "If we start doing serious business with the Kazakhs, there is nothing the Americans can do about it." Honarvar believed it was this frustration that motivated Washington to opt to send troops to Central Asia, his theories culminating in the conclusion that the U.S. government itself was behind the terror attacks of September 11, 2001, to create a pretext for the war in Afghanistan, and military deployment in the region.

As elsewhere in the Arab world, such suspicions are rife in Iran. However, just why the American government—supposing it accepted the killing of thousands of its citizens, and the humiliation inherent in the collapse of the World Trade Center—would intentionally attack its own Department of Defense, Honarvar was at a loss to explain with any plausibility. He was convinced, though, that "Iranians are a danger to the United States because we are the only people in this region not to put up with American domination. The sanctions against us hurt us less than they hurt the American economy itself." In his view, Kazakhstan was on the verge of liberating itself from American colonization, whereas Iran's northern neighbor Azerbaijan was still under Washington's thumb. Candidly, Tehran's oilman conceded, "There has not been much I could do. All my missions to Baku to discuss oil swaps with the Azeris have failed." Azerbaijan has pinned all its hopes solely on the pipeline to Ceyhan, which Honarvar predicted will end up as the greatest industrial ruin in history, hinting that Tehran would have ways and means to thwart the pipeline plans. He declined to elaborate, arguing that he was not involved in pipeline politics. He did, however, write down a name and phone number on a piece of paper and slipped it into my hand. "Go and see this man in Tehran and tell him I sent you. Maybe he will tell you more."

The traffic in Tehran is legendary. As I step out of my hotel the next morning, I am overwhelmed by a cacophony of honking cars, yelling drivers, and trucks that come to a screeching halt one moment, only to rumble off again the next. Nearly every one of the city's fourteen million inhabitants seems to own a Peyhan car and use it to drive across the city all day. Peyhan is Persian for "arrow," which is slightly absurd in light of the permanent gridlock on Tehran's streets. On Ferdosi Avenue, which the taxi from the airport raced down the previous night, all vehicles are now condemned to noisy inertia. In the rare event of a foot-wide gap opening up, several Peyhans from various directions attempt to rush into the space, their drivers swearing at each other. A motorcyclist shoots forward, going in the wrong direction. He wears a mask to protect himself against the nauseating exhaust fumes.

A mild breeze drives the otherwise unbearable smog out of the city. Visibility is good enough to make out the enormous snow-capped Alborz Mountains to the north. It is one of the first days of spring, and the sun shines warmly on the people strolling past shop windows on Ferdosi Avenue. The cherry trees between the buildings are just beginning to bud.

At the end of the avenue, in the center of a roundabout, is a splendid monument to the national poet Ferdosi, the Persian Homer. When Persian culture became increasingly Arabized in the tenth century, Ferdosi deliberately chose the Farsi language for his poems, and for that reason alone he is seen as its savior today. For thirty years, the poet worked on his famous opus *Shah-nameh,* the "Book of Kings." With fifty thousand verses, it is eight times the size of Homer's *Iliad,* filled with stories of Aryan-Persian heroes and their deeds prior to the Islamic conquest. When the mullahs came to power in Iran after the 1979 revolution, Ferdosi's statue was one of the few they did not dare pull down. Though they rightly considered the poet's pagan heroic epics un-Islamic, they could not eradicate his role as one of the founders of the national culture.

Twenty years later, with the momentum of the Islamic revolution long stalled, the *Shah-nameh* has long since made it back onto the compulsory reading lists of Iranian students. More than ever, Ferdosi represents what the French nationalist Charles de Gaulle, who never referred to the Soviet Union as anything but "Russia," would have called the "eternal Persia."

Of course, the Islamic revolution has provided Iranians with their own heroes. Along the main roads, larger-than-life portraits of Ayatollah Khomeini adorn nearly every available house wall, looking stern and dignified. By comparison, the bespectacled face of Ayatollah Ali Khamenei, who succeeded Khomeini as supreme spiritual leader after Khomeini's death in June 1989, seems pale and uninspiring. Next to these portraits, walls have paintings of martyrs and bloody scenes from the Iraqi war, which from 1980 through 1988 cost the lives of one million soldiers. With large and somewhat accusing eyes the *shuhada*, the dead heroes, look at passersby as if to remind them of their fate.

At the entrance to Tehran University, the flags of the United States and Israel are painted on the sidewalk so that students can step on them every day. Most of the young men and women passing through the gate this morning, whether consciously or not, walk around the faded national colors. Hardly anybody pays attention to a banner on a fence that reads "Death to the USA!" On the spacious campus, whose water fountains and trees make it look like a park, students sit in groups on benches or on the lawn. Some chatter excitedly, others peruse books in preparation for upcoming exams. Among them are a surprising number of young women, who make up the majority of all enrolled students. In some faculties, such as natural science or mathematics, up to 70 percent of the student body is female. However, the different sexes are taught in strictly segregated buildings.

All young women on campus wear the chador, the black robe that covers the entire body from head to toe. Underneath, however, many wear fashionable sneakers and blue jeans. Trendy and expensive sunglasses are as commonplace as mobile phones. The headscarf, with which women in Iran are required to cover their hair, is often worn very liberally. Many female students have pulled it back from their foreheads, showing plenty of long, beautiful hair. This was unthinkable only a few years ago, when the religious police handed out whiplashes as punishment for every visible curl of hair. Today, the women on the streets of Tehran are testing just how far the headscarf can slide down onto the neck. Many young women also wear makeup, particularly generous amounts of eye shadow. Such behavior is still not without its risks, though. Women who in the eyes of security forces go too far are routinely arrested and fined. In July 1999, police stormed the university residence halls and randomly attacked students, killing one young man. To prevent such incidents in the future, the Majlis, the Iranian parliament, decided a year later that police need to ask the dean for permission before entering university premises.

Despite many setbacks, the blossoming faces of Iranian women are an unmistakable sign that the country is changing. This began in 1997 when the moderate Mullah Mohammed Khatami was surprisingly elected president with 69 percent of the votes. His supporters were mostly young people dissatisfied with the country's economic and cultural ossification under the mullah regime. Half the Iranian population was born after the revolution, and are no older than twenty-four years. A quarter of them are unemployed. Those countless young people crowding the streets in Tehran know no system other than the current one. They cannot judge their leaders' policies by comparing them to the brutal rule of the shah regime they never experienced. Since coming to power, Khatami has initiated liberal reforms in order to curb the worst excesses of the Islamic revolution. Religious laws have been relaxed, creating more democratic rights for the citizens. In 2001 Khatami was reelected by a wide majority.

However, the president faces a powerful opponent in the supreme spiritual leader Khamenei, supported by the Council of

Guardians of archconservative mullahs who condemn any cultural liberalization as Western decadence. Controlling the country's security forces, the Council of Guardians has so far blocked all laws and governmental decisions that it deemed too progressive. In the largely nationalized economy, the mullahs occupy all positions of power. Dozens of reform-oriented newspapers have been banned, and editors have been arrested. Since 1998, several intellectuals sympathizing with Khatami have been murdered. Iran is arguably the only country in the world where the opposition is headed by the country's sitting president. Meanwhile, the bitter power struggle between the two parallel governments has reached a stalemate, increasingly paralyzing Iran's political and social systems. Ultimately, the headscarf can be moved backward only so far. It either remains there or drops altogether. At present, no Iranian woman would yet dare to do the latter in public.

For Amir Loghmany, the headscarf is also a yardstick for the country's mood. The longtime political editor of *Hamshari,* Iran's biggest daily newspaper, recalls, "In the old days, under the shah, many young women deliberately put on headscarves to express their support for the revolution. Today, they want to get rid of them again." Loghmany, one of the country's most respected political analysts, watches a group of four giggling girls applying red lipstick to one another's lips nearby. "The country is alive and thoughts are turning around. After all, that is why our heads are round, not square."

We are in Darband, a popular destination for excursions north of Tehran. Up here, at the first foothills of the Alborz range, the air is fresh and unpolluted by city smog. It is Friday, the holy day, and thousands of young people hike up on narrow paths alongside a mountain creek into a gorge. Many of them have come here in expensive all-terrain vehicles; they are the sons and daughters of the wealthy, long-established families from the posh northern parts of town. "They come up here into the mountains to have fun," says Loghmany, whose slightly mischievous face and gray, longish hair give him an uncanny resemblance to Abolhassan Bani-Sadr, the first president of Iran after the revolution. "The higher they climb up, the more they can do what down in the city would be strictly forbidden. No mullah has the courage to come here." On a wooden bridge across the roaring creek a young couple, looking very much in love, hold hands. The girl's headscarf hangs loosely around her neck; she has braided her full, dark hair. Loghmany smiles. "Another two hundred yards further up and they can kiss. And if they manage to find a secluded spot behind a rock somewhere, who knows?"

Behind the couple, a group of young men walks past, dressed in jeans and leather jackets. One of them carries a stereo on his shoulders blaring loud rock music. It is their faces that distinguish these young rebels so conspicuously from their 1970s Western counterparts. They are all clean-shaven. In Iran beards are worn by the rulers. More than 75 percent of all Iranian youths do not pray, according to a recent poll commissioned by the government itself. There are far fewer mosques in Tehran than in Cairo or Amman, and only rarely a muezzin's call to prayer can be heard. "The young people do not put up with everything anymore, and they turn their backs on Islam. In reality, Iran is a secular society. Not even the mullahs still believe in what they preach," observes Loghmany. "By elevating Islam to a political state ideology, it has been practically destroyed as an authentic religion in Iran."

For fifteen years, from 1963 to 1978, Loghmany, the son of a wealthy doctor and diplomat, studied and worked in Würzburg, Frankfurt, and Basel. In Frankfurt, he studied political sciences and discovered the Frankfurt School, attending lectures by Theodor Adorno and Max Horkheimer. "We were all idealists in the 1960s but then none of what we believed turned out to be true," the fifty-five-year-old says of his past as a 1968 rebel. Yet he still remembers clearly and fondly the parties, bars, and girls in Frankfurt's residence halls. "It was a wild time." Like the oilman Honarvar in Texas, the young Loghmany soon joined the opposition in exile against Reza Pahlavi, much to the chagrin of his monarchist father. When the shah paid a state visit to Germany in 1967, Loghmany was among the thousands of demonstrators in Berlin. Only a few feet away from him, the student Benno Ohnesorg was shot dead by police that day.

As a Ph.D. in political science, Loghmany visited Ayatollah Khomeini in his exile in Paris. "He was very inaccessible and always had a mysterious air about him," he recalls. At the end of 1978, Loghmany returned to Iran in order to give support to the popular uprising against the shah. "Our revolution was social, not religious. I guess we wanted to create paradise on earth. But then it all went way too fast and an entirely unnecessary mass hysteria broke out. That was when we handed control to the mullahs, and until today they have not relinquished it again." Loghmany remained in the country and began to work as a journalist. During the war against Iraq in the 1980s, he often reported from the frontlines, narrowly escaping death during an Iraqi gas attack on the Kurdish town of Halabja. "Never have I seen anything more horrific than the sight of women and children suffocated outside their houses."

After the war, Loghmany reentered politics, working as an adviser to President Rafsanjani and Ayatollah Khamenei inside the centers of conservative power. Only in the mid-1990s did he begin to use his position at the liberal *Hamshari* newspaper to support the presidential candidacy of Khatami, who at the time was politically sidelined as the head of the national library. Today, both men know each other personally. "The liberalizing change in Iran cannot be reversed anymore," Loghmany believes. "It is as if we have just come out of the cinema, just after the showing of the mullah film. The outside daylight still blinds us but under no circumstances do we want to go back into the darkness."

Loghmany cautions against hoping for an imminent counterrevolution, though. As the young generation is not prepared to take the risk of an armed uprising, any change would have to evolve in a gradual and peaceful manner. He sees comparisons with the fall of the communist regimes in Eastern Europe in 1989 as inappropriate. "The mullahs remain dangerous," he says. "Unlike the communist leaders of 1989, they have by no means lost their belief in their own moral legitimacy." Many journalists like Loghmany have had to experience this firsthand. Whoever questioned the conservatives too openly was arrested and sentenced to long prison terms. President Khatami looked idly on as the freedom of the press, budding after his election, soon withered away. "For a short while we believed we could write everything," Loghmany recalls. "But we were wrong."

The outcome of the domestic power struggle in Iran will be very important for the new Great Game. Should the reformists behind President Khatami prevail, Iran could free itself from its international isolation and open itself more to the West, to the benefits of Iran's traditional ties with Europe. Whether this would reduce the rivalry with the United States in the region remains doubtful. Both countries are currently too incompatible in their strategic and economic interests.

"It is entirely up to the government in Washington to improve its bad relations with us," says Loghmany while we stroll down the splendid, chenar-lined Valiasr Avenue, past the shah's old summer palace. "But it is under the influence of the powerful Jewish lobby in America. The Jews need Iran as a foe in order to justify their brutal policies against Palestinians." Nobody in Iran is anti–American, Loghmany stresses. Only a small militant minority shout slogans such as "Death to the USA!" while the majority have long seen through that show. Washington could talk about any issue with Tehran, he believes, as long as there was mutual respect. "We want to be treated on an equal basis. We are Persians, a proud and haughty people, and our culture is thousands of years old."

Inevitably, President George W. Bush's dictum of the "axis of evil," which is formed by Iran, Iraq, and North Korea, arises. Loghmany acts nonchalant: "We just laugh at that. You cannot take seriously whatever this uneducated Texan cowboy says." He repeatedly fiddles with the lapels of his loden jacket, then lights a cigarette, his fine, well-groomed hands shaking slightly. "What an insult to compare us with a totalitarian regime like North Korea!" Loghmany suddenly bursts out. "The Americans and their double standards: We Iranians have a more open democracy than any of the Arab sheikhdoms with whom the Americans are aligned!"

For many Iranians, Bush's vitriolic speech was an egregious insult. Tehran had supported for years the Afghan opposition against the Taliban regime and the terror network Al Qaeda. In doing so, Iran sought revenge for the killing of Iranian diplomats in Afghanistan by the Sunni Taliban, who brutally persecuted the Hazaras, the Afghan Shiite minority. Tehran also wanted to stem Pakistan's and Saudi Arabia's influence in the region, both of whom supported the Taliban. The Iranians supplied weapons and money, and thousands of Northern Alliance fighters were trained in camps in eastern Iran. The country accepted about two million Afghan refugees.

On the evening of September 11, 2001, many people in Tehran spontaneously lit candles to express their shock and solidarity with the American terror victims. Iran quietly supported the anti-terror campaign of the U.S. forces in Afghanistan, even promising to help rescue any downed American pilots. Now the U.S. government has accused Iran of meddling in Afghanistan's internal affairs. There is no reason to doubt that Iranians feel threatened by a Bush administration, which has an avowed doctrine of preemption, and has already shown in Afghanistan that it means business. Washington's threats also unwittingly play into the hands of the conservative mullahs, who use the resulting fear in their power struggle with liberal reformers. "Only the 'American as foe' image still keeps the regime in power," Loghmany says. "They use it again and again to refute demands for greater freedom."

In fact, many Persians fear that the true American intention in Afghanistan is to encircle and attack Iran. Even Washington's efforts to remove Iran's archenemy Saddam Hussein from power in Iraq offer no comfort in Tehran. The objective of the United States' new aggressive policy is, many believe, the elimination of Iran as a rival power in the Middle East and the Caspian. Washington has looked on with increasing alarm since the end of the Cold War at how the "mullah state" has extended its political power into ex-Soviet Central Asia. Tehran seeks to profit economically from the ancient ties of Persian culture and language reaching all the way to India, although the declared foreign policy goal of exporting the Islamic revolution has in practice long been relegated to the back burner. Whatever the short-term outcome, Iran can no longer be excluded

as a powerful player from the new Great Game. "It does not matter
what the Americans do," Loghmany says. "They cannot keep us out
of the region. We have to be reckoned with in Central Asia."

The town of Mashhad lies in the strategically important northeast
corner of Iran. The borders with Turkmenistan and Afghanistan
are only a two-hour drive away. For centuries, goods and arms
have passed through this junction in all directions. The main roads
are in excellent shape, and a new railway line to Ashkabad, the
capital of Turkmenistan, just 200 miles to the northwest, has just
been opened. Not far from Mashhad, training camps were run for
years by Afghan mujahideen, fighting first the Soviets and then
the Taliban. With the Taliban's overthrow, Mashhad is now at the
center of a crucial battlefield in the new Great Game.

Contrary to the increasingly secular and liberal Tehran, Mashhad is still firmly under the mullahs' control. Many black-turbaned
clerics walk the streets, and not a single hair slips out from under
any woman's chador. Three years ago, Mashhad made headlines
in the international press when the bodies of several prostitutes
were found brutally murdered. The holiest city in Iran, it is home
to the tomb of the eighth Imam Reza, the only successor of the
Prophet to be buried in Iran. The tomb is the country's most important Shiite place of pilgrimage, with more than twelve million
worshippers of the "party of Ali" every year stepping into the
shrine of Reza, who in the ninth century was poisoned by Sunnis
on orders from the Abbasid caliph Ma'mun. The split between
these two factions of Islam dates back to the question of who
should succeed Mohammed after his death. The Shiites chose Ali,
the Prophet's son-in-law, to become the first imam, who was to
be followed by eleven others. The Sunnis rejected the idea of spiritual leaders and elected Mohammed's father-in-law to be the first
of four secular caliphs.

A great golden dome, flanked by two smaller emerald ones,
towers above the enormous shrine. On a roof, a black flag reminds
all pilgrims of Muharram, the Islamic month of mourning. All the

major streets in this city of two million inhabitants lead to this holy site. At the entrances—separate ones for men and women—armed guards check all clothes and bags, a warranted precaution for in 1994, a bomb killed dozens of people on the grounds.

The entrance opens up to a confusing yet harmonious complex of mosques, *madrassas,* and other buildings grouped around the holy site. Hundreds of people mill over the courtyard in front of the shrine, in a relaxed and joyful atmosphere. Groups of men and women sit on carpets that cover the cold marble floor. They pray or sing, while others quietly read the Koran. Still others have taken along food for a picnic, amiably chatting while eating flat bread and drinking green tea. Three small boys chase each other across the square, brandishing plastic revolvers. One of them nearly bumps into a group of men hurriedly carrying a coffin out of the shrine. The men rush along so fast that the open wooden box, which they support with only one hand each, sways like a trawler on a stormy sea. The corpse, covered in a white cloth, is thrown back and forth in the box. In a corner of the court the procession stops, and the men place the coffin on the floor and form a circle around it. A dozen women, all dressed in black, stand behind them, some convulsing with crying fits. A black ribbon has been tied around the corpse, indicating that the deceased is a woman. An imam approaches the group. He starts to intone a loud prayer and the men join in. No sooner has the cleric finished than one of the bereaved hands him some banknotes. The carriers lift the coffin and rush to the exit. There they nearly collide with another group of mourners who, shouldering a coffin, head straight for the shrine.

At a fountain in the middle of the square, pilgrims wash themselves in the last of a series of ablution rites conducted by Muslims before entering the shrine. Then they walk barefoot to the tomb of Imam Reza. To get there, one passes through twisting hallways and vaults where long-bearded clerics preach to kneeling pilgrims. All ceilings are decorated with countless glinting mirrored fragments, reflecting each ray of light a million times over. The massive wooden doors between the rooms are covered with golden fittings, which the believers kiss and touch with one hand before proceeding further toward the inner sanctum. The sarcophagus appears, slightly elevated and placed inside a gigantic silver cage. Waves of people struggle to get close enough to touch the bars of the cage. Totally enraptured men climb up the bars and stretch out their arms toward the sarcophagus, shouting praise and prayers. On the other side of the tomb, separated by a balustrade, waves of wailing black women swell and recede like the tide. The pilgrims throw sacrificial offerings, mostly banknotes but also some jewelry, onto the tomb.

The donations will later be collected by the leaders of the Astan Quds Razavi Foundation, which administers the shrine. Like many other religious organizations in Iran, the foundation has acquired great power and wealth over the past twenty years. The partly state-owned economic empire owns mines, factories, weaving mills, dairies, and the famous carpet manufacturers of Mashhad. The foundation's president, an ayatollah and good friend of Khamenei, is one of the most powerful mullahs in the country. On his orders, the shrine complex is currently being expanded so drastically that in just a few years it will comprise one-tenth of the entire city. More and more new sacral buildings and minarets rise from construction sites cleared of their previous residential use. Meanwhile, a new tunnel for the city highway is being dug directly underneath the holy site, where a subterranean town complete with a shopping mall will be created.

"The mullahs are corrupt, the foundations only serve their self-enrichment," whispers Ahmed, a man with whom I strike up a conversation after evening prayers in front of a mosque. Like most Iranians, Ahmed, a retired English teacher, speaks bluntly when criticizing the clerics: "Who knows how much money from the donations at the tomb the leaders of the foundation stuff into their own pockets?" A deeply pious Shiite who misses no morning or evening prayers at the mosque, he once supported the Islamic revolution but now feels that only thieves and power-obsessed people occupy the state's top positions. "Luckily, the Shiite belief obliges man to rise up against unjust government."

Shiites are considered to be more inclined to political uprisings than Sunnis. Apart from the issue of the Prophet's succession, another crucial belief separates the two Muslim factions. While Sunnis naturally assume a just God who legitimizes any worldly order, the Shiites explicitly state that Allah must be just. As a consequence, they believe that every Muslim has the duty to resist against unjust worldly rulers and false preachers, if necessary by martyrdom. The same Shiite proclivity for rebellion that brought the mullahs to power in 1979 may soon also spell their downfall.

Back in Tehran, I take out the piece of paper on which oil agent Hamid Honarvar had jotted down the phone number of Seyed Reza Kasaei-Zadeh, the planning director of the National Iranian Oil Company (NIOC). "Ah, yes! I have been informed," says a deep voice on the other end of the line. "Come to the following address, today at five o'clock."

Near the meeting point is the former U.S. embassy, where radical students, among them Hamid Honarvar, kept American hostages for more than a year. The sumptuous compound lies in a vast park studded with pine trees. The slashed remains of the national coat of arms still hangs on the front gate, and next to it, a banner proclaims "Death to the USA!" Two soldiers gaze down on pedestrians from a watchtower above the gate, as the Iranian military has moved into the former embassy. The compound's outer walls are adorned with political murals and slogans. "The day America praises us we should mourn," one of them reads. An artist has drawn the Iran Air passenger plane shot down for no apparent reason by the American battleship *U.S.S. Vincennes* in 1987, where more than 250 people lost their lives. "We will make America face a severe defeat," reads a prophecy by Ayatollah Khomeini, next to a painting of a skull grinning from the Statue of Liberty.

The state oil monopolist NIOC is located in a high-rise office block of central Tehran. Planning director Zadeh's office is handsomely appointed, with portraits of Khomeini and his successor Khamenei hanging behind his desk, though President Khatami's portrait is conspicuous in its absence. From Zadeh's eighth-floor vantage point, he can survey the entire city, including the thirteen-thousand-foot peaks of the Alborz range and, just underneath the shadow of the NIOC, the American embassy. "Today we just call the embassy the American den of espionage," Zadeh laughs.

Unlike his colleague Honarvar, the soft-spoken and elegant Zadeh was never a revolutionary but already had held high office in the administration of the *ancien regime*. After the shah's ouster, the trained oil engineer rose in the NIOC ranks and took over the management of the Abadan refinery in the south of Iran. The British had built the plant, which until about twenty years ago was one of the world's biggest, right on the Iraqi border. It became a primary target for Iraqi missiles when Saddam Hussein invaded Iran in 1980. "When we heard the first rumors of an attack I immediately stopped operations," Zadeh recalls. "But naturally there was still a lot of oil on the premises. When the Iraqi planes bombed the storage facilities, it all flowed into the river and exploded. It was hell, literally." Many of his workers died, and Zadeh barely escaped with his life. Soon thereafter, he took over the management of all nine refineries in the country.

The Iranian oil industry is currently not in great shape. As in other sectors of the economy, many state-owned plants and facilities are out of date. The NIOC lacks hard currency reserves for the necessary investments in modern production techniques, such as gas reinjection. Iran sits on proven oil reserves of 93 billion barrels, or about 10 percent of the world's resources, but production is falling, from 4.3 million barrels in 1978, the last year of the shah regime, to 3.7 million barrels in 1997. Over the same period, the share of crude for export has dropped from 88 percent to 67 percent.[2]

Zadeh, however, is in a joyful mood. He also took part in Honarvar's successful negotiations with the Kazakh government in Almaty. "We agreed on a very good deal. Now we are preparing everything for the oil swap." An added terminal has already been built at the Caspian port of Neka, and twenty-six miles of a new 32-inch pipeline to Tehran have been laid. Additionally, the NIOC has built two new refineries north of the capital where up to five hundred thousand barrels of Kazakh oil are to be processed every day. These are preparations that have undoubtedly been going on for years. The Kazakhs and Iranians have obviously planned a resumption of oil swapping for a long time. In light of this, I ask Zadeh if the Kazakh crude for swapping would also come from the Tengiz field. Leaning back in his leather armchair, Zadeh says with a smile, "What sources the oil will come from is not yet certain." Perhaps some companies, such as ChevronTexaco or ExxonMobil, will also participate (albeit illegally) in the swap? Zadeh folds his hands, a precious and beautiful Aghigh ring glinting on his left hand. "No, we have no contact whatsoever with any private companies. We deal only with the Kazakh state," Zadeh replies. If intermediaries for the oil concerns are indeed involved in the deal, as was the case in the first oil swap of 1997, Zadeh would not reveal this even on his deathbed, the risk of American intervention being far too great.

"The oil does not just come from Kazakhstan but also from Turkmenistan," Zadeh continues, pointing to a glass cube on top of a television set in a corner of his office. A plaque on the cube bears the inscription: "In commemoration of the first oil swap agreement between the Islamic Republic of Iran and Turkmenistan in February 2000." Years ago, the Turkmens, despite protests from Washington, built a small pipeline to northern Iran. Behind the plaque, a few brown drops of the first Turkmen delivery are enshrined inside the glass, bombastically described as "the first drops of crude of the Third Millenium."

On the subject of the Caspian pipelines, Zadeh says, "Besides the oil swaps, we are going to offer an alternative pipeline in competition to other plans—after all, our network is already fully developed." He points to a large map of Iran on his office wall on which existing pipelines are represented by small rubber tubes. The planned route will run from Kazakhstan along the eastern Caspian shore, through Turkmenistan, and on to the Iranian border. From there the pipeline would continue across the eastern part of the country, down to the port city of Bandar-é Abbas. "We can get the Caspian oil to the markets at much lower costs than the Baku-Ceyhan pipeline," Zadeh says confidently as I leave his office. "And there is nothing America can do."

In October 2002, Iran urged Caspian oil producers to ignore U.S. sanctions and to pipe their oil through Iran. "My message is, and I would like to emphasize, less politics but more economics," said Mahmood Khagani, the Iranian energy ministry's director for Caspian affairs. "The 'golden gate' from the Caspian Sea to the Persian Gulf is now open," he added. "Companies working in the Caspian Sea can be sure their resources will be delivered in the international markets."[3]

Sanctions against Iran have thus far discouraged American oil corporations from accepting the Iranian pipeline offer. The Persian route would be—as even American oil executives concede privately—shorter, cheaper, and safer than any of the other planned pipelines through Russia, the south Caucasus, or Afghanistan. And while European companies active in Iran also face heavy fines in the United States, very few of them feel similarly bound by the U.S. sanctions. In September 1997, when the French corporation TotalFinaElf and the Russian oil giant Gazprom struck a two-billion-dollar deal with Iran to develop the huge offshore gas field of South Pars in the Persian Gulf, Washington issued thinly veiled threats to fine the company's branches in the United States, but Total's CEO Thierry Desmarest remained unimpressed. "Nobody recognizes the extraterritorial character of the law, which goes against the principle of sovereignty in relations between nations. We reckon that we are free in our movements," he concluded. Desmarest was seconded by Lionel Jospin, then French prime minister, who noted that "no one accepts that the United States can now impose their laws on the rest of the world."[4] The Clinton administration acquiesced, assuring Total that it would not face legal consequences in this case.

European companies have taken advantage of the absence of American competition on the Iranian oil market. Total is currently conducting a feasibility study for the Iranian pipeline. "We support the company in this," says a French diplomat I interview in Tehran. "We continue not to accept the sanctions of the United States. We generally reject the American logic that Iran must be isolated." France, along with other European countries, seeks instead to integrate Tehran economically, in an effort to support liberal reformers led by President Khatami in their embittered power struggle with the conservative mullahs. And while the theocrats are still unwilling to open the country to direct foreign investments, trade between France and Iran grew by 50 percent in 2001 alone.

The U.S. government's policy on European countries dealing with Iran is intractable. "They will have to put up with being punished by U.S. courts, and European managers may be barred from entering the States," a high-ranking U.S. diplomat once told me. None of that will change as long as Iran continues to support international terrorism. As evidence, the official cited an alleged arms delivery by Tehran to the Palestinians, discovered on a vessel in the Mediterranean a few days earlier. The Kazakh government's declared intention of accepting the Iranians' pipeline offer visibly annoyed the diplomat. "The Kazakhs think very schematically—they use a ruler and draw the shortest line to the Persian Gulf. We try to point out to them that from a security standpoint this idea is far from ideal." From a strictly economic perspective, the diplomat conceded, the pipeline through Iran would be the most attractive of all Caspian routes. "In a purely commercial sense the Iranian route is great—but not under strategic criteria."

In its efforts to keep the United States out of the Caspian region, Iran has found an unexpected ally in Russia. American activities in this region have led both countries to temporarily set aside their centuries-old enmity. Now that they no longer share a common border after the fall of the Soviet Union, their relations have grown almost cordial. Despite sharp criticism from Washington, Moscow encourages Russian companies to sell arms to Iran, and to assist the country in building its first civilian nuclear power plant at Bushehr. The $800 million project, expected to be completed by 2004, has been a major concern for American officials and nonproliferation experts who fear that Iran could convert nuclear waste from the plant into weapons-grade radioactive material, thereby accelerating its efforts to develop its own nuclear weapons. The Russian assistance to Iran has now become the biggest stumbling block in the current U.S.-Russian rapprochement.

One of the principal architects of this new alliance between Moscow and Tehran is Alexander Maryasov, the long-standing Russian ambassador in Iran. We have agreed to meet for tea at the Russian embassy, which is located within such vast grounds that Maryasov arranges for me to be picked up by a car at the gate. The limousine slowly cruises through the park, studded with palms and pine trees. Behind a small artificial lake, the palatial embassy appears, built in the bombastic style of the 1930s. The embassy's many rooms are so intimidating they remind me of the Romanian dictator Nicolae Ceauşescu's megalomaniac Palace of the People in Bucharest. The distance between the parquet floor and the stucco ceiling measures at least twenty feet, and all the rooms are deserted.

I wait for Maryasov in a room the size of a gymnasium. The walls are covered with paintings of battle scenes, and the floor with Persian carpets. Three clusters of low 1970s-style armchairs are spread throughout the room, a strange mismatch with the other objects.

Ambassdor Maryasov is a tall, gaunt man with severely parted jet-black hair and huge, horn-rimmed glasses. His lean features lend his face a stern and aristocratic elegance, as if he were an old-school diplomat from a time far before Russia's Soviet period.

"Do you know which historical event took place in these halls?" he asks after a welcoming handshake. "Here, Stalin, Roosevelt, and Churchill came together for the Tehran Conference in December 1943." The gathering was the first of four major war conferences by the Allies fighting against Nazi Germany. With the war's tide gradually turning against Hitler, the Allied leaders met to discuss their strategies. Originally, the meeting was to be held at a place in the West, but Stalin refused to leave the Soviet sphere of rule. Persia, which was at that time occupied by British and Soviet troops, seemed a good compromise. It was the first time that Stalin personally met the two Western statesmen, who had both taken long and risky travels to get there. Stalin urged them both to open a second front in the West to help the Red Army in its desperate struggle. "This is where they sat and debated," says Maryasov, pointing at a polished mahogany table in the room next door. "Stalin sat there, and Roosevelt and Churchill there and here," the fifty-four-year-old continues, almost as if he himself had been present. "Then there were warnings that German agents, of whom there were many in Tehran back then, were planning to assassinate Roosevelt. Therefore, the American president did not go back to his embassy but spent the nights with us."

There is hardly a Russian who knows Iran as well as Maryasov. In 1969, he was first dispatched to the country as a consul. The Muscovite speaks fluent Farsi besides French and English. During the revolution of 1979 the diplomat was also accredited in Tehran. "Khomeini viewed us Soviets, like the Americans, as evil Satans. He was afraid of communism." After the hostage-taking of U.S. diplomats, the Iranian foreign minister, as Maryasov remembers, also suggested an occupation of the Soviet embassy. It would not have been for the first time. In 1829, a furious mob stormed the Russian embassy in Tehran, hacking to death ambassador Alexander Griboyedov and his entire staff. The reason was that at the conclusion of a successful campaign against the Persians, the ambassador, who was also a poet and close friend of Alexander Pushkin, had dictated harsh capitulation terms to the shah. The killing, behind which St. Petersburg suspected the Persians' British allies, made Griboyedov one of the most prominent victims of the Great Game. Exactly 150 years later, however, Ayatollah Khomeini was wise enough not to confront both superpowers simultaneously.

For 444 days, Russian diplomats were left to watch the fate of their captured American colleagues and rivals in the Cold War. "Of course, we liked the anti-imperialist element of the revolution. It was a blow to the United States and we thought that was very good," says Maryasov with a vicious sparkle in his eyes.

After the Soviets invaded Afghanistan in December 1979, relations between Moscow and Tehran soured. During the 1980s Iran funneled arms and money to the mujahideen to support their struggle against the Red Army, which in 1989 withdrew from the Hindu Kush beaten and humiliated.

"Since we no longer have a common border with Iran, we share many identical views on political issues," Maryasov explains.

"Particularly in Central Asia, where Iran has demonstrated flex-
ibility and common sense, we have many goals in common."
Maryasov praises Tehran for not attempting to export the Islamic
revolution to the former Soviet republics. In the civil war of the
Tajiks, who are by ethnicity closely related to the Persians, Iran
mediated talks calmly and pragmatically.

The basis for the new trans–Caspian alliance lies in Maryasov's
"identical views" with Iran, upon which he is happy to expand. "We
are in agreement with Tehran that no other great foreign power
should gain influence at the Caspian Sea." He initially mentions no
country by name, but criticizes American support for the Baku-
Ceyhan pipeline across the formerly Russian South Caucasus. "We
are against this project because behind it lie political and strategic
motives." Their shared opposition against the Mediterranean pipeline brings Iran and Russia, unequal partners and rivals on the oil
market, ever closer together.

"A pipeline routed through Iran would be supported by
Russia," says Maryasov, though he is quick to add, "but only, of
course, when all Russian pipelines operate at full capacity." At the
same time Moscow fears that Tehran could exaggerate its saber-
rattling vis-à-vis its little-loved neighbor, Azerbaijan. "This could
easily serve as a pretext for a foreign power to enter the region,"
says Maryasov. "Azerbaijan could ask the United States to intervene and send troops to the Caucasus."

Maryasov sharply rejects American accusations of Russia
providing Iran with weapons of mass destruction and the technology to build nuclear bombs. "We sell conventional arms to Iran,
just as the United States does to other countries. There is abso-
lutely no evidence that nuclear warheads have been traded." The
assistance given by Russian engineers in the construction of the
first Iranian nuclear power plant at Bushehr, he stresses, is subject to regular control by the International Atomic Energy Agency.
"It is all open and transparent," he says; "nobody is building any
secret bombs there." Like many Western diplomats in Tehran, the
Russian ambassador shakes his head at President Bush's claim
that Iran is part of an "axis of evil." "Such double standards," he
insists. "Israel's lobby in Washington is behind all of this. Until this

day, the Americans have not learned anything in their relations with Iran. They are narrow-minded, they do not look closely enough, and they do not listen."

Dropping his diplomatic reserve entirely, Maryasov says, "Now the Americans have moved troops into Central Asia. There can be no partnership between us and the United States if the Americans always act unilaterally without even consulting us. We will get to a point where we feel our national security is endangered." Asked what he thinks American interests in Central Asia are, Maryasov does not mince his words. "The U.S. military has used terrorists in Afghanistan as a pretext to penetrate Central Asia. For the Americans this is about economic interests, especially the Caspian oil."

The ambassador is convinced that the Central Asian power struggle with the United States is far from decided. "As soon as our economy regains its strength, we will reestablish our old relations with Central Asia and the southern Caucasus, and reassert our sphere of influence in that region." Maryasov's frank words underscore just how strong an opposition inside the Russian power structure President Putin's pragmatic and cooperative course with Washington could still face.

For the six-hundred-mile journey from Tehran to Baku, any traveler of sane mind and sound budget would travel by air. I opt for the road, not wanting to miss out on the drive along Iran's northern coast. Idyllically squeezed in between the water and the steep slopes of the Alborz range, it is one of the most beautiful stretches of the entire Caspian Sea coast. For the long journey, Loghmany tracked down a 1977 Chevrolet Nova. Relics of the pro–Western shah era, a few of these American cars still roam the streets of Tehran. Extravagant 1960s Cadillacs, these days only seen in American films, are also very popular with Iranians. The Chevy Nova, though, remains the favorite. "I'd rather repair it for the hundredth time than scrap it," says Homayoun, my driver, as we leave the suburbs of Tehran in the early morning. In the fifteen years he has driven this car, the slightly built Homayoun has reset the hundred thousand mileage counter twice, he says, perhaps even three times. Turning right from the main road, we cruise up the Alborz Mountains. "You will see, this car can cope with any climb." An hour later, we are swerving around in a frightening snowstorm at an altitude of nearly twelve thousand feet. Visibility is barely ten yards. Five inches of snow cover the road. Tehran's springlike warmth is a distant memory.

After a four-hour white-knuckle struggle along slippery, spine-chilling abysses, Homayoun lets the car roll down to the coast. Here, the sun returns, and the vegetation is green and lush. Pine trees grow on these humid northern slopes. In Chalus, we hit the coastal road, which follows the shoreline for hundreds of miles. The beach is disappointing. Seaweed, debris, and dead birds rot in the sand. High tides, indicating treacherous currents, break right on the shore. Nearly all the coastal villages have been devoured by ugly modern developments. Detached villas, most of them derelict, cloy the shoreline. Others were built too close to the waves and are now submerged by the rising water level.

"In the old days, things were happening here," Houmayoun says in fluent English. "We partied all night long. The first discos opened here, and the most beautiful girls from Tehran sunbathed on the beach." Today, men and women bathe on the beach in strictly separate sections, and women are not allowed to take off the chador. Homayoun points to a villa in a small pine forest at the beach. "This used to belong to us, that is where I spent my summer holidays as a child."

Houmayoun grew up in northern Tehran, the son of a four-star general in the Iranian army. "We were very wealthy. My sisters and brothers and I had nannies and a servant." As their father was a member of the shah's general staff, two military guards took the children to school every morning. "Sure, not everybody had such a good life as we did back then, but the shah was a good man. At no point did he care as little about the people as the mullahs do today."

We reach Ramsar, once the coast's most exclusive holiday resort. Here, the Middle Eastern jet set partied through the 1970s.

King Hussein of Jordan spent his summer holidays in Ramsar. On a hill above the small town, the splendid hotel where the Shah used to stay comes into view. "I always wanted to work there, as a hotel director," the forty-eight-year-old Homayoun recalled. When he had finished school, his father sent him to London to study hotel management. One day his father took him along to a reception at the shah's palace and the ruler asked the young Homayoun why he would not become an army officer. "I told him that I would rather work in the hotel business. At this, he laughed and promised me that after my studies he would give me a hotel. The problem was that when I returned from London to Iran, the shah was gone." The new rulers imprisoned his father, by then eighty years old, for twelve months. Shortly after his release he died. The family no longer had sufficient funds to pay for the villas and the staff. Homayoun never found a job in hotel management because his family was too well-known and ostracized. "We were once one of the great families—today we are nothing." He laughs, but without any trace of bitterness in his voice.

Dusk is falling as we reach Astara, the border crossing to Azerbaijan. During the entire ten-hour journey through Iran, supposedly a police state, we were not stopped by a single patrol, or forced to pass a single checkpoint. Inside the small border post, an official slams an exit stamp onto my passport. Before dawn, I will have reached Baku to catch the ferry to Turkmenistan, my next and, by all accounts, a very mysterious destination.

Stalin's Disneyland: Turkmenistan

The *Professor Gül*'s two chimneys belch black smoke when the captain orders the boat's engines to go to full power. "All clear," a sailor shouts in Azeri, and after almost a week's delay in Baku I am on my way to Turkmenistan. Baku had lived up to its Persian name of "windy city," as a storm raged over the bay for three days. First the wind blew from the south with a warmth that felt like spring, then overnight the wind shifted northeast, carrying with it from Siberia a bitter cold. Then all was calm for a few early morning hours, and our captain decided to risk the crossing.

Named after an Azeri scientist and about 450 feet in length, the rusty *Professor Gül* serves as a cargo ferry for trucks, tanker cars, and for fifty dollars, foreign passengers. A few dollars buy an upgrade from a worn Pullman seat to a cabin on the upper deck. Though far from spacious, it has a bunk bed, two chairs, a fridge and even a full-fledged bathroom with shower and toilet. A massive lock is attached to the porthole. As the only passenger on the entire ship, I wander through a maze of passageways and staircases until I run into Avaz, the ship's second mate. In his jogging suit and plastic sandals he looks more like a tourist than a sailor. "Only last year we had about five hundred passengers on each trip, most of them traders from Azerbaijan," Avaz recalls. "But then the Turkmen government raised the price of a visa to ninety dollars. Nobody can afford that."

Built in a Yugoslav shipyard in the 1980s, the *Professor Gül* endured a long odyssey through the Black Sea, many Russian canals, and the Volga River to end up in the Caspian Sea. The ship's very high sides are, in the Caspian, a constant liability. "This may work in the calm Mediterranean. But here, the storms are too strong. With every strong gust the ship tilts to the side, which means that we have steer against the wind at full speed—and that is dangerous." When I arrived at the wharf, I saw a locomotive pushing about twenty railcars into the ferry's hull. To prevent the cars from rolling back and forth, the sailors merely placed iron slabs under the wheels.

No sooner has the *Professor Gül* reached the high sea than the wind and waves grow stronger. The restaurant on board has been shut down, but in the galley on the lower deck a rather destitute-looking woman offers to fry a chicken. After dinner, I walk back to the upper deck to smoke a cigarette in the black and starless Caspian night.

It was somewhere on these waters that on July 23, 2001, Azerbaijan and Iran came to the verge of an armed conflict over oil. An Azeri exploratory vessel from Baku operated by BP Amoco had ventured into the southern part of the Caspian Sea to test drill a suspected oil field. Aboard the ship were geologists and engineers. Around midday on July 23, two Iranian fighter jets suddenly roared over their heads and circled above the ship for two hours. An Iranian gunboat appeared. A naval officer radioed the BP vessel's captain to immediately cease all drilling operations and leave Iranian territorial waters. When the Azeri ship did not change its course immediately, the Iranian gunboat repeated its demand, adding that there would not be a third warning. The BP vessel turned around and sailed back to Baku.

"Our people were more than a hundred sea miles away from the Iranian coast," commented BP spokesman Steve Lawrence after the incident. "But the Iranians were armed, there was nothing we could do." BP has played down the incident so as to not put at risk potential future post-sanctions business deals with the country, for the Iranian foreign ministry declared, "If any company carries out any operations in [Iranian territory] the Islamic

Republic will stop their operations and will not do any business or sign any contracts with them in the future."[1]

The Azeri government and American diplomats protested vigorously against this gunboat diplomacy. Relations between Baku and Tehran were already strained because of the very sizable Azeri minority in Northern Iran. Tehran justified the armed intervention on the grounds that the BP vessel had been in a part of the Caspian Sea that Tehran considers part of Iran. "After the Azeris simply ignored all our earlier diplomatic notes, we had to use military means," an Iranian government official said. "Now they have understood that we are serious."

The confrontation raised a much larger question that has never been adequately resolved. The five littoral states—Russia, Kazakhstan, Turkmenistan, Iran, and Azerbaijan—have not come to an agreement on the territorial division of the Caspian Sea. At first sight, the disputed issue is a simple one: is the Caspian Sea a sea or a lake? It would be a rather academic problem if billions of tons of oil were not also at stake. How that oil will be distributed depends on the definition of the world's largest inland body of water. If the Caspian Sea is a lake, each nation would merely control a strip of several nautical miles stretching out from its respective coastline. The large central part of the lake would, however, be international waters whose shipping routes, fish stocks, and natural resources would have to be used communally in a condominium. The states would have to agree on how to develop the oil fields and how to split the profits.

If the Caspian Sea is defined as a sea, however, the entire seabed and surface would then be divided among the countries like a pie. Most legal experts interpret the UN Convention on the Law of the Sea in such a way that has determined the Caspian Sea is not a lake. However, for decades the Soviet Union and Iran have treated these waters differently. Two bilateral treaties stipulate that ships from both countries could freely navigate the entire body of water, and that all resources were to be shared. However, at the time the treaties were signed this clause pertained primarily to fish stocks and not to natural resources such as oil and gas.

Since the collapse of the Soviet Union, the three new independent nations on the Caspian Sea, off whose coasts the greatest
resources happen to lie, no longer feel bound by the old treaties.
With American support, they want to divide the seabed and
its natural riches into five unequal sectors corresponding to the
coastal length of each country. The Russians repeatedly rejected
such a solution until they discovered oil reserves in their own
sector. Moscow has since insisted that only the seabed be divided
and not the surface. That way ships, including naval forces, would
continue to freely navigate the Caspian without encountering armed
border patrol vessels. This would be primarily to the Russians'
advantage as they could easily move their large Caspian fleet close
to the shores of the former Russian territories.

Iran insists on falling back on the old treaties with the Soviet
Union, maintaining that the Caspian Sea is a lake whose natural
resources should be exploited together. Conceding that this would
pose absurd practical problems, the Iranians have claimed a 20 percent share of the Caspian, from the sea bottom to the surface. The
ensuing nautical border that would be created is already being
patrolled by vessels of the Iranian navy. The mullah regime suspects that the United States could use the activities of American
oil companies as a pretext for a military presence, allowing the
U.S. Navy to threaten Iranian coastline no longer only from the Persian Gulf. Tehran's demands conveniently overlook the geographic
fact that Iran's coastal strip is relatively short, entitling the country, according to international law, to a mere 14 percent of the surface. Iran's desired 20 percent share would include many of the
oil fields that for decades had been developed and exploited by
Soviet Azerbaijan.

Iran's gunboat diplomacy with Azerbaijan raises tensions in
a border dispute that could easily escalate into what *The Economist* has called a "scenario for a third world war."[2] Azerbaijan
and Turkmenistan are also locked in a dispute over the distribution of oil resources. The Azeris want the sector boundary to
run in a wide arch to the east, parallel to the bulging Apsheron
peninsula. The Turkmens instead insist on a strictly vertical

borderline, drawn from north to south, through the 750-mile-long sea, allowing it ownership of at least half of all natural resources now claimed by Azerbaijan.

One of the disputed oil fields is the giant BP Amoco-operated Chirag field, estimated to contain up to seven billion barrels of crude oil. The *Professor Gül*'s route leads right past the Chirag gas flare's colossal flame, which is visible from a distance of more than thirty nautical miles. Reminiscent of the great Pharos lighthouse in antiquity, the fire conjures red clouds in the sky and shimmering crests on the waves up to the ship's bow. To the west of Chirag, the lights of Neft Dashlari ("Oily Rocks"), the world's largest offshore oil rig, shimmer in the distance. Constructed in 1949 by Soviet engineers as a city on stilts linked by sixty miles of roads, Neft Dashlari was once considered a marvel of Soviet engineering, the pride of a country that a few years before had stopped the Nazi armies' advance to the Caspian oil fields. Now more than fifty years old, these hopelessly obsolete installations are falling apart like those of Sandy Island off the Baku coastline. Many of the six hundred derricks have sunk into the sea, while accidents claim the lives of many workers.

The next morning, shortly after sunrise, the water is placid off the Turkmen coastline. I have already packed my travel bag to disembark when I hear a loud rattling sound. The *Professor Gül* drops anchor. The crew gathers on the upper deck and starts to play volleyball. To keep the ball from going overboard, a sailor attaches it to the net with a fishing line. "We will have to lie at anchor until tomorrow morning, if not longer," Avaz says. "The Turkmens don't allow us into the port right away. That's how they are. Their president is cross with our president because Azerbaijan nicked all the good oil fields."

Nearly twenty-four hours later, at three o'clock in the morning, we finally sail into the port of Turkmenbashi. Several uniformed men appear on the wharf. Against the blinding glare of spotlights, I can see only faceless silhouettes with guns bulging out from their belts. These are Turkmen border guards. "No fooling around with those guys," Avaz advises me. "Whatever you do, my friend, be humble now. Otherwise you are looking at a very long night."

It took more than four weeks to obtain a visa for Turkmenistan, one of the world's most isolated countries. The embassy in Berlin referred me to an obscure travel agency in southern Germany, the only company authorized to provide a visa support letter. To obtain the letter, I had to book a package holiday, which I then canceled at the last minute. The cost for the four-week tourist visa was $150, a record for this region. Apparently the Turkmens, who only eighty years ago lived as nomads riding horses through the Central Asian steppe, have retained a healthy mistrust of foreigners.

The border guards shove me aside. Only after they have inspected the documents for each and every railcar in the cargo room, which takes an hour and a half, am I permitted to present my passport and disembark.

Turkmenistan is probably the only country in the world where a taxi to the airport is more expensive than the ensuing flight. "No, sir, this is not a mistake. The ticket costs thirty-five manat," affirms the attendant at the Turkmenistan Airways counter at the small airport in Turkmenbashi. For little more than two dollars, I can fly to Ashkhabad, the capital, some five hundred miles away, in a brand new Boeing 757. Many brightly dressed women are on my state-subsidized flight, on their way to sell fruits and fish from the Caspian Sea at the bazaar in Ashkhabad. In the evening, they will return home on the last flight back to Turkmenbashi with a nice net profit, as travel expenses are negligible.

Turkmenistan is often called the new Kuwait on the Caspian Sea. The ex-Soviet desert republic, independent since 1991 and roughly the size of California, sits on prodigious riches. The proven gas reserves of one hundred trillion cubic feet are among the top ten in the world, with the Energy Information Administration estimating possible reserves of up to 260 trillion cubic feet. Add to this the largely untapped oilfields off the Turkmen coast whose size nobody has been able to estimate. Its raw materials make Turkmenistan one of the most valuable prizes in the new Great Game.

There is only one problem: Turkmenistan's president, Saparmurat Nyazov. Better known as Turkmenbashi, the "leader of all Turkmens," as Nyazov has called himself for years, the former head of the Communist Party in Turkmenistan has turned the country into his own personal khanate. In no other former Soviet republic has the Stalinist system survived as authentically as in Turkmenistan. Traveling abroad is impossible for most of the five million Turkmens, and the old KGB police apparatus still exercises, albeit under a slightly different name, absolute control over the population. Appointed lifelong dictator by a rubber-stamp parliament, Nyazov is convinced of his own divinity, and has reinvented his country as a gigantic theme park, with the only theme being himself. Almost every street corner in the capital has multiple portraits of the sixty-year-old stocky man with a soft and somewhat simple face. On some he looks like Burt Reynolds, on others like a genetic blend of Leonid Brezhnev and the German politician Franz-Joseph Strauss. All public buildings are decorated with banners proclaiming the state slogan, *Halk, Watan, Turkmenbashi* ("One People, One Fatherland, One Leader").

"It all reminds you a bit of Kim Il Sung in North Korea but is a lot weirder," says a Western diplomat whom I will call Elizabeth. She accompanies me on a walk through Ashkhabad. A diplomat in Turkmenistan for six years, she starts the tour in the center of town with a triumphal three-pronged arch, boldly combined with a 220-foot victory column. It supports a giant statue of Turkmenbashi himself, made of pure gold. His coat billows in an imaginary wind, and his arms are stretched out. Gazing down on his subjects, Turkmenbashi rotates like a revolving restaurant, making a full turn every twenty-four hours. "That way his gilded countenance always faces the sun—or vice versa," Elizabeth comments sarcastically. In the days that follow, I count no fewer than thirteen statues of Turkmenbashi, likewise all made of gold. The triumphal arch, whose three curved legs make it look like a spaceship, is dedicated to Turkmenistan's neutrality, a political stance close to the ruler's heart. In December 1995, the General Assembly of the UN, urged on by the Turkmen delegates, officially acknowledged in a vote that the Central Asian republic was a neutral country. This status ensured that Turkmenistan remained strictly impartial in the war against the Taliban regime in neighboring Afghanistan. It was the only ex-Soviet republic in Central Asia to reject all American requests for assistance and to not offer any bases to the U.S. Air Force, although it allowed many humanitarian aid missions to cross the border into northern Afghanistan.

Next to the Arch of Neutrality, the dictator has erected a monument to commemorate a catastrophic earthquake in the early hours of October 6, 1948, which in only one minute completely devastated the city. More than 110,000 people, more than one-third of the population, perished. Among the dead were Nyazov's mother and brother. (His father had died in World War II.) As none of his relatives were prepared to take care of the young boy, he grew up in an orphanage. "The fact that he still succeeded in his life must have convinced him that he belongs to the chosen," Elizabeth believes. The monument, almost the size of a small house, suggests this. The earthquake is symbolized by a wild bull bouncing a globe off his horns. Into a gaping abyss falls the dying mother, still holding up with her last ounce of strength the little boy (made of gold, of course); a natural catastrophe as the advent of a savior.

Turkmenbashi's dead family members have also been immortalized in imposing monuments. His mother has the special honor of holding Justitia's scales in front of the palace of justice. The statue is guarded by police who patrol every street corner in Ashkhabad. Opposition is tolerated only in exile but persecutions are rare in Turkmenistan, which is the only country in the region to have abolished the death penalty. "From what we know, under Nyazov there is only one political prisoner in the country, and that guy had the wrong friends," Elizabeth says as she confirms the police state's unexpected humane streak. "Turkmenbashi is not a tyrant. He is more like a child, and a pretty nutty one at that."

We approach the president's palace, whose colossal gilded dome shines in the sunlight. The building was constructed on a small hill to allow limitless amounts of water to cascade down the slope into a moat. A neon green light floods the grounds at night. "A few years ago, this was a residential area but Nyazov had it torn down," recalls Elizabeth. "The residents were told to move to relatives and be proud of their sacrifice for the fatherland." Like all official buildings, the palace's walls are made of white marble imported from Italy. Even the façades of many Soviet-era concrete monstrosities, such as the central post office, have been upgraded with marble slabs.

Obscure anecdotes about Turkmenbashi abound in Ashkhabad. "The other day he must have wondered in his palace if the people really loved him as much as his ministers assured him. So he glued a false black beard to his face and drove to the outskirts of the city to ask common men in the street for their opinion." Needless to say, nobody in Turkmenistan dares to publicly express their true views on political issues. "Even less so if the interviewer arrives in the president's armored, dark Mercedes limousine, and has a false beard dangling off his chin."

That was not the first time that the eccentric dictator drove himself in his car, which he had once received as a gift from Mercedes-Benz. Unlike any other statesman in the world, he refuses on principle to be chauffeured. "The other day a new building in town was officially inaugurated," Elizabeth remembers, trying not to laugh. "The entire diplomatic corps was more or less assembled at the site. Only the president was still missing. And sure enough, there he came, racing up in his Mercedes. He parked it, got out, locked the doors, put the keys in his pocket, sauntered over to us and said merrily, 'All right, let's start the show!'"

Taking a taxi to the edge of town, we pass the new football stadium that, like thousands of other buildings, streets, and the Caspian port town, has been named after the president. On the side of the road, a Turkish company has constructed high-rise buildings with luxury flats that stand empty. "Nobody is going to move in there," Elizabeth remarks. "Turkmens earn an average salary of 50 dollars a month; they cannot afford such flats. Plus, the buildings are not earthquake-proof." The same is true for a dozen luxury hotels that Nyazov had built along one road in expectation of numerous international petroleum businessmen.

We arrive at Turkmenbashi's latest grandiose project, the water fountain park. Although his country is essentially one large desert, water games are Nyazov's greatest obsession. Over several square miles of previously fallow land, labor brigades set up numerous water fountains of all sizes and fantastic designs. Every fountain has animal figures, flamingos, tigers, fish, spewing water. Pebbled paths, lined with palm trees and exotic conifers, crisscross between the fountains. The imported palm trees are wrapped in blankets because the Turkmen winters, with temperatures dropping way below zero, are too chilly for the tender plants. Sprinklers water the newly sown lawns.

The men and women who labor by the hundreds to tend the luxury park seem to lack motivation; most are dressed in rags. "As in the Soviet Union," Elizabeth explains, "nearly all adults in Turkmenistan work for the state. Most of them are employed in the realization of their boss's large-scale projects." Numerous soldiers also work as part of the labor gangs. In Turkmenistan, soldiers can be hired by private people for gardening or for household chores. "Last month, we went to the army and applied for three recruits to help us move our office," Elizabeth says. "We got them."

The site is of pharaonic dimensions. From its center rises what is supposedly the world's largest water fountain, a dark marble pyramid no less impressive than those at Giza. Water cascades down the steps. As we move closer to the grandiose marble block, the roar of the water becomes deafening. "For this spectacle, only drinking water of the best quality must be used," says Elizabeth, shaking her head. "The temperature in Ashkhabad rises to more than 110 degrees in summer, and of course all the water evaporates and there is nothing left for drinking."

In an effort to ease the plight of his hard-working subjects, the dictator has introduced myriad obscure holidays. "The most fun is the day of the melon in autumn," Elizabeth says. "On that day soldiers pile up one big mountain of tens of thousands of melons in the city, and until dark the people can eat as many melons as they can take."

Turkmenbashi also offers spiritual guidance to his people. He recently declared that neither the Koran nor the Bible contained enough moral lessons. So he wrote a religious book and called it *Ruhnama,* or the "answer to all your questions." As Turkmenbashi himself explains, "The never-ending spiritual source for a true Turkmen, who continuously ponders on his spiritual world, who really worries about his well-being, who is self-conscious, alert, and careful about enhancing his intellectual, physical and spiritual capacities, should be the *Ruhnama.*" Every government office has a weekly study hour to discuss its collection of fables and country lore, and the pink-covered book is part of the mandatory curriculum for all schools and universities. The *Ruhnama* has become the centerpiece of the country's education system, while many other disciplines have simply been eliminated.

The authorities have also restricted access to other sources of information, shutting down Ashkhabad's few Internet cafés, cutting off cable television feeds from Russia, and stopping subscriptions to Russian newspapers. Instead, the state television channels broadcast daily *Ruhnama* readings, reminiscent of oriental fairy tales. On a canvas behind a female speaker wearing the traditional Turkmen folk dress, a half-moon shines and falling stars race across a dark sky. The logo of the three state TV channels, inserted in the upper right-hand corner, is a brilliant golden bust of the president.

Cabinet sessions are also regularly televised live, the proceedings reminiscent of a primary school. Before answering Nyazov's questions, his ministers need to stand up. The TV broadcasts are not about democratic transparency, Elizabeth says. "The boss wants to demonstrate to the people what idiots all the other politicians in the country are."

That night, Elizabeth and I get a dramatic taste of Turkmenbashi's methods of rule. We are on our way, on foot, to a restaurant in the center of town. It is dark, and most buildings are floodlit in yellow, blue, and pink, making the capital look like an oriental version of Las Vegas. The streets are deserted, even more so than during the day. I suddenly hear a deep voice and turn around, as it seems to come from somewhere close behind me. Then the voice moves somewhere else. "That is Turkmenbashi," Elizabeth says. "There are loudspeakers that they put everywhere in the city." She walks up to a tree and after a brief search, points at a small Sony speaker that has been fixed in the branches. Thin cables run along the trunk and disappear into the ground. A sound system for the entire center of the city. "For the president to be heard at all times," Elizabeth explains, laughing.

As we cross the large parade ground in front of the presidential palace, Turkmenbashi speaks to his people from a giant video screen on the edge of the square. Apart from us and two military guards, no other subjects have gathered to listen. The ruler, in a dark suit, looks unhappy. His words come at a deliberate and sluggish pace, for after decades of climbing the party career ladder in Moscow, Nyazov still does not speak his native tongue fluently. "Something odd is going on here," Elizabeth says, cause for concern in a city riddled with odd sights.

Nyazov turns to his immediate audience, sitting in rows of chairs before him, and calls a tall and grim-looking man forward. "That is Mohammed Nazarov, the head of the KGB, the most hated man in the country," Elizabeth observes. After what appears to be a robust public humiliation by Nyazov, the secret service general begins to speak himself, his head bowed and his voice shaking. "A self-criticism session! Just like under Stalin," Elizabeth whispers. "The boss has called on Nazarov to publicly criticize himself in front of everyone. That is his end."

We follow the spectacle that reminds me of Russia's show trials in the 1930s, or those during Mao's Cultural Revolution. "He has fired him, live on television," Elizabeth says. "He reproached him that his secret service had meddled too much in people's private lives. That's not bad. That will make Nyazov more popular with the people." The diplomat gets out her phone and calls a colleague at the embassy to discuss this news.

Sometime after my visit, Turkmenbashi renames the days of the week and the months of the year after himself, the *Ruhnama*, his mother, and anything else he likes. Mondays are now called *Turkmenbashi*.

*   *   *

As entertaining as the Turkmen ruler's whimsical antics are, it is very difficult for Western governments and companies to gain political and economic influence in this country of abundant natural resources. Unlike the situation in other key states on the Caspian Sea, such as Kazakhstan and Azerbaijan, foreign investment in Turkmenistan, particularly in the oil and gas sector, is far from encouraged. The president's arbitrary absolutism prevents any clear legal standards of ownership and effective protection from corrupt officials. "This is how the first traders must have felt when they travelled to the court of the emir of Bukhara in the nineteenth century," a British businessman tells me one evening in a bar. Like Elizabeth, he prefers not to be identified for fear of negative consequences. "For example, the Turkmens could simply tear up our existing contracts and expel me."

The only benefactor from the difficulties Western rivals face is Turkmenistan's former colonial overlord Russia. It was only just over a century ago that Tsarist troops defeated the last nomadic bandits of Turkestan in the battle of Geok-Tepe in January 1881. Yet even after the collapse of the Soviet Union, the small country has not ended its dependence on Russia. Turkmenistan, out of necessity, continues to export its main cash product, gas, through the old pipelines to Russia. There are no others except for a small new pipeline to Iran, which hardly reduces the country's dependence on Moscow. Gazprom, the Russian gas giant, has repeatedly and arbitrarily shut down its pipelines, blocking the flow of gas. During the mid-1990s, the Turkmens in response came up with the bold plan to lay a pipeline underneath the Caspian Sea to Azerbaijan, where it would be linked to a pipeline to Turkey. The project was enthusiastically embraced by the American government seeking to free Turkmenistan from Russia's grip, and as in the case of Azerbaijan, the best step toward that goal would be an east-west pipeline avoiding Russia.

The Shell Corporation joined the project and conducted feasibility studies. Shell's director general in Turkmenistan is Pius Cagienard. His office is located in a luxury hotel, which also houses the small embassies of Britain, Germany, and France. "We wanted to do it. The feasibility studies showed that the pipeline would make absolute sense, both technically and commercially," says Cagienard, looking at photographs of the day in 1999 when Shell managers and President Nyazov signed preliminary contracts. "The project became caught up in a geopolitical struggle between the United States and Russia, and Moscow came out on top," the Swiss recalls. "The Russians put so much political pressure on President Nyazov that he no longer dared to offend them by signing a final contract." The opportunity for a second export route was lost, as Turkey has since concluded supply contracts with Iran and Russia. Ironically, the Russian pipeline, named the "Blue Stream," will be laid under the Black Sea to the Turkish coast.

Profiting from Shell's failure, the Russian energy concern Itera—a close partner of the gas giant Gazprom—stepped in. Igor Makarov, Itera's CEO and one of Moscow's powerful oligarchs, grew up in Ashkhabad. In his business dealings, Makarov was able to rely on his long-standing friendship with President Nyazov. In early 2002, the two men agreed that Turkmenistan would deliver 1.4 trillion cubic feet of gas to Itera, through the old northbound pipelines. Makarov is the temporary winner in the scramble for Turkmen gas, and his rise to the top is one of those wondrous careers forged out of post-Soviet transitional chaos.

When the USSR disintegrated in 1991, Makarov started a lucrative trade in food to Turkmenistan. Soon the demand for meat and butter grew so great that Makarov needed loans in order to purchase more products. He turned to some casual acquaintances in Florida who provided venture capital for the upstart business. In 1992, Itera was founded and registered in Jacksonville, Florida. Two years later, the Turkmen government informed Makarov that it would no longer be able to pay cash for future food deliveries. Instead it offered a barter of 142 billion cubic feet of gas. It was an enormous amount, but without value unless Makarov managed to sell it. So he went to the monopolist Gazprom, which, then as now, controlled all gas pipelines in Russia. He asked to be allowed to export the Turkmen gas through the big Drushba ("friendship") pipeline to Europe. After World War II, the Soviets had laid that pipeline to occupied East Germany. As early as the 1980s, in the wake of détente, Drushba began to supply Western European markets and has since become one of Russia's most important sources of hard currency income.

Gazprom's bosses refused Makarov's request but offered another plan. Instead of Western Europe, they would pump his gas to Ukraine. The catch was that Makarov could not expect much in payment from the cash-strapped Ukrainians. Makarov ultimately agreed, because in lieu of paying cash, the Ukrainians could supply food directly to Turkmenistan. Makarov began his trade in gas, and nine years later, the Itera group has expanded into one of the biggest raw material empires in Russia, reporting in 2000 a turnover of $3 billion.

Itera has recently been plagued with allegations of massive fraud. Makarov apparently knew how to develop his first contact with Gazprom's higher echelons into a very profitable relationship. Under the banner of privatization in the 1990s, the gas monopolist handed over to Itera several production facilities worth hundreds of millions of dollars. Among them was the Siberian gas field of Achimovsk, with an estimated 12.5 trillion cubic feet of gas. For his 49 percent share in Achimovsk, Makarov did not pay the market price of $500 million but the ludicrous sum of $265,270. Market observers believe that Gazprom executives secretly own Itera shares, and if these allegations trigger criminal charges, the billion-dollar deal with Turkmenistan could fall apart.

Before my journey to Turkmenistan, I flew to Moscow to meet with Vladimir Martynenko, a member of the Itera board and Makarov's right-hand man. A dynamic dark-haired man with a nice tan, the forty-nine-year-old had returned to Russia the night before from an energy conference in Houston. "Everybody who is anybody in the energy business was there," Martynenko recalled. "Good deals were made."

Martynenko refused to comment on the corruption charges against Itera, but that did not stop him from fetching a long black guitar case and pulling out a red Rickenbacker electric guitar. "John Lennon once played on it," he said in awe. "I bought it at an auction in Houston, for very little money." Since the 1960s, when he served as a Soviet diplomat in China and India, Martynenko has been a self-professed rock fan and aspiring guitarist. Hooking up to an amplifier, he played fairly decent Bob Marley and Jimi Hendrix covers for the next fifteen minutes.

After reluctantly agreeing to continue our interview, he commented on the gas deal with the Turkmens: "We are very satisfied that we have come to an agreement. We are planning great investments in Turkmenistan." His upbeat mood was justified. At $43 per ton of gas Itera pays, compared to the common European price of $100, a dirt-cheap rate, to be remitted in part with natural produce. Was it an advantage for Itera that the Turkmens had no alternative to the Russian pipelines, I ask. "No, not at all," Martynenko countered. "This is a fair price, everybody is happy. We are not taking advantage of the pipeline situation." No political obstacles, he maintained, had caused the alternative plan of a trans–Caspian pipeline to go nowhere. "The Russian government did not exert pressure at all; the blame for the pipeline's failure is only on the Azeris." Martynenko believed Baku boycotted the pipeline and would not allow enough gas to transit the country to make it profitable. Washington exerted pressure, he said, as did Moscow. "But it was not enough to make the Azeris cave in. That is how the project died," Martynenko insisted. Escorting me out to the corridor, he casually remarked that Itera acted as a sponsor for the national karate team. "Three of our security guards at the exit are world champions in karate—be careful on your way out."

Buoyed by Itera's success, Russian President Putin has suggested that Turkmenistan and other ex–Soviet states join Russia in a "Eurasian alliance of gas producers." Similar to OPEC, this gas cartel would set production quotas and fix prices. Market observers see this proposal as an attempt by Moscow to control potential competitors in the "near abroad." Russia, the world's biggest gas producer, also needs the Central Asian states as suppliers because it already has difficulties fulfilling its supply commitments to Europe.

The Central Asians have so far reacted cautiously to the cartel proposal, viewing it as a ploy to draw them back into the Russian orbit. Despite the failure of the trans–Caspian pipeline project, the Turkmens still hold out hope for a second big export route for their gas: through Afghanistan. The idea, which has far-reaching geopolitical implications for Central Asia, is not new. As early as the mid-1990s, the Argentine energy company Bridas and later the American oil corporation Unocal had planned to build two pipelines from Turkmen oil and gas fields through Afghanistan to Pakistan. Both rival companies hoped to annually supply about seven hundred billion cubic feet of gas to a country in desperate need of energy resources. Benazir Bhutto, the Pakistani prime minister at the time, traveled on many occasions to Ashkhabad and personally lobbied for the project. Enthusiastically embracing the idea, President Nyazov signed an agreement with Unocal managers in New York City on October 21, 1995. While no Afghan had been invited to the ceremony, former U.S. Secretary of State Henry Kissinger was present, acting as an adviser to Unocal.

The American government was informed of Unocal's plans and it supported them. In Afghanistan, the civil war had entered its sixteenth year, but the Taliban troops were on the advance and seemed finally posed to pacify the country, with massive support from the American allies Pakistan and Saudi Arabia. When the radical Islamists took Kabul in 1996, the Clinton administration stated that this would lead to stability in the Hindu Kush. Robin Raphael, assistant secretary of state for Southeast Asian affairs, said at a congressional hearing that the Taliban represented a peaceful political process. The Clinton administration's primary interest was to use the anti-Shia Taliban further to isolate Iran and contain its influence in the region.

With the chances of pipelines being built through a Taliban-controlled corridor from Herat to Kandahar rising, Unocal trained hundreds of Afghans in a Kandahar school to construct and operate a pipeline. In February and November 1997, two Taliban delegations accepted an invitation by Unocal and traveled to Washington and Houston for talks with government representatives and Unocal executives. At Unocal's expense, the mullahs were accommodated in a five-star hotel and visited supermarkets, the zoo, and

NASA headquarters.[3] High-ranking Unocal managers also repeatedly traveled, along with Turkmen government officials, to war-ravaged Afghanistan to meet with the Taliban and their Northern Alliance enemies and to gain their support for the pipeline project.

"We told both sides that we would supply gas to the transit towns, build schools, and give jobs to their people, and the Afghans were impressed," Gozchmurad Nazdianov remembers. The Turkmen oil minister from 1994 to 1998 met with me in Ashkhabad to talk about the Afghan pipeline. In charge of the project from its inception, Nazdianov negotiated the contract with Unocal and participated in each of the sensitive missions to Afghanistan, which lies just south of Turkmenistan. "The Afghanistan pipeline was a great idea. All feasibility studies conducted by Unocal show this," he says, his enthusiasm for the project apparent. "The pipeline was cheap and short. It would have long been built if it were not for that crazy civil war." As long as fighting continued, Unocal bosses were well aware that no bank in the world would finance a loan for the project.

Nazdianov and the oil managers, among them Unocal Vice President Marty Miller, flew to the Hindu Kush on four separate occasions. The plane was provided by the United Nations, with all costs and expenses paid by Unocal. "Actually, we were not going on mere business trips anymore, but rather on peace missions," Nazdianov says. "We made it clear to both parties in the war that for the pipeline to be built they would have to make peace first." As long as the Taliban were not recognized by the West as a legitimate government, Unocal was unable to secure loans from international financial institutions.

Both the ruling Taliban and the Northern Alliance were very much interested in the pipeline project and sent high-ranking ministers to receive the Unocal managers. The radical Islamist Taliban treated the Americans cordially even though Americans were officially condemned as infidels. "We did not discuss religion. If big money comes into play, even Koran students quickly forget about their faith," Nazdianov grins. The Taliban, according to the former oil minister, demonstrated a well-honed business sense and immediately started negotiating transit fees. In their negotiations, they were constantly in touch with their leader, Mullah Omar, via satellite phone. "They quickly realized the enormous profits they could make from the pipeline. We offered them $250 million per year in transit fees," he says, adding that he knew of no direct bribes being offered to the Taliban.

The anti–Taliban forces initially supported the pipeline project, too. Led by the Tajik General Ahmed Shah Massoud and viewing themselves as the country's legitimate government, they appointed a special minister for energy, the notorious Uzbek General Rashid Dostum. Nazdianov had known him since the Soviet occupation of Afghanistan in the 1980s when Dostum had fought with the Russians as a Communist officer. In 1992 he betrayed the pro–Moscow regime in Kabul and defected to the mujahideen. From his northern stronghold of Mazar-e-Sharif, he rose to become one of the country's most powerful warlords during the civil war, and was feared for his brutality.

"The Northern Alliance, too, knew exactly what this business deal was about," Nazdianov recalls. "Compared to the Taliban there was only one difference in the negotiations with General Dostum. All night long, we drank vodka with him." It helped that Dostum also spoke fluent Turkmen. Unocal's managers were less favorably impressed with the warlord. "Dostum is a big and strong man, and all his fighters were armed to the teeth. That scared the Americans," Nazdianov remembers, shaking with laughter. "The Unocal guys would not touch a single glass of vodka but sat frightened in a corner. They thought they were surrounded by bandits."

Yet all of Unocal's efforts were in vain. The Northern Alliance refused to make peace with the Taliban for the sake of the pipeline. Standing behind this decision were the Northern Alliance's powerful supporters, Russia, India, and Iran. All three countries had reasons for trying to prevent the Unocal pipeline. Moscow had no interest in seeing the Turkmens obtaining an export alternative to the Russian pipelines. That is why Unocal failed in its attempts to enlist Gazprom's support for the Afghan project. India did not want its enemy Pakistan to extend its influence in the region, and Iran sought to export gas to Pakistan itself. With the help of British companies, Tehran plans to build a $3 billion 850-mile pipeline from the South Pars field in the Persian Gulf to the Pakistani port city of Karachi; this would be in direct competition to the Afghan pipeline. Afghanistan's neighboring countries ruthlessly waged their struggles of interest on the backs of the Afghans so that in late 1998, UN Secretary General Kofi Annan warned of a "deeper regionalization of the conflict," in which Afghanistan would be degraded to a mere "stage for a new version of the Great Game."

Ultimately, the Unocal delegation came away with nothing. Neither side in the war was ready for peace, and the fighting raged on. During their last visit to Afghanistan, the joint Turkmen/Unocal delegation came under fire at Kabul airport. Unocal also came under attack at home. After vigorous protests by American feminist groups against the oppression of women in Afghanistan, the U.S. government sought to distance itself from the Taliban regime and Unocal's pipeline plans. Unocal abandoned the project entirely when, in August 1998, the United States attacked Osama bin Laden's Afghan training camps with Cruise missiles, retaliating for the Al Qaeda bomb blasts at U.S. embassies in Kenya and Tanzania. Nazdianov remains disappointed. "We were devastated. We tried to convince other companies such as Shell and Elf Aquitaine to take the lead in the consortium. They were interested but without American support and peace in Afghanistan it could not work." Nazdianov himself had also failed, and that same year Turkmenbashi fired him as oil minister. Today, Nazdianov works as a professor of Russian language at the University of Ashkhabad.

In hopes of one day seeing the pipeline built, the Turkmen government maintained relations with both sides in the Afghan civil war, the only ex–Soviet Central Asian republics to do so. Now with the American victory over the Taliban regime, the Afghan pipeline corridor has been opened up again. The project is once again gaining political momentum. At a state visit to Turkmenistan in early March 2002, Afghan President Hamid Karzai discussed reviving the pipeline plans with Nyazov. Ex-minister Nazdianov, who was present at the talks, is enthusiastic about the pipeline's future. "Everybody agreed that the pipeline would easily be feasible now." So far, no new investor has contacted the Turkmen government. "But as soon as the U.S. troops have brought the situation in Afghanistan under control and peace exists," Nazdianov says, "the oil companies won't be slow in coming forward."

While its oil and gas wealth allows Turkmenistan to preserve its neutrality in the Great Game between the United States and its rivals, the war in Afghanistan dramatically forced Turkmenistan's three Central Asian neighbors in the east to take sides.

The Yankees Arrive:
Uzbekistan and Kyrgyzstan

I n the early dawn of October 6, 2001, a few hours before the first American bombs fall on Afghanistan, a huge black plane is seen in the sky some eighty miles north of the Afghan border. It lands at Chanabad, a derelict airbase in the desolate steppes of Uzbekistan. The inhabitants of the nearby small town of Karshi immediately suspect that the plane is not one of the ancient Soviet Antonovs that routinely roar over their houses. It is a U.S. Air Force C-131 transport plane, the first of hundreds to fly in to Uzbekistan over the coming days and weeks. The rumors of the past week are true: The Yankees are here.

Aboard the planes are two thousand elite infantrymen of the Tenth Mountain Division, New York, as well as special forces from Fort Knox, Kentucky. Their official task is to fly humanitarian missions over Afghanistan and to rescue any downed U.S. pilots. For this, the Uzbek government has put Chanabad, one of the biggest Soviet airbases during the war against Afghanistan, at the coalition forces' disposal. The infantrymen are the first American troops to be deployed on the territory of the former Soviet Union, ten years after the end of the Cold War.

Three days after the first American plane's arrival, I attempt to get from Karshi to Chanabad by taxi, but Uzbek soldiers block the way. They strictly enforce a six-mile no-go zone that they have created around the base. Heavily armed special units of the Interior Ministry block all access routes to Chanabad, which lies just out of sight in a depression of the steppe. A few international journalists wait around at the outer checkpoint where the Uzbeks have piled up oil drums and barriers to create insurmountable obstacles. The day before, three reporters who ventured too close to the base were detained and taken away. My CNN colleagues are particularly disappointed: they had taken access to the U.S. military base for granted. The TV crew had even gone through the trouble of bringing in an expensive satellite dish for live broadcasts.

"Just turn around and get out of here," I am told when I ask an Uzbek soldier if anyone is getting onto the base. "There are no Americans around, anywhere." At that moment, another U.S. Air Force Hercules transport plane roars up from the depression behind us, but the Uzbek guard's poker face remains intact.

The locals in Karshi are equally mystified by what is going on at the base. Their only clues are, literally, up in the air. Two men in a teahouse tell me that helicopters, possibly Chinooks or Black Hawks, had taken off for the first time from Chanabad on the day before. "The pilots were doing test flights," one assumes. The men do not know what the mysterious base looks like. "For years nobody from here has been allowed to go there." Locals were banned after an arsonist burned down half of the base in the early 1990s. "Now there are no jobs available anymore, not even in the canteen or in cleaning. It is all done by the military personnel." Security measures are so strict that Uzbek civilians, hired by the Americans as interpreters, are not allowed to leave the base. Only one young translator from Tashkent, whom I track down later, has quit his job after two weeks because his wife is expecting a baby. He was released after he promised not to divulge any details of military activities at the base. He keeps his word—almost. "All I can say is this: The Americans are settling in as if they intended to stay for a very long time."

Stationing United States troops and those of its allies in former Soviet Central Asia has ushered in a dramatic fresh chapter in the region's new Great Game. The Americans' coup signified arguably the most amazing *renversement d'alliance* since the end of the Cold War. Ten years after the collapse of the Soviet Union, its former constitutive republics Uzbekistan and Kyrgyzstan, and to a lesser degree Kazakhstan and Tajikistan, have made a serious effort to extract themselves from Russia while moving under the protective umbrella of the United States. Washington's search for allies after September 11, 2001 offered them an ideal opportunity. By the end of that month, a close succession of high-ranking U.S. diplomats, military officers, and finally Secretary of Defense Donald Rumsfeld flew to the Uzbek capital of Tashkent to meet with the government behind closed doors. Both sides refused to disclose what these talks were about, well aware that there was an invisible third participant sitting with them at the negotiating table—Russian President Vladimir Putin. There was one issue on the minds of all diplomats in the region: Will Russia allow significant military cooperation between the United States and the ex-Soviet republics?

The first signals from Moscow were not promising. It would not be necessary for a campaign in Afghanistan to send American troops to Central Asia, declared Minister of Defense Sergei Ivanov. While other influential Russian politicians made comments along similar lines, Putin dispatched a special envoy to the region's capitals for urgent consultations. The Russians realized that too dominant a posture might push the Central Asian republics even further into the Americans' arms, so the explosive issue was settled at the highest level, in a direct phone call between Putin and President Bush.

Few details of their conversation leaked out, but insiders described the mood as very constructive. Bush acknowledged that Putin had been the first foreign statesman to offer his condolences on September 11. For his part, Putin knew that Moscow could no longer afford to be seen as uncooperative in Central Asia, and realized that Russia had much to gain from a joint war against terrorists. The economically crippled country had long been struggling to stem by itself the rising tide of both the illicit Afghan drug trade and radical Islamic groups in Russia's soft southern underbelly. Having the world's only remaining superpower offer to take over that task made things easier for Putin. He also counted on the West for viewing Chechen separatists as terrorists from then on, along with ignoring Russian forces' outrageous violations of human rights.

A few days after that Bush-Putin phone call, the Uzbek government announced it would open its airspace to the U.S. Air Force and put military bases at its disposal. Both governments signed a classified agreement. Similar offers by all of Uzbekistan's neighbors followed over the next days and weeks, without triggering a single official objection from Moscow.

Long before September 11, 2001, officials in Washington had begun to see the ex-Soviet republics in Central Asia as ideal allies in the struggle against terrorists in Afghanistan and its neighboring countries. As early as the autumn of 1997, then again in September 2000, American and other NATO troops took part in joint military exercises in Kazakhstan under the auspices of NATO's Partnership for Peace program, which included many CIS states. A small Russian contingent was invited to join, stemming any potential protests from Moscow. As part of these exercises, some American bombers flew to the war games directly from the United States. With midair refueling, the planes did not need to land anywhere along the way, allowing Washington to demonstrate to the Central Asian countries that it was able at any time to mount a military defense of its interests and those of its allies. In February 2001, American forces made another appearance, this time for a special antiterror exercise in Kyrgyzstan.

When only several months later the Pentagon mobilized its war machine after the attacks in New York and Washington, it was left with little choice for attack bases but the ex-Soviet republics. America's traditional partners in the region bristled at the thought of supporting an American campaign against a Muslim country. Saudi Arabia and Egypt, in particular, fearing political unrest at home, refused to let any American warplanes take off from their territory for combat missions in Afghanistan. Pakistan, whose secret service helped to create and later supported the Taliban, also appeared at first as a wholly unsuitable base for U.S. troops. On a daily basis, violent anti-American protests by radical Islamic groups broke out in various Pakistani cities. The country's military dictator Pervez Musharraf's official renunciation of his support for the Taliban offered little reassurance, for this overnight foreign policy about-face only increased the popular pressure on the regime. The Bush administration had good reason to worry that its troops would land directly inside enemy territory.

In contrast, no such fears existed in Uzbekistan. The country is firmly under the iron control of dictator Islam Karimov. Like nearly all presidents in the region, Karimov was the head of the republic's communist party until 1991. When the ossified system collapsed, the Uzbek transformed himself overnight into a national patriot in order to hold on to his power. So far, this strategy has worked extremely well. Any opposition is either in prison or underground, the parliament rubber-stamps all laws, and the media are strictly controlled. Recently, Karimov delayed presidential elections on the grounds that Uzbeks had other worries than politics. Few sectors of the country's ailing economy have been privatized. Uzbekistan ranks at the top in the world in only one area: human rights violations. Karimov has chosen one of history's worst mass murderers as the new national figure for his police state, Timur Lenk, also known as Tamerlane. In every Uzbek town, pompous equestrian statues of the medieval emir have replaced the old busts of Marx and Lenin. His name "Timur the Lame," rather unusual for a ruler, dates back to a leg injury that Tamerlane is said to have sustained in his early days as a horse thief. Despite his physical handicap, this last great nomadic ruler of the Central Asian plains mounted thirty-five campaigns from 1370 to 1405 and succeeded in building an empire stretching from present-day Egypt to the Great Wall of China. His cavalry evoked fear and horror wherever they rode because Tamerlane was extraordinarily ruthless. Like his predecessor Genghis Khan two centuries before, he had countless towns burned down and more than a million people massacred. Many more were maimed, raped, and enslaved. After a battle, Tamerlane had the gruesome habit of ordering the skulls of his victims to be piled up in huge pyramids.

Tamerlane was also known as a pious Muslim and a promoter of art. In his capital, Samarkand, now in Uzbekistan, he commissioned some of the most spectacular Islamic architecture ever built, such as the splendid Registan Square. Tamerlane is not only morally questionable as a role model, but he was not even Uzbek, but a descendant of Mongols and Tajiks who, in fact, often mocked the Uzbek people. Evidence of this could be found in some of Tamerlane's remaining letters until Karimov ordered them to be destroyed.

Uzbekistan's terrible human rights record is unlikely to have been of any consequence in the autumn of 2001, as U.S. forces were faced with the challenge of positioning troops close to the Afghan borders. An alliance with Uzbekistan made strategic and diplomatic sense. As early as the mid-1990s the United States began establishing a special relationship with Tashkent. Trade between the two countries increased eightfold between 1995 and 1997, with Uzbekistan being the world's second largest producer of cotton and the fourth largest gold producer. The Pentagon has also confirmed that in the summer of 1999, Green Berets units went to Central Asia to train Uzbek officers and special forces. The eighty-thousand-strong Uzbek army is the biggest in the region.

Uzbekistan's strength reflects the leading role the country claims in Central Asia. Its population of twenty-five million far exceeds second-ranking Kazakhstan's fifteen million. The rivalry between these two countries over leadership in the region leads each to look for powerful partners. Uzbekistan's relations with Russia have deteriorated further than those of any other Central Asian country. Apart from neutral Turkmenistan, Uzbekistan is the only republic not to renew its membership in the CIS security pact.

Ten years ago, an equal number of Russians and Uzbeks lived among Tashkent's two million inhabitants. Now the Slavs constitute only a small minority in the country, and the government has replaced the Cyrillic alphabet with Latin letters. Since the clan-minded Uzbeks increasingly distribute jobs and positions of power among themselves, many ethnic Russians have choosen to emigrate. The only place mass gatherings of people can be witnessed in Uzbekistan is in front of the Russian embassy in Tashkent, where ethnic Russians line up to obtain visas, though in this regard Uzbekistan is by no means unique. Enormous migrations are taking place in all Caucasian and Central Asian countries. Although this mass exodus has so far been nonviolent, the Slavs' fate is reminiscent of the French inhabitants of Algeria in the early 1960s.

"What we are going through is a painless genocide," a Russian woman in Tashkent once told me.

Aside from Uzbekistan's relative independence from Moscow, the country was attractive as a U.S. military base by virtue of the fact that there has never been a single political demonstration under Karimov's rule. Anti–American protests were anyway not likely because unlike the millions of ethnic Pashtun Pakistanis, hardly any Uzbeks saw the predominantly Pashtun Taliban as anything other than godless and dangerous criminals. This was especially true for the ethnic Uzbeks in northern Afghanistan who were sworn enemies of the southern Afghan Taliban. The notorious Uzbek general Rashid Dostum, whose power base lay in the northern Afghan town of Mazar-e-Sharif, for years enjoyed financial and covert military support from Tashkent.

Religiously motivated solidarity with Afghan Muslims would be hard to find among Uzbeks. While mosques have appeared all across the country since the end of Soviet rule, and some underground Muslim movements, such as Hizb ut-Tahrir, are gaining in popularity, seventy years of atheist policies have left an indelible mark in Uzbekistan. Muslim vows of abstinence have yet to make a dent among vodka drinkers, and many women in Tashkent wear no veils but favor makeup and miniskirts. "The Taliban would have to work hard to make us quit our bad habits," a taxi driver in the capital once put it to me.

The only serious threat to American troops is the Islamic Movement of Uzbekistan (IMU). With supposed ties to Al Qaeda, the IMU has in the past operated from hidden bases in the mountains of Tajikistan. Ravaged by a civil war in the 1990s, Uzbekistan's impoverished neighbor provided an ideal base for terrorists. Central Asian dictators, most of all Karimov, have pointed to the chaos in Tajikistan in order to justify their own iron-fisted rule. No regime allows any Islamic party to associate openly.

The IMU was founded and led by the infamous warlord Juma Namangani from the Fergana Valley, Central Asia's most densely populated and ethnically diverse hotbed, where the borders of Uzbekistan, Tajikistan, and Kyrgyzstan meet in a convoluted way. Little is known about Namangani, who has refused to be interviewed or have his picture taken. According to associates, Namangani rediscovered his Muslim roots during the 1980s while fighting in Afghanistan as a Soviet Army conscript. He later founded the IMU, which is blamed for a series of bomb attacks that rocked Tashkent in February 1999. Dozens lost their lives, and Karimov himself barely escaped assassination. A year later, Namangani traveled to southern Afghanistan, where he met with Taliban leader Mullah Omar and Osama bin Laden to obtain from them money and military supplies. The IMU, by then developing into a pan-Islamic force, was also heavily involved in the smuggling of Afghan opium through Tajikistan. Funded and equipped by Al Qaeda, Namangani's guerrilla troops launched several incursions into Uzbekistan and Kyrgyzstan in 2000, killing more than fifty soldiers in both countries. The IMU then moved to bases in the Afghan cities of Mazar-e-Sharif and Kunduz, assisting the Taliban in their war with the Northern Alliance. After the September 11 attacks, Mullah Omar appointed Namangani commander of the 055 Brigade of foreign Taliban fighters. He was fatally wounded in late November when American warplanes attacked a convoy near Kunduz. The IMU militants who survived are suspected of regrouping in the Afghan border regions.

When the IMU launched its first attacks, the Uzbek regime struck back by arresting thousands of alleged terrorists, many of them innocent citizens, who were then arbitrarily sentenced to long prison terms or death. Human rights organizations have reported horrific conditions in Uzbek jails, where prisoners are systematically tortured to death. Justifying his brutal crackdown against suspected terrorists, President Karimov once said in the Uzbek parliament, "Such people must be shot in the head. If necessary, I will shoot them myself."

Muslims are not the only ones singled out for persecution. As the post-Soviet renaissance of Islam appears to threaten the secular establishment, authorities have severely restricted freedom of religion. In May 1998, the Uzbek rubber-stamp parliament passed the Law on Freedom of Conscience and Religious Organizations, which radically curtailed the freedom of worship. Today, all Muslim organizations and mosques have to be registered, and imams require a government-issued work permit. Pious Muslims who pray outside the state-sanctioned mosques and wear long beards, traditional turbans, or the *hijab,* risk arrest and harassment by the police. The regime's across-the-board repression has done little to stamp out Islamic militancy, and is more likely attracting more recruits.

The United States has condemned Karimov's totalitarian methods in the past. Pointing to Uzbekistan's abysmal human rights record, the Clinton administration rejected Uzbek pleas for more economic assistance. Intense international pressure led the Karimov regime to free thousands of prisoners in an amnesty on the tenth anniversary of Uzbek independence on September 1, 2001. Just ten days later, however, the new need for an alliance led to a radical erosion of previous American policy. The U.S. Department of State quietly removed Uzbekistan from its annual list of countries where freedom of religion is under threat. At the same time, the Bush administration quadrupled its economic and military aid to a total of $220 million in 2002, not including the estimated one hundred million dollars of rent to be paid for the Chanabad airbase.[1] This largesse is a clear sign that the Bush administration conveniently ignores Uzbekistan's human rights abuses. As the writer Ahmed Rashid has pointed out, "Uzbekistan is using its acceptability within the Western alliance as a means to intensify repression against its own people."[2]

On the evening of October 6, 2001, American air strikes against Taliban and Al Qaeda positions begin. CNN shows only blurred green night vision images similar to those used to document the American attack on Baghdad in January 1991. In a speech to the nation, President Bush announces a long war against terror. The next day, I drive down to the southern town of Termez, right on the Uzbek border with Afghanistan. The journey through the flat Uzbek steppe is long and tedious. On the road, the Uzbek army has set up several checkpoints. The soldiers, dressed in patchy desert camouflage and armed to the teeth, frisk every driver and examine their car trunks. A most-wanted list is fixed to a pole with mug shots of about fifty sinister-looking and mostly dark-bearded suspected IMU terrorists. A short distance away on a wall is one of the countless and omnipresent propaganda banners extolling, in a quote from President Karimov, the stability and peace in independent Uzbekistan.

We reach the shore of the Amu Darya River that marks the present-day border with Afghanistan. A half-mile wide at this point, the ancient Oxus River flows sluggishly. After years of drought in the region, the water level is very low. In 1888, the future Lord Curzon, then still a twenty-nine-year-old Tory parliamentarian, undertook an adventurous journey straight through the heartland of the Great Game. When he arrived at the fabled Oxus River, he wrote excitedly: "There in the moonlight gleamed before us the broad bosom of the mighty river that from the glaciers of the Pamir rolls its 1,500 miles of current down to the Aral Sea."[3]

Along the riverbed, women in garish headscarves pick cotton, Uzbekistan's main export product. From tall watchtowers, soldiers look over at the Afghan shore. In the haze, I make out the contours of an old factory. The situation is calm but tense. A few days earlier, the Taliban regime threatened its northern neighbor with an attack, supposedly moving eight thousand fighters to the border. Tashkent responded by putting its army in a state of alert.

The only way to cross the Amu Darya is via the famous Friendship Bridge. It was across this steel bridge that Soviet tanks and troops invaded Afghanistan on Christmas 1979, only to cross it again in defeat ten years later. The border crossing has been closed for years to keep out the chaos of the Afghan civil war. For refugees it is virtually impossible to sneak across the border at this point. Over the previous days, additional concrete slabs and armed vehicles have been moved to the bridge to block it. "We have orders to let nobody across the river," a border guard says.

We drive into town, an unattractive settlement of low-rise apartment blocks. In a teahouse not far from the classically Soviet "red square," a group of old men sit and discuss the outbreak of the war. They report that on previous nights they heard several explosions beyond the river, probably from the town of Mazar-e-

Sharif, some twenty-five miles south of Termez. The sounds of battle there are nothing new for Termez's twenty thousand inhabitants because the Taliban and the Northern Alliance have been fighting over this strategically important region for years.

"But last night, the booms were louder than usual. That must have been Cruise missiles," says one of the men. His gaze falls on the walls of the town's garrison, where a dozen rusting tanks and artillery pieces from the first Afghan war have been put on display. Their barrels are directed straight at passersby who hurry past. "Hopefully, the noise will always stay that far away."

In the big, blue-tiled mosque of Termez, hundreds of people have gathered for afternoon prayers. Despite the official ban, the men wear *tupetaika* caps and heavy caftans, and the women's veils are embroidered with flowers. The imam, Sheikh Abdullah Hafiz, asks the congregation to pray for peace. His white turban and *chapan* robe complement his long snow-white beard. After the prayers, he steps out onto the courtyard in front of the mosque. In a gesture of reverence, many believers bow to the mullah.

A few days before, he had returned from an urgent meeting with other national Muslim leaders in Tashkent. "We are very upset about the war," says Sheikh Abdullah while two police officers on either side of him crane their heads and listen attentively. Cautiously the cleric expresses his congregation's feelings about the American attacks on Afghanistan: "It is necessary to fight terrorists, but to kill innocent civilians, women and children, is a terrible sin. It is very difficult at the moment not to feel for our Afghan brothers." The officers frown but keep quiet. Their authority seems limited around here. As in the Fergana Valley, Islam has seen a strong renaissance in southern Uzbekistan since the end of Soviet dictatorship. "In the old days, we had two mosques and about two hundred practising Muslims in the Termez region—now we number about one hundred thousand and we worship in seventy-six mosques," Sheikh Abdullah says proudly.

How do strict Muslims in Uzbekistan view the American military deployment in their country? In search of answers I drive to Bukhara, the once fabled town on the Great Silk Road, the main route for traders' caravans on the way between Europe and China in the Middle Ages. In the nineteenth century, the emirs of Bukhara ruled over a vast independent khanate, a terra incognita separating the imperial armies of Russia and Great Britain. Agents of both sides undertook dangerous journeys to the town, showering Emir Nasrullah with gifts and promises in an unsuccessful effort to lure him into their fold. The ruthless ruler detained the British officers Colonel Charles Stoddart and Captain Arthur Conolly, both seasoned veterans of the Great Game, in a vermin-infested pit for years. On a June morning in 1842, the two Englishmen were beheaded on the square in front of the Arc, the emir's citadel, but not before they had been forced to dig their own graves. Their execution, one of the darkest chapters of the Great Game, triggered no retribution. For the shocked British Empire, Bukhara remained beyond reach, while it would take another twenty-five years for Russian troops to conquer the town.

From the Arc I walk through the restored but eerily deserted small streets of the old town. As Bukhara is theoretically only a three-hour car drive from Taliban positions, the tourists have vanished. Even the carpet dealers around the splendid Kalyan minaret have packed up their wares. In the old days, not only the muezzins but also the emir's henchmen used the tower. On his journey through the town in 1888, Lord Curzon witnessed an unusual execution. "The public crier proclaims aloud the guilt of the condemned man and the avenging justice of the sovereign. The culprit is then hurled from the summit and, spinning through the air, is dashed to pieces on the hard ground at the base."[4]

Across the square from the minaret is the façade, richly decorated with majolica mosaics, of the famous Mir-Arab Madrassa, the oldest and most prestigious Koran school in Central Asia. Its director has permitted me to spend a day with the students.

When Asadullah closes his Koran, he looks relieved. Class is over. Hurriedly, the nineteen-year-old and his fellow students tie thin cords around their books and notepads, briefly bow their heads to the teacher and rush out through the low door of their classroom. "It is important to read the words of the Prophet," says Asadullah as he walks out onto the sunny courtyard. "But there are other things in life, too." Thus, Asadullah's conversation with his friends during their lunch break, in the shade of the sixteenth-century azure blue domes, is not entirely pious, least of all the jokes about the corpulent female kitchen helper who is the only woman in the building.

The neat-looking young men in their white shirts, black jackets and traditional *tupi* caps seem a world apart from the wild-eyed Koran students in neighboring Afghanistan who, if the television images are to be believed, spent their days madly reciting Koran verses. "No, no. We are different. What we are learning over here is a loving Islam," says Asadullah, stroking his thick dark hair. "We do not prepare for the jihad—just for our exams." Although only 150 miles south of Bukhara bombs and missiles rain down on the neighboring country, the young Uzbek Muslims have little sympathy with the besieged regime of the Taliban, graduates of fundamentalist Koran schools in Pakistan. "We have nothing in common with them. The Taliban are not true Muslims but terrorists," Asadullah claims, in politically correct post–September 11 language, but with obvious conviction.

Founded in the early sixteenth century, the Mir-Arab Madrassa was the only Muslim school in the entire Soviet Union that the communist rulers were unable to shut down for any extended period of time. It was only under Stalin when its doors remained closed from 1930 till 1946. Upon reopening, the Mir-Arab resumed churning out the red empire's Muslim elite, including nearly all of its leading imams and mullahs. The communists approved none of the other *madrassas,* which numbered fifty in Bukhara alone. In a typical Soviet move, the grandiose Kalyan mosque opposite the Mir-Arab, in which up to ten thousand worshipers used to pray before the proletarian revolution, was transformed into a warehouse. Even under the emphatically secular Karimov regime, only ten state *madrassas* have been allowed to reopen, while all independent schools and mosques remain banned. Behind the thick walls of Mir-Arab, about 150 young men undergo an elite four-year training program. Inside the tiny ground-floor classrooms, located immediately underneath their Spartan sleeping areas, they study the classic disciplines of Arabic, rhetoric, logic, and the Koran, but also secular subjects such as natural sciences, geography, and

English. The school's administration has also set up a modern language lab, equipped with recording gear and headsets.

"If we taught them nothing but religion, as we used to in the old days, the boys would become ignorant robots, like the Koran students in Afghanistan," says Mullah Muhiddin Namonov, Mir-Arab's headmaster. His students observe the required five daily prayer sessions in the college's mosque, but Namonov stresses, "Religion has to adapt to modern times and keep up with scientific progress." In his dark suit, the clean-shaven thirty-five-year-old himself cuts a rather secular figure. His office is equipped with a state-of-the-art computer and television set, complete with satellite dish. From a portrait on the wall, President Karimov gazes down benevolently on us. "What we teach here is very different from what is being taught at *madrassas* in other countries such as Pakistan or Iran," Namonov continues. "Our students have to understand that the Taliban are just trying to hide behind the shield of Islam. They are sinners because they kill and deal with drugs." The Mir-Arab Madrassa, which has experienced five hundred years of bloody Central Asian history, is not a place where people get overly excited by current events. The presence of American troops on Uzbek soil, however, seems to annoy Namonov. "It would be better if Muslims themselves would wage a jihad to purify Islam from the Taliban and other terrorists."

The next day I drive to Samarkand, some 200 miles north of Bukhara. The name of the city evokes the wild romance of the Silk Road, spellbinding the British diplomat and writer Fitzroy Maclean when, in the late 1930s, he ventured to Turkestan, then a forbidden zone for foreigners. "I climbed by a narrow twisting stairway to the top of the Shir Dar and from there looked down on the sun-baked Registan and beyond it on the fabled city of Samarkand, on the blue domes and the minarets, the flat-roofed mud houses, and the green tree-tops. It was a moment to which I had long looked forward."[5]

Like the old town of Bukhara, the majestic Registan Square lies deserted in the warm autumn sun. Only a handful of guards stroll past the azure blue majolica mosaics of the three *madrassas,* the most precious examples of Central Asian architecture. Here, in the sixteenth century, the Orient's most respected scholars studied and taught. Near the Registan I meet up with Ozod Jalulov, a Soviet veteran of the first Afghanistan war. The short, lean man takes me to his small artisan shop where his friends Ahmed and Aziz are already waiting for us. In the 1980s, all three fought in the same unit in Afghanistan. "If American troops go into Afghanistan, they will sooner or later find themselves in hell on earth," says Ozod. His friends nod in agreement. "For me, Afghanistan was the worst time of my life. They were always hiding in the mountains, those mujahideen. They knew each and every damned path and cave. It was perfect for one ambush after the other on our convoys." Ahmed, too, has not forgotten what it means to fight against invisible partisans. "They were watching us at all times," the former infantryman says, recalling an attack in which his best friend was killed. "We were sitting together on top of a tank, our rifles cocked in hand, staring at the rocks above us. Suddenly my friend said: 'I think I saw one.' I turned around to him, and there he was, already with a red hole in his forehead and falling off the tank."

Those who survived attacks struggled with a brutal climate, sandstorms, and epidemics such as typhus. When the Soviets withdrew from Afghanistan in 1989, the world's largest army had lost its air of invincibility. It was only then, in the course of Mikhail Gorbachev's glasnost policy, that the Soviet regime first published an official casualty count. Nearly fifteen thousand Soviet soldiers had died. Only five years earlier, Moscow would concede the death of a mere twenty men. Some estimates of Soviet servicemen sent home in sealed zinc coffins run as high as fifty thousand, which is approximately how many Americans lost their lives in Vietnam.

"I hope the Americans know what they are letting themselves in for," Ozod continues. "Their situation today is actually quite similar to ours back then. We, too, were told that we would hunt down criminals and bring peace and stability to the country. But the Afghans did not want us to help them." The invasion of its southern neighbor, regarded in the West as a brutal attempt to expand the Soviet empire, is still seen by many veterans as a well-intentioned attempted liberation. Though Ozod and his veteran

friends do not envy the U.S. soldiers their task, they have not forgotten what many in Central Asia regard as a bitter irony of history.
"The terrorists whom the United States now want to eliminate were
armed trained as mujahideen by the Americans in the 1980s—
when they were fighting us," Ozod remembers, adding with a slight
hint of *schadenfreude,* "America now reaps what it sowed during
the Cold War."

In the following weeks, the concerns of many Uzbeks that the
Afghan war might spill over the border prove to be unwarranted.
At the end of October, the Taliban evacuate from Mazar-e-Sharif,
and the Uzbek General Dostum retakes the town. After much pro-
crastination by the Karimov regime, the "Friendship Bridge"
across the Amu Darya is reopened to deliver humanitarian aid to
suffering Afghans in early December 2001. The Afghan war has
almost come to an end when Washington and Tashkent agree on
a new seven-year lease for the Chanabad Airbase in Karshi.

About two months after the Taliban's fall, on a clear morning in
February 2002, two American Humvees drive into a village somewhere amid the craggy mountains of Kyrgyzstan, Uzbekistan's
northern neighbor. Some villagers, mostly children or elderly men,
stare at the Humvees. The first vehicle stops. Staff Sergeant Chad
Bickley again reminds his men in desert camouflage battledress
of the patrol's mission, "Don't forget, guys: we're out here to make
friends. We will shake hands, wave and hand out candies, okay?"
"Yes, sir!" the soldiers respond, grab their black M-16 rifles, and
get out of the Humvees to win the hearts and minds of the villagers.

Bickley approaches a group of old Kyrgyz men. "Hi, my name
is Chad of the U.S. Air Force. I just wanted to check on you and
see how you are doing in this village." A local interpreter translates his words. The men remain silent. Eventually, one man replies, "Good, thanks." Meanwhile, Captain Todd Schrader kneels
down in front of two small boys, shoulders his M-16 and offers
them a sip from his bottle of Kool-Aid. The children are not interested, perhaps finding it a bit unhygienic that Schrader first drank

from the bottle himself. He then shows them how to consume sherbet powder, using his hand, tongue, and plenty of saliva. He holds out the small package to the boys. They do not move. "They are still a bit shy," Bickley explains. "After all, they have never seen American soldiers."

They will, however, have noticed the numerous U.S. Air Force planes that, from mid-December onward, land and take off on a twenty-four-hour schedule from the nearby Manas airport of the Kyrgyz capital of Bishkek. These planes transport troops of the 376th Air Expeditionary Wing as well as supplies for the latest military base set up by Washington in Central Asia. The U.S. government has rented the civilian airport from Kyrgyzstan, the smallest of the five Central Asian republics to emerge from the Soviet ruins. After Chanabad airbase in Uzbekistan, and a smaller camp in Tajikistan, Manas is the third and largest U.S. base in ex-Soviet Central Asia. Up to three thousand troops are being stationed here, including allied units from France, Spain, and Denmark.

Before Staff Sergeant Bickley and his group left the camp for a tour of the surrounding villages, they replicated a worst-case scenario in a small birch wood. "Guys, usually the villagers like us but we have to be prepared for everything," Bickley told his men. For half an hour they practiced what to do in case of enemy contact, throwing themselves onto the frozen ground, shouting "Bang, bang, bang!" and crawling behind trees for reloading. Captain Schrader was the marksman in charge while Airman Michael Alberson emptied his entire magazine. Bickley lobbed imaginary smoke bombs from behind, while the radio operator called for help from the Quick Reaction Force who had stayed a few miles behind. Warmed up by the mock battle, the soldiers jumped into the Humvees and drove off. On the main road, their convoy overtook a fully occupied Lada whose frightened driver almost veered off into a ditch.

The real patrol later passes without incident. The only serious threat Bickley and his men face are from two Kyrgyz scalawags lobbing snowballs at them. They respond to this attack with candies. "We give some candies and toys to the kids, and occasionally some cigarettes to the adults," Bickley says while he and his soldiers march through the village in loose formation. He keeps the barrel of his rifle pointing to the ground, so it won't appear intimidating. "We talk to the villagers to find out what they think of our presence. We have never encountered any mistrust or hostility, just curiosity at times. The people here like us. Through our patrols we give them security and protection from thieves." When a dog barks at him from a driveway, Bickley turns around. "Hey dog, if only I knew your language I could explain our mission to you as well, and you would stop barking."

Yet the villagers remain skeptical. Speaking to my interpreter in an unobserved moment, one man complains: "Why do the Americans have to run around with such big rifles? Who knows what could happen? We are worried about our children." The man's neighbor has forbidden her children to accept any sweets from the soldiers. "How do I know if these candies are edible or not?" asks the Kyrgyz woman. "And what is more, our village is not a zoo where you can feed children like animals."

After an hour, Bickley and his men end their patrol in Uchkun and climb back into their Humvees. Driving out of the village, the soldiers wave at the locals. A small boy sitting on a tall brown stallion stares down at the uniformed men, motionless. Nobody waves back. Bickley does not seem fazed, nor does he know the name of the village we just left. "I cannot remember, it is too hard to pronounce. We just call it 'downtown'."

We arrive at "Peter J. Ganci Base," which is written on a sign rising out of a pile of goat skulls at the main gate. Air Force Captain Richard Essary, who will take me on a tour of the base, explains, "Ganci was a firefighter who on September 11 saved nearly a hundred lives in the World Trade Center's South Tower before he was killed himself." Essary, a pudgy twenty-nine-year-old from Salt Lake City, softens. "When our commander heard the story of that hero he decided to name this base after Ganci. In fact, our commander said, it was God who named the base that way."

The extent of American commitment, just in terms of hardware, is impressive. The huge C-17 and Boeing 747 transport planes of the U.S. Air Force on Manas airport's tarmac dwarf the few Tupolev airplanes of Kyrgyzstan Air. With the help of dozens of excavators, bulldozers, and cranes, a pioneer unit erects a new hangar for the F-18 Hornets and Mirage-2000 fighter jets that are soon to arrive. Soldiers are busy hammering and supervisors scream instructions, while a concrete mixer disgorges its gray liquid into the foundation ditches of the new building.

Behind the rundown terminal are the living quarters of the base, which extend over some two hundred acres: about 220 Harvest Falcon and Force Provider tents stand side by side in long rows, providing shelter for nearly three thousand soldiers. The sight reminds me of the U.S. base Camp Bondsteel in southeast Kosovo. Starting out as a tent city after NATO's war against Yugoslavia, the camp grew into a veritable small town.

Squads of soldiers march across the inner yard, their bright combat boots grinding on the loose chippings. Underneath their desert covers, many of the men don narrow reflective sunglasses. "We wear dashing and clean uniforms because, after all, we are ambassadors of the United States," Captain Essary says. "We want to make sure that we are good guests and that we show our best side." Before joining the military, Essary, whose home base is in Montana, studied political science and international relations, yet in all these weeks in Kyrgyzstan, he has never heard of Almaty, the Kazakh city of a million inhabitants barely 250 miles north of Bishkek. "Oh well, we did not really learn a whole lot about Central Asia at college," he confides.

We step into one of the crew rooms, created with simple steel containers. One of them houses a cinema, which this evening is showing *American Pie,* followed by *Runaway Bride* with Julia Roberts. In the game room, soldiers play cards, while others type e-mails home on computers. A television set shows the Armed Forces Radio and Television Service (AFRTS), the station for all U.S. forces around the world. At that moment fanfare music blares from the TV, reminiscent of German propaganda newsreels in the 1940s. Superimposed over a billowing American flag, the name of the next show appears on the screen, *Our Leaders.* The speaker is Undersecretary of Defense Dov Zakheim. Talking directly from the Pentagon, he assures the men and women fighting the war against terror that the people back home fully support them. "This is a war on two fronts, and the second front is the home front. It is of great importance to this government and we will do whatever is necessary."

Another fanfare blares from the TV to announce another leader, but Captain Essary continues our tour. "Back there, I have something very beautiful to show you." He takes me to a table piled with cardboard boxes filled with red envelopes. They contain thousands of greeting cards sent by American school children to the soldiers. "Operation Valentine's Day" is written across one of the boxes. Captain Essary fishes out a random letter, with a big heart taped to it, and reads it out loud. "Dear soldier! We hope that you will soon catch bin Laden. I was in New York when it happened and I was very scared. Love, Rachel." In another letter a boy named Andy from Virginia thanks the soldiers for protecting him "against the evil" out there in the world. "That is so beautiful, isn't it?" utters Captain Essary.

As we leave the recreational facility, I notice notes pasted next to the door. On it somebody has written common Russian phrases and their meanings, such as "Good afternoon!" and "Good evening!" The Russian expressions are so badly misspelled that they are barely recognizable. The "Russian phrase of the day" reads "pa-zhah-lus-ta" which was translated into "you are welcome!" Aigul, Captain Essary's Kyrgyz interpreter accompanying us to translate between him and locals working on the base, clarifies. "Actually, the word rather means 'please!', as in a request." Checking to make sure Essary is out of earshot, she whispers, "But then that is a word the Americans don't use very often with us."

Her unexpectedly snappy remark surprises me. Only a few minutes ago, the university-educated translator explained to me how happy she was about the arrival of the American troops. "All my friends envy me this job," she said proudly as she earns fifty dollars a day, more than most Kyrgyz make in an entire month. Captain Essary takes us to the camp's canteen, where up to five hundred people can eat at the same time. All food is flown in from the United States or Europe, predominantly in the form of sealed food rations for instant consumption. Local products do not appear on the troops' menus, to the irritation of many Kyrgyz farmers who had hoped for a new market. "For us hygiene and health are number one priorities," Captain Essary explains. He grabs a pack of biscuits from the counter and offers it to Aigul. She declines. "If you don't want our food, then we don't want yours, either." Captain Essary laughs off Aigul's comment.

We take a jeep to the base commander's tent near the Manas airstrip. Before we are allowed near, we have to stop and get out so Alsatian sniffer dogs can check the vehicle for explosives. Captain Essary gives me some last-minute instructions for the interview. "No foreign policy questions," he warns. "And please do not mention the story of the firefighter Peter J. Ganci. Otherwise the commander would probably cry." Brigadier General Chris Kelly, a wiry man with steel-blue eyes and a regulation crew-cut of graying hair, does not appear to be the sensitive type. His handshake could crush an uncooked potato. Playing with his bulky Air Force Academy graduation ring, Kelly defines his mission in clear terms. "We are building this base in order to fulfill General Franks' mission to eradicate all Taliban and Al Qaeda in Afghanistan." General Tommy Franks is the commander-in-chief of the U.S. Central Command in the war against terror. Kelly's demeanor speaks of his determination to fight, underscored by a black skull-and-crossbones flag flying in front of his tent.

Yet when General Kelly talks about the day in December 2001 when his C-17 plane landed at Manas, his voice sounds less resolute. "We arrived here with considerable fear because we were flying directly into the unknown. We looked around and there was nothing! I was afraid of making mistakes and not getting the support from the locals." The fifty-year-old never thought in his twenty-eight years of military service that he would set foot on former Soviet territory on a combat mission. "Not even for five minutes," he says.

I remind General Kelly of the rumors in the Central Asian press that American troops are pursuing strategic goals in the region other than the fight against terrorism: "There is nothing secret and nothing sinister about our mission," he responds sharply. "We simply cooperate with those nations who share our vision of what the world should look like. I can understand that some people are scared by the fact that we are staying on ex–Soviet territory. But the Cold War is over, the Soviet Union no longer exists. In Operation Enduring Freedom we cooperate with a multinational coalition. Kyrgyzstan is an independent country, and after all, it was the Kyrgyz who invited us. So what is the problem?" When I ask Kelly how long the U.S. troops would remain in the country, his failure to mention the Kyrgyz is notable. "We will stay as long as General Franks needs us here. There is no time limit. We will pull out only when all Al Qaeda cells have been eradicated. We are fighting for a noble cause. General Franks executes the will of the world."

For the governments of the five former Soviet republics in Central Asia, the American commitment appears to be the greatest boon since the end of the Cold War. In 2002, Washington's economic and military aid for the region more than doubled, to $400 million. The exact sums paid by the Pentagon to impoverished Kyrgyzstan for the Manas airbase are treated with discretion by both sides but the Kyrgyz government does pocket some seven thousand dollars for every American plane taking off or landing, certainly the steepest airport tax in the world. The city of Bishkek, until ten years ago named after the Bolshevik general Mikhail Frunze, could use a cash infusion. Dreary Soviet-era concrete buildings sprawl around a tall bronze statue of Lenin, whose right arm, as always, leads the way to revolution. Only a few shops liven up the gray streets. This is supposed to change with American help. In fact, during the first four months of the base's existence, according to government claims, some $14 million has flowed from there into the local economy. The men and women of the Air Force have allegedly spent more than $1 million on souvenirs and entertainment in the city. That sum is somewhat astounding as alcohol consumption, prostitution, and gambling are strictly forbidden to the soldiers.

Captain Essary has kept a special surprise for the end of our tour of the base: the arrival at Manas of the first three French Mirage-2000 fighter jets. We drive to the airstrip, where Essary is shocked to discover that the French press officer, Lieutenant Bertrand Bon, has already invited the entire local media to witness the event, including press, radio, and television. More than fifty excited Kyrgyz journalists arrive in two buses; many of them see the base for the first time, as the U.S. Air Force has restricted access to local media. Taking his French colleague by the side, Captain Essary hisses, "What the hell did you bring all these people here for?" With a haughty air, Lieutenant Bon retorts, "I figured that they should have something nice to look at, finally." General de Gaulle, though probably dismayed at the sight of French units under American command, would have been pleased.

The loud roar of engines announces the arrival of the Mirage jets. Excitedly, Lieutenant Bon points to the horizon while the Kyrgyz cameramen and photographers bring their equipment into position. Three planes thunder across the sky in an arrow formation. Instead of landing, they roar above our heads at a fairly low altitude. At the end of the airfield, two Mirages veer off to the sides in artistic arcs while the third pilot jerks his jet up steeply into the air. Minutes later, all three planes touch down in a harmonic sequence. A perfect display of Gallic pomp, the only thing missing is *tricolore* smoke from the engines. The Kyrgyz are impressed. Lieutenant Bon beams while Captain Essary and the other American officers present try to look decidedly bored.

After a thorough examination of the jets, the journalists gather around Lieutenant Bon and Captain Essary to ask questions. A young woman asks Essary if he believes that most Kyrgyz are happy about the presence of American forces in the country. "Of course, otherwise your government would not have invited us, right?" Many of the journalists cannot stifle giggles at this answer. Essary is confused: "Why are you asking? Do you doubt this?" The young woman replies: "Of course not, sir. Just a silly question, just wondering." Afterwards, I speak to the journalist, Fatima Gayazova, editor-in-chief of a local TV station. "They are giving us a nice show here," she says. "But it is not true that we Kyrgyz are happy about the Americans moving in here. The people do not want our country to sacrifice to another great power the independence it has only just gained."

Polls commissioned by the government show that the majority of Kyrgyz do not want to accept the American soldiers as neighbors.

According to one study cited in the local press, 77 percent of the population oppose the presence of U.S. troops, while 62 percent of all interviewees state that the relationship with Russia could worsen. "Many are suspicious and they believe that the United States only wants to control Central Asia," Gayazova says. Domestically, the government's decision has led to tension. The regime of President Askar Akayev, the only Central Asian head of state who is not a former top communist, was long considered to be the strongest democratic hope in the region. Lately, the liberal course has turned into repression. Shortly after my visit, police forces crack down on an opposition rally, killing six people. Opposition leaders accuse the regime of abusing the presence of American troops to suppress democratic movements.

With a member of the president's family controlling all fuel sales at Manas airbase, the population's opposition to the U.S. troops is likely to increase. "The people in Central Asia like neither American culture nor the behavior of the United States. The Americans believe they could simply buy us," Gayazova says. "The Americans will stay here as long as they like. An unstable Afghanistan will always serve as a perfect pretext."

The American advance into Central Asia also worries the national-conservative elites in Moscow, who still regard the region as Russia's strategic backyard. "Russia does not approve of the establishment of permanent U.S. bases in Central Asia," declared Russian parliament speaker Gennady Seleznev, who traveled to Almaty only days after the landing of American troops in Kyrgyzstan. Pointing to the CIS security pact, the politician insisted on a veto right for Moscow. "They [the Central Asians] must not take decisions without joint consultations in the framework of the treaty." Shortly thereafter, the Kremlin disowned Seleznev and declared that it was up to Kyrgyzstan whether or not to accept U.S. troops. Both viewpoints reflect the fact that the Russian state, ten years after its creation, has still not found a uniform foreign policy.

To find out how much President Putin's official lip service to the antiterror alliance is really worth in Central Asia, I fly to Moscow to meet with Victor Kalyuzhny, the Russian deputy foreign minister and Putin's special envoy to the Caspian region. In a move typical of Russian bureaucracy, the Foreign Ministry spokesman had declined my interview requests for weeks. Then one morning an e-mail from Minister Kalyuzhny himself invited me to come to his office a few days later.

The foreign ministry on Smolenskaya Square is a Stalinist-era skyscraper whose towers are still emblazoned with a large hammer-and-sickle symbol. Dating back to 1951, the building is reminiscent of a giant birthday cake, its granite façade studded with thousands of small windows. The antennas and radio poles linking the government with its embassies all over the world, fixed up and down the one hundred or so floors, crawl like spiders over the building. Some shake threateningly as a storm gathers across Moscow.

At the main entrance, two black marble obelisks flank a set of colossal bronze doors decorated with hammers and sickles, as well as the names of the fifteen Soviet republics. The lobby is an equally dazzling array of white marble and golden chandeliers, dwarfing the many pallid-faced diplomats shuffling past the security barriers. The antechamber to Minister Kalyuzhny's office, in contrast, still breathes the stuffy air of the Brezhnev era. Two male secretaries sit opposite each other at wooden desks, working mechanically through stacks of files. The walls are paneled a dark wooden color, while the floor is covered with stained brown carpets. Ruched yellowed nets and heavy beige curtains almost entirely cover the window.

Victor Kalyuzhny, a tall, portly man with snow-white hair, invites me to sit at a conference table. The walls of his office are decorated with watercolors of Moscow street scenes, each lit by its own gallery light. On a small table in the corner is a signed portrait photograph of Vladimir Putin. I make a few polite comments about the ghastly Moscow weather when the diplomat interrupts. "Your first question, please!" he says brusquely.

Raised and educated in the Siberian town of Ufa, Kalyuzhny rose to become president of the Eastern Oil Company in the wild postcommunist 1990s, acquiring great wealth along the way. The oil baron, who is a close friend of the petrol oligarch Victor Chernomyrdin, entered politics. Kalyuzhny first became involved in the new Great Game when, in his capacity as oil minister under President Boris Yeltsin, he was one of the fiercest opponents of the Mediterranean pipeline through the southern Caucasus. President Putin then appointed Kalyuzhny as his special envoy to the Caspian region, instructing him to end the territorial disputes among the littoral states.

This is by no means an easy task, as Kalyuzhny himself concedes. "The greatest obstacles are greed and stinginess on the part of the countries involved, except Russia, of course." Each littoral state tries to create a deal to its own advantage, but he considers the Iranian demands wholly unjustified. He recalls the Iranian-Azeri gunboat incident in July 2001. "We must find a solution soon; otherwise, the demands could lead to military conflicts in the near future." Would it not be a first step toward peace to demilitarize the Caspian Sea, I ask. "There is no way Russia is going to get rid of its Caspian fleet," Kalyuzhny retorts. "Particularly not now that American troops are based in Uzbekistan and Kyrgyzstan!"

Kalyuzhny has touched on the real issue sooner than I thought he would: "We have a saying in Russia. If you have guests in the house there are two times when you are happy. One is when they arrive, and one is when they leave again." I point out that the American troops are not guests of Russia but of the independent Central Asian republics. "Kyrgyzstan and Uzbekistan are CIS member states and are bound by security treaties with Russia," Kalyuzhny insists. "The Americans have to pull out of Central Asia as soon as they have caught bin Laden."

Kalyuzhny acknowledges that Russia has fought with sincerity alongside the United States against terrorists, and it would continue so to do. "We have got a common problem and a common tragedy. But this tragedy did not begin on September 11, 2001," the diplomat says, referring to a series of bomb attacks in 1999 when terrorists blew up apartment blocks in Moscow, killing hundreds of people. The perpetrators of those attacks were never caught, and though the Russian government blames

Chechen terrorists, there are persistent rumors that the attacks
were masterminded by the Russian secret service in order to create a casus belli for the second Chechen campaign.

"If the West had listened to our warnings of Islamic terrorists back then, the attacks of September 11, 2001 would have never
happened," Kalyuzhny believes. "But people only seem to learn
from their own mistakes." He has registered with satisfaction that
Western criticism of Russian actions in Chechnya has since fallen
relatively silent. "The Chechen rebels are terrorists and bandits,"
Kalyuzhny says, and stresses that the Russian constitution still
applies to the secessionist republic. Were Moscow to let Chechnya
secede, other republics such as Tatarstan or even Siberia could
strive for their own independence. "In the United States it would
not be possible, either, for one state simply to break away," he
adds.

The cooperation between the United States and Russia in the
struggle against terrorism has surprised many observers to the
extent that the media have begun to hype a "new strategic partnership" between the two countries. I ask Kalyuzhny on what basis
such a durable alliance could be formed. Again, he replies with
unexpected clarity. "After all, Russia is a nuclear power that one
should not mess around with. That is why the Americans try to
win us over as partners." Both superpowers' common responsibility for the world, he says in very Soviet language, requires bal-
anced policies marked by mutual understanding between the
partners. "We are interested in peaceful coexistence with the
United States and we have unilaterally destroyed many of our
nuclear weapons. But we expect sincerity from the Americans."
In Central Asia, he adds, healthy competition is an option, but it
would be wrong for one side to seek the destruction of the other.
"Guests should know that it is impolite to stay for too long."

As I step out into the rain-swept Smolenskaya Square, my
doubts about the longevity of Russian-American rapprochement
have only grown stronger. Instead of a genuine strategic partnership, it is a temporary tactical marriage of convenience. For
the majority of the Russian establishment it is unthinkable to per-
manently cede the political, economic, cultural, and territorial

hegemonic claims on the Caucasus and Central Asia. Nor are they prepared to accept a permanent presence of U.S. troops in Kyrgyzstan or Georgia, in the same way Americans would not tolerate Russian troops in Mexico.

Putin has managed to convince his generals that a cooperative, hands-off policy makes sense in the short term because it allows the desperately overstretched Russian forces to regroup and regain their strength. Once the battered economy has recovered with the help of Western capital, Moscow will hardly be kept from reasserting a more dominant role in the world.

Recent developments show that Russia has decided not to wait much longer. In December 2002, President Putin made an unexpected visit to Kyrgyzstan, signing a new security pact with his Kyrgyz counterpart. Russia then deployed a squadron of Su-25 and Su-27 fighter jets, bombers, and other aircraft to an airbase in Kyrgyzstan. They were the vanguard of a force that will ultimately comprise more than twenty aircraft and up to one thousand troops, making it one of the most significant deployments of Russian military in the region since 1991. The planes and soldiers will be joined by troops from Kazakhstan and Tajikistan to form a new joint rapid-reaction force.

Moscow's move is widely seen as an effort to reassert its military influence in the region it once controlled. Defense Minister Ivanov bluntly stated the purpose of the new force: "In case of aggression . . . the air force unit will be employed for its direct purpose—to bomb and wipe out the enemy."[6] The airfield in Kant where the Russians have set up their latest foothold in Central Asia lies only thirty-five miles away from the Manas airbase, where the American troops are stationed.

China also reacted to the American presence on its borders by holding joint military exercises with Kyrgyzstan, which was the first time servicemen of the Chinese People's Liberation Army ever took part in a maneuver abroad. The two sides subsequently signed an antiterrorism pact and discussed the possibility that Beijing may station troops in Kyrgyzstan.

Alarmed by the Russian and Chinese moves, Uzbek President Karimov declared that the presence of military bases in Central

Asia could be regarded as positive only where they served to ensure security, peace, and stability. "Military rivalry between the great powers in an overheated region is counterproductive," he said.[7]

A few weeks after my visit to the U.S. troops in Kyrgyzstan, I travel south to Tajikistan, where more than twenty thousand Russian regular army troops and border guards are stationed, forming a counterweight to the increasing American presence in Central Asia. Though the former Soviet republic of Tajikistan in the Pamir Mountains north of Afghanistan has been a nominally independent country since 1992, the Russian influence is still very strong. As Moscow's largest military force outside the Russian borders, most of the troops were sent here as CIS peacekeepers in 1997 after a disastrous five-year civil war had turned Tajikistan into a failed nation. More than fifty thousand people, most of them civilians, died in the fighting between the post-communist government and Islamic factions.

Today, the pro-Moscow government of President Imamali Rakhmanov has made some progress toward a more stable situation and national reconciliation, but Moscow refuses to withdraw its troops. The 201st Motorized Division, which is currently building new headquarters in Dushanbe, would stay for at least another fifteen years, Russian Defense Minister Sergei Ivanov has routinely stated. The Russian border guards stationed along the mountainous 850-mile Tajik border with Afghanistan are unlikely to pull out any sooner.

"We are protecting the southern flank of the CIS against Afghan terrorists, arms dealers and, most importantly, drug smugglers," says Lieutenant Colonel Pjotr Pjotrovic of the Russian border guards, at their headquarters in an imposing nineteenth-century villa in the tree-filled center of Dushanbe. "In a sense we are the first bulwark of Western Europe, where most of the heroin ends up after all." Pjotrovic, a plump middle-aged man, extinguishes a cigarette between his thumb and index finger and says, "The drug smuggling has got much worse. The Afghans must have had a bumper harvest over there." In 2001, his colleagues confiscated 1,200 kilograms of heroin. Tajik dealers pay up to $3,000 per kilogram, a price that later rises dramatically along the transport routes to the European market, reaching $100,000 per kilo in London.

Similar to the scramble for Caspian oil, the $25 billion Afghan narcotics trade shapes Great Game politics in Central Asia, causing misery on a stupendous scale. For two decades, opium-based drugs have been exported from Afghanistan to the rest of the world. Today, about 80 percent of all heroin used in Western Europe originates from the Hindu Kush.

The smuggling routes for Afghan drugs have shifted markedly in the recent past. Only a few years ago, most of the Afghan heroin and opium was taken to the other two countries of the "Golden Crescent," Pakistan and Iran, to be smuggled on to Western Europe. Yet the large-scale heroin traffic led to catastrophic drug problems in Pakistan and Iran, with millions of young people having become addicted. As a result, both countries have massively stepped up their controls at their respective borders with Afghanistan.

The smuggling gangs have therefore moved to the "silk routes" through the former Soviet Union, where porous borders and corrupt security forces facilitate the drug traffic. From Tajikistan the heroin gets to Russia and on to Western Europe via either Uzbekistan or the Kyrgyz city of Osh in the Fergana valley. With Kazakhstan getting more serious about combating the drug trade, smugglers have begun to take a new detour from Osh via Xinjiang to Russia. Though mainly a transit country, Russia itself has been terribly affected by Afghan drugs. The number of heroin addicts has grown from three million to five million in recent years, which also causes Russia to struggle with one of the world's highest growth rates in HIV infections.

One-third of all drug smugglers arrested in Russia are from Tajikistan. "Just the day before yesterday we detained two *kontrabandisti* and confiscated thirty-two kilograms of heroin," Lieutenant Colonel Pjotrovic tells me. Detained? I ask. "Oh, well. There appears to have been an exchange of fire," Pjotrovic replies, shrug-

ging his shoulders. "In the course of it, the criminals were eliminated, I believe." Three photographs on the wall show shackled
and blindfolded Afghan prisoners being led away on a field. I ask
Pjotrovic how many smugglers have so far been shot dead at the
border this year. "More than thirty," he replies. "But one border
guard was killed, too."

The next day, I take the plane from Dushanbe to the border
town of Khorog in Tajik Badakhshan. In Soviet times this was the
only flight route in the entire country where Aeroflot pilots had a
danger bonus added to their salaries. For a hair-raising hour, the
small Fokker plane darts through the Pamir range's narrow gorges
and past snowy peaks, the wings nearly touching the rocky cliffs.
The view over the "roof of the world," as the Pamir is called, is magnificent. To the north lie its two highest peaks that still bear their
Soviet-era names, Pik Kommunizma and Pik Lenina, both rising to
23,000 feet.

Below is the Badakhshan region, divided into Tajik and Afghan
parts. The artificial border was finally drawn in the early twentieth
century as part of a compromise between the British and the
Russians to end the Great Game. As a buffer zone, the diplomats
carved out the eastern extension of Badakhshan, a long narrow
stretch of territory known as the Wakhan Corridor. Today, it also
borders China and Pakistan. For the sake of keeping the two empires apart, the Badakhis were separated and hence drawn into
two very different orbits. Ironically, the post–Soviet chaos in both
Tajikistan and Afghanistan has allowed Badakhis on both sides to
reach out to each other again, restoring long-lost kinship ties. This
has facilitated the cross-border flow of drugs.

Khorog lies on a narrow high plateau at 7,000 feet, squeezed
between craggy snow-covered mountains. Almost all of its twenty
thousand inhabitants are unemployed, as the infertile alpine
wasteland is unsuitable for agriculture, and the only factory in
town, a textile plant, was shut down years ago. The university,
whose excellent reputation in Soviet days lured settlers to this
bleak spot, is still open. Thus, even bazaar vendors often hold academic diplomas and speak several foreign languages. Since many
young men died during the civil war or moved away in search of

work, the gender ratio in Khorog is slightly tilted. For every man, there are about eight women.

"And they are very beautiful, which makes life a bit more tolerable," Ruslan grins. The young man is one of the lucky few to have found a part-time job at a Western aid organization in town. Asked about the Russian border guards stationed in Khorog, his face darkens. "They behave like colonial rulers, they want to suppress us Tajiks." In Ruslan's view, the Russians use the fight against drug smuggling as a pretext for their military presence. "The Russians deal with drugs more than anyone else," says Ruslan. "A few weeks ago, a Russian general was arrested in Tajikistan with eighty kilograms of pure heroin in his bags."

Ruslan tells me that Russian border guards at a checkpoint recently shot five local Tajiks dead after allegedly catching them with heroin. "That was murder," Ruslan says. "I grew up with those guys. They were no drug smugglers, no way. The Russians are lying. They were drunk and just killed the guys for fun." The families of the dead have unsuccessfully demanded an investigation of the tragedy. "The packs of heroin presented by the Russian authorities to the public after the shooting were planted in the men's pockets after they were killed," Ruslan says. "After all, the Russians have got plenty of that stuff."

The barracks of the Russian unit responsible for the killing lie an hour's drive south of Khorog, along the thundering Panj River marking the official border between Tajikistan and Afghanistan. It is strewn with enormous boulders, making it easy to cross from one country to the other by foot. Bleak mountain slopes rise on both sides, and the narrow valley is dotted only with a few poplar trees. At the base's main gate, the Russian soldiers look at me askance. To enter the premises, an officer tells me, I would need an official letter of permission from the ministry in Moscow. I already know this, but my countless faxes to the ministry before my journey elicited no response at all. Fortunately, as Russian soldiers go by the book only when they really have to, it takes me only a few minutes of persuasion to get inside the base.

In a tree-shaded courtyard, an officer barks loud orders at twenty newly arrived recruits from Russia who are undergoing their first drill. Every two seconds, the shaven-headed men stand upright and drop back to the ground. They practice disassembling and reassembling AK-47 assault rifles, and move on their bellies over the concrete ground, past a new stone monument commemorating the barracks' existence from 1918 to 2001. Chiseled into the stone and painted red is the outline of the Soviet empire, stretching from Vilnius to Vladivostok, as if the newly independent republics such as Tajikistan did not exist.

I find Captain Oleg, the leader of the patrol squad that killed the five Tajiks, in the officers' building. "It was shortly before midnight when I received a radio call from a patrol a few miles downriver that they had spotted two Afghan men," recalls the thirty-four-year-old Muscovite who joined the border guards eight years ago. "The men were carrying a rope and a tractor tire," typical smuggling gear to transport drugs to the Tajik side of the river, where accomplices take over the load. "They could not be far," Oleg continues. "Suddenly, this white Lada appeared on the road in front of us." The situation reminded the Russian of an ambush by Afghan *kontrabandisti* into which he and his comrades had walked years earlier. After the attackers had fired hundreds of rounds from their AK-47s, eight of Oleg's comrades had lain dead next to him. With one bullet stuck in his thigh, Oleg had been the only survivor. Oleg pulls up his trousers to show me the scar where the bullet penetrated.

"When the Lada pulled up to us, we acted in accordance with the rules," Oleg continues. "We asked the passengers of the car twice to get out with their hands up. But then we saw their guns. In such a situation we shoot to kill. That is the way it is," he says, his right hand stroking the dark fur of his Doberman, Deutscher, his closest friend at the base, whose name reminds Oleg of his Cold War service in a Red Army unit in Magdeburg, Germany.

Oleg dismisses rumors that corrupt Russian officers cooperate with Afghan drug smugglers. "Of course, a few soldiers here and there might stuff a few grams into their pockets, one cannot prevent that," he says, lighting a cigarette. "As for officers, though, the KGB makes sure that this does not happen. We are all being strictly controlled."

We walk out to the courtyard, passing a large plaque that proclaims, "To the heroes of the Soviet Union who gave their lives in the fulfillment of their internationalist duty." The photographs show the faces of fallen Red Army soldiers, many bearing the caption "Afghanistan" and a date in the 1980s. "We have added a few heroes from Chechnya," remarks Oleg, adding that he is tired of the rough life in the barracks. Not having seen his wife and daughter for months, he wants to go *damoi,* back home.

We climb onto a watchtower at the far end of the base, from which a guard behind a machine gun watches the narrow river valley. On the Afghan side, a man drives a donkey along a mountain path, and two men are busy felling a young poplar right on the shore. "Behind those mountains the Afghan opium farmers work their poppy fields," says Oleg.

Though drugs are currently Afghanistan's one big cash crop, the reasons Great Game players are trying to gain control over the country lie elsewhere: terrorism and pipelines.

Pipe Dreams: Afghanistan

The engines of the Khan's approaching convoy are still only barely audible, yet some of the roughly two hundred bearded mujahideen stop talking, grab their assault rifles, and stand at the ready, smoothing creases in their combat fatigues. Behind the mujahideen, hundreds of people mill about in a small pine tree park—children, graybeards with turbans, women wearing cornflower-blue *burqas*, silken head-to-toe coverings.

It is Navroz, New Year's Day in the Persian sun calendar, 1381 years after the birth of the prophet Mohammed. The inhabitants of Herat, the biggest city in western Afghanistan, spend the day—March 21 on the Western calendar—with traditional outdoor picnics and visits to relatives' graves. This is the first time Afghans have celebrated Navroz since Taliban rulers banned all New Year's customs as un–Islamic, and reason enough for Ismail Khan, the legendary mujahideen warlord and returned ruler of Herat, to reinaugurate the park. Heavily armed guards climb onto the roof of a pavilion, one of them carrying a grenade launcher; just a few days earlier, the park had been cleared of mines. The guards are there to ensure the safety of *amir sahib,* as Khan is called by his subjects.

It has been several months since the Taliban regime collapsed, with most of its fighting units simply dissolving into the countryside and the big cities. About ten thousand U.S. troops and an additional thousand allied soldiers now occupy the country at the Hindu Kush, battling against scattered pockets of Taliban and Al Qaeda resistance in the mountainous border regions with Pakistan. While Osama bin Laden and Mullah Omar have mysteriously vanished and gone underground, a five-thousand-strong non–American International Security Assistance Force (ISAF) patrols the streets of Kabul. A new Afghan government under President Hamid Karzai has begun to rebuild a country devastated by twenty-three years of war.

Progress is slow in Afghanistan, though, because only a fraction of the $4.6 billion promised by the international community has so far reached Kabul. Regional warlords, some of whom are on the CIA's payroll as anti–Taliban allies, still rule most of the fragmented country. Commanding militias of about seven hundred thousand men under arms, the warlords severely limit the central government's authority, causing Karzai to be scornfully nicknamed "the mayor of Kabul." Ethnic conflicts have arisen between the Pashtuns in the south, most of whom supported and joined the Taliban, and the northern Tajik and Uzbek tribes, who supported the forces of the anti–Taliban opposition. President Karzai is a Pashtun, as is the eighty-nine-year-old former Afghan king Zahir Shah, who returned to Kabul some thirty years after his overthrow; however, most power is being wielded by a group of Tajiks from the Panjshir Valley north of Kabul. These men are the closest associates of the legendary mujahideen leader Ahmed Shah Massoud who had led the anti-Taliban Northern Alliance, a motley coalition of tribal-based guerrilla forces officially called the United Islamic Front for the Salvation of Afghanistan, until his assassination by alleged Al Qaeda fighters on September 9, 2001. The Panjshiris and their opponents are constantly engaged in a behind-the-scenes struggle for power in Kabul.

Amidst this instability, General Khan, the "Lion of Herat," has emerged from his hiding place in the mountains once again as one of Afghanistan's most powerful provincial leaders. The *amir sahib* rules like an absolute monarch in Herat with little concern for the central government in Kabul. So far, he has refused to be appointed governor by the comparatively inexperienced Karzai. This independent stance has angered the Bush administration, which views the Sunni Tajik as an ally of Iran, whose border runs a mere ninety miles west of Herat. For years, the Iranians have supported the mujahed, often granting him exile, and there is suspicion that through Khan Tehran is meddling in internal Afghan affairs. Washington fears that Khan is trying to set up an independent province, literally a modern khanate. Iranians have reportedly funneled arms and money toward the warlord's guerrilla army, leading to a bitter struggle over control of the town. Its strategic location on the main roads to Iran and Turkmenistan could be crucial for the outcome of the new Great Game in Central Asia. The routes of two long-planned pipelines for gas and oil from the Caspian Sea to the Indian Ocean lead directly past Herat.

The emir's brown Toyota Land Cruiser skids through the park, closely followed by three pickup trucks full of fighters toting Kalashnikov assault rifles and rocket launchers. Though he is surprisingly short, Khan would remind every Western child of Santa Claus with his massive snow-white beard, save for his black and white spotted turban. The *amir sahib* is only in his mid-fifties, but in a country haunted by two decades of civil war many men and women, Khan included, seem to have aged much quicker.

"*Allahu akbar!*" the crowd shouts three times. "God is great!" The men bow their heads to the warlord in reverence and put one hand on their chests, in a sign of sincerity and loyalty. Many here have been his close allies since 1979, when Khan, then a major in the Afghan army, called for jihad. The son of a poor rural family, Khan attended the Askari military school in Kabul and returned to his hometown a lieutenant. Deeply conservative, Khan witnessed how communist putschists in Kabul pursued a radical modernization of the country after 1978, dispatching an increasing number of Soviet advisers, officers, and engineers to Herat. He did not like what he saw.

In March 1979, Khan led an uprising of the town's garrison against the new rulers and ordered hundreds of Soviet advisers and their families slaughtered. In retaliation, Moscow dispatched three hundred tanks and shot the three-thousand-year-old city of Herat to pieces. Government troops massacred the town's population, killing about twenty-four thousand people in a single week.

Most of the victims were civilians who died in bombings by Soviet
fighter jets and helicopters in what was Russia's first open intervention in Afghanistan. Bulldozers shoved the mangled bodies
of the dead into mass graves on a hill above the town. Khan and
sixty rebels fled to the mountains and embarked on a partisan
struggle.

Shortly thereafter, the Red Army invaded Afghanistan. Soviet
jets pummeled Herat with daily carpet bombings while on the
ground, Soviet troops and Khan's mujahideen engaged in a brutal
cat-and-mouse game that lasted for years. Unlike Kabul, Herat was
never "pacified" and became one of the most inaccessible places
on earth. Herat's Soviet commander, General Andrushkin, wrote
in a letter to Khan that he should expect the same fate as the
Basmachi leader Ibrahim Beg, the legendary guerrillero who had
fought the Bolsheviks in Central Asia in the 1920s but was finally
defeated and killed. "You Russians still remember Ibrahim Beg
seventy years later," Khan taunted in his reply. "I will make sure
that you will not forget me in two hundred years."

Khan's units committed far fewer horrific acts of brutality
during the civil war following the Soviet withdrawal in 1989 and
the fall of the communist puppet regime in Kabul in 1991. As the
province's self-appointed governor, Khan provided a degree of
security, education, and food supply unrivaled in the rest of the
country. After initially holding back the superior Pashtun Taliban
troops, the Tajik suddenly evacuated Herat without a fight and fled
to Iran with his most loyal troops by his side. When he returned
later on a clandestine mission to Afghanistan, an Uzbek general
betrayed him to the Taliban for $12 million. Khan was imprisoned
in a dungeon in the southern town of Kandahar for three years,
both his hands and feet bound by shackles. Khan would probably
not have survived the end of the Taliban regime if he had not, with
the help of a prison guard, miraculously escaped to Iran. There,
he resumed fighting.

Along with exile, Iran provided arms, money, and training for
Khan's best mujahideen soldiers by the *Sepah-e-Pasdaran* (Revo-
lutionary Guards), the archconservative wing of the Iranian army.
Khan himself oversaw the training camps near the town of Mash-

had in eastern Iran. During the Taliban's reign, Iran accepted more than two million Afghan refugees, who are now being gradually repatriated by the UN.

The journey for many Afghans returning to their homeland often runs from Mashhad to the border post at the small town of Dogharun. To cross over into Afghanistan, one has to walk through half a mile of a bleak no-man's-land. During my trek, the hot March sun scorches a ground parched from four years of drought, while wind gusts blow sand devils across the freshly tarmaced road. On either side, people loiter and beg, among them cripples, blind men, and war invalids, along with countless children whose bodies are afflicted with festering wounds and eczema. One boy, his hair tousled and his face thickly covered with dirt, walks on crutches because a mine had torn off one of his legs.

An Afghan border guard wearing an oversized, outdated uniform beckons me into his little hut, where he neatly enters my passport details into a bulky, leatherbound book. Pictures of Ahmed Shah Massoud and Ismail Khan hang on the wall. After stamping my visa, the guard takes my hand, holds it for a long time, and welcomes me to his country. Directly across the road from the border guard's hut is the field office of the UNHCR, the United Nations' refugee organization. Its head, an Afghan named Zia Ahmad, watches my arrival. "From the Taliban you would not have got such a reception," he laughs and invites me in for lunch. With his coworkers we sit down on a carpet around big bowls filled with traditional pilaf made of goat meat, rice, and tomatoes, along with green tea to drink.

For years, Ahmad has worked in this office, looking after Afghan refugees on their way to Iran. Now he sees them returning to their country. "Every day, about four hundred refugees come back from Iran. They hope that this time it will be forever," Ahmad says, though unemployment, poverty, and famine await them at home. "And yet what counts for them is that the war is over. We help them by giving ten dollars and grain seeds to every family," he says. Over the following weeks the UNHCR plans to bring up to fifity thousand refugees back to their old villages in buses and trucks.

Through a window, we watch the constant traffic at the border post. "Under the Taliban, things were very quiet here. And on the roof of each building there were pieces of artillery, directed at Iran," Ahmad recalls. "Today, Iranian trucks come through every two minutes." Outside, a long line of trucks is forming to get across the border. I ask Ahmad about their potential cargo. "Yes, yes, many arms, people say," he replies. "But personally, I have never seen any. So far, I have only noticed food and building materials." Iran has pledged to donate as much as $500 million to the Afghan government for reconstruction in the next five years, a sign that Ahmad does not necessarily interpret as meddling in Afghanistan's internal affairs. "My country needs help. So I don't care where that help comes from."

From the border post, it takes about four hours to cover the ninety miles to Herat. The road through the Kara Kum desert to Herat is essentially a patchwork of small islets of asphalt peeking out from the sand. On a state visit to Tehran in March 2002, Afghan President Hamid Karzai received an offer from the Iranian government to construct a new paved road from the border to Herat. Work had already begun when the project stalled. American diplomats in Kabul quietly intervened against the construction, fearing the new transport link would reinforce Iranian influence in western Afghanistan, while among Afghans rumors spread that Iran insisted on the new road being named after Ayatollah Khomeini.

On what is left of the road to Herat, the transition from the modern, urbanized Iran to the archaic world of Afghanistan is abrupt. Against a backdrop of craggy mountains, villages cluster around the few remaining sources of water in the desert. Wrapped in robes and turbans, villagers drive donkeys between mud huts whose walls have been eroded and hollowed by wind. Then the first signs of the long war, blown-apart and burned-out iron skeletons of Russian tanks, appear by the side of the road, sand drifts forming around them.

Stopping off at a kiosk to have tea, I notice a man sporting a rich, full beard who was playing with a hand grenade, which he offered to give me by throwing it at me. I decline the offer politely. On the edge of the settlement lies a *sarai,* an old mud fort, where armed mujahideen have gathered around a vintage antiaircraft gun on the roof. Nearby, a Soviet "Stalin Organ" (a Katyusha multiple rocket launcher) that could very well have already been used to repel General Paulus' Sixth German Army at Stalingrad rusts in the sand.

After a four-hour drive, Herat's five gigantic minarets emerged from the shimmering heat in the valley of the Hari Rud River, remnants of the magnificent *madrassa* of Sultan Husain Baiqara and the *musalla* built by the Timurid Queen Gauhar Shad. In 1885, these exquisite fifteenth-century palaces of worship fell victim to the first Great Game when British military advisers ordered the *musalla* and the *madrassa* to be torn down, lest potential Russian invaders, who had advanced up to the oasis of Pandjeh north of Herat, exploit their strategic positions. Only nine minarets were left standing, three of which later succumbed to an earthquake. The Russian invasion one hundred years later led to an additional minaret being destroyed by a bomb.

Jan Malekzade, a political adviser to the UN in the province, gives me an initial tour of the city. He invites me to a guesthouse located in a quiet quarter of the town filled with trees. Behind the high walls fortified with barbed wire, UN employees relax in a well-tended, irrigated garden that feels like an oasis. After the Taliban fell, Malekzade moved here from his previous base in Tajikistan. Since his father is Iranian, the young Austrian gets along well in Herat where people speak Dari, a dialect related to Farsi. "In Herat, the Americans and the Iranians really confront each other for the first time," Malekzade says excitedly. "The town is chock-full of agents. Casablanca must have been like this in the early 1940s. Every week, the Americans strengthen their presence here, and they observe every move the Iranians make."

Herat's old town, whose narrow streets are alive with a medieval hustle and bustle, are filled with donkey carts and men in turbans and *shalwar kameez,* the traditional baggy trousers and long-tailed tunics worn by most Afghan and Pakistani men. They sell fruits, nuts, and vegetables. Groups of women in cornflower-blue *burqas* stroll past the stalls and haggle with the bazaar vendors. Their presence is a small move toward freedom, as they were not even allowed to leave their houses without their husbands under the Taliban. In another sign of remodernization, a boy wheelbarrows a battery-operated stereo through the streets, which blares once-banned rock music at top volume. Some thirty afghani, about one dollar, buy one of the Persian or Pakistani music tapes the boy offers for sale.

Several big-wheeled carriages come trundling toward us, their horses decorated with red bobbles and bells that jingle with each step. Behind the coachmen, groups of veiled women huddle together. A Toyota pickup truck skids around the corner and, honking wildly, parts its way through the crowd. Riding on the flatbed, young men brandish Kalashnikov assault rifles and grenade launchers. Nobody in the bazaar pays them any attention.

"At the UN, we know of several truckloads of brand-new, semi-automatic MP-5 rifles that arrived in Herat," Malekzade says. "On top of that, Ismail Khan's soldiers received new uniforms from the Iranians." He believes that Khan is working his contacts in the Iranian *Sepah-e-Pasdaran*, the Revolutionary Guards, who supported him for years in his resistance against Russians and Taliban. In Malekzade's view, the mullahs want to prevent a liberal and secular regime from coming to power in Afghanistan, which would then push for democratic reforms in Iran. There are rumors that Persian mullahs are sending money to Khan so that he can continue to pay for his troops' loyalty. "Whether Ismail Khan is really going to place them under the authority of the central government is very uncertain. Actually, he is currently enlarging his army," Malekzade says. "They have already clashed again with Pashtuns on the border with the Kandahar province."

We reach the famed Blue Mosque, whose azure domes and ceramic-tiled minarets resemble those of the mosque at the Holy Shrine in Mashhad. Both temples were built in the fourteenth century by Queen Gauhar Shad, daughter-in-law of the bloodthirsty ruler Tamerlane, when Herat was the cultural and political capital of Central Asia. Under the Timurids architecture flourished, as did painting, poetry, and music. Herat is often culturally considered a Persian city that has produced many important writers and artists.

Cultural legacy aside, many Heratis view the close relationship between Ismail Khan and Iran with suspicion. They watch Iranian television, have relatives across the border, and from a trading standpoint are closer to Tehran than to the Afghan capital Kabul, but Iranians have traditionally looked down on Afghans as impoverished cousins. "Iran did accept more than two million refugees and, unlike Pakistan, it did integrate them into society. However, the Iranians often abused them for dirty work and paid them badly," Malekzade says, adding that the level of education of returning refugees is still much higher than that of the locals, guaranteeing them positions of power. "The returnees will strengthen the ties with Iran and there will be many Iranian agents among them." And yet, he stresses, this would not inevitably increase Iran's political influence in the region around Herat. "People in Afghanistan have learned by now that outside interference is rarely to their advantage."

American activities in Herat are likewise viewed with skepticism. While no uniformed U.S. military personnel are present, many Americans in civilian clothes implausibly claim to be working for obscure humanitarian organizations. "That's true as long as you define Operation Enduring Freedom as a humanitarian mission," jokes a European Red Cross worker. American intelligence activities are so out in the open that members of the French organization Médecins sans Frontières (MSF) have decided to boycott the weekly expatriate parties at the Red Cross building in Herat. "We are a nonviolent organization and do not wish to be seen in the company of American military personnel," an MSF employee told me.

Meanwhile, it is common knowledge that the CIA has set up its regional headquarters in a guesthouse that once belonged to Ismail Khan. Located on a mountain slope directly above the amir's residence, it overlooks the entire oasis town, lying indefensibly in the wide Hari Rud river valley. Before Leonid Brezhnev's troops, the armies of Alexander the Great, Genghis Khan, and Tamerlane marched through this valley. The river emerges from the eastern Paropamisus Mountains, only to disappear somewhere in the western Kara Kum Desert. In clear weather, CIA reconnaissance might just be able to see the Iranian border.

*   *   *

My plan in Herat is to speak to Ismail Khan, who has once again become a regional key figure in the new Great Game. Just like the emir of Bukhara in the nineteenth century, Khan enjoys being wooed by two powerful rivals. Since it was not possible to approach the emir during the inauguration ceremony of the park on Navroz day, I pay a visit to his *chef de cabinet* in the governor's palace. Laughing at my written request for an interview, he says, "Today is the first day of school and His Excellency will speak at a grammar school in town in an hour's time. Go there and give the letter to him personally. Maybe you are lucky and His Excellency will receive you afterward."

The first day of school in Herat and throughout Afghanistan is a significant day. For the first time, girls—who for six years had been denied any kind of education by the Taliban—will be allowed to return to school. Cause for even greater excitement are the rumors that women will take advantage of the occasion and shed their much-hated *burqas*. As in most places in post-Taliban Afghanistan other than Kabul, women in Herat are still required to be covered head to toe in public, and run the risk of being punished by the religious police if they fail to comply. On television, the archconservative Khan himself exhorts women never to go uncovered in the streets. Teachers wishing to take off the *burqa* were told that they would lose their jobs. Most women lack the courage to be the sole person showing an uncovered face, and see their only chance is a common act under the protection of a large crowd.

Roughly half of the three hundred guests who show up for the official ceremony in the grammar school's assembly hall are women. My interpreter Yovid arranges a talk with a female teacher. "We want to get rid of the *burqa*," the woman says. "But every one of us is scared of what they might do to us. It is such a humiliation." There are reported cases of Afghan women resisting the dress code who then were beaten up by men, or had acid poured over their faces. During my talk with her, I find it very difficult to communicate through the *burqa*'s small window. Her eyes are practically invisible. Only her hands and her feet, in black high-heeled shoes, give some indication as to her age and appearance.

I ask Yovid to tell the woman about my discomfort. "You are not talking to a woman," she replies sadly. "You are talking to a nothing. I have been reduced to a nothing."

Seconds after we have said good-bye, I lose track of her, no longer distinguishable from the other blue women in the room. "You have to pay attention to the feet," Yovid says. "They tell you everything." He tells me how for four weeks he courted his young bride without ever seeing her face. Her voice, body movements, hands, and feet had been enough to intrigue him. I recall the story of a French reporter who dressed up as a woman during the war in order to slip into Afghanistan. The Taliban captured him immediately; he had kept his hiking boots on.

One by one, the women ascend the dark staircase to the assembly hall, passing rows of soldiers. None of them dares to take off the *burqa* yet, though a few women stumble on the stairs for lack of being able to see. Upstairs, women and men are segregated into two seating areas, with a middle aisle keeping them apart.

The crowd rises to their feet when Khan arrives. An entourage of several other dignitaries, including a UN representative and workers of the children's fund UNICEF, trail behind him. Khan drops into an armchair near the podium. Suddenly, as if on cue, dozens of women pull their *burqas* over their heads. Others stick their faces through slits they have cut into the head sections. Young female students emerge, as well as older teachers and mothers. All of them have covered their hair with dark *hijabs,* as do the women in Iran. A deathly hush descends on the hall. Some of the men, mostly turbaned graybeards, shake their heads at the ignominy. Other men, including some elderly, openly look at the women and smile at them. Unperturbed, Khan keeps his eyes fixed on the ground.

After a children's choir has sung Afghan songs, the emir approaches the podium. The entire audience rises respectfully. A father holds up a young girl who throws blossoms onto the ruler's head. "*Allahu akbar!*" the men roar three times. Khan begins his speech by exclaiming "*Bismillah-ir-Rahman-ir-Rahim,*" in the name of Allah, the kind and merciful. The warlord makes no comment on what we have just witnessed. Instead, his message is about education. "Our enemies have tried to keep us in the dark, without education. This is what a nation does when seeking to destroy another nation," he says, a thinly disguised barb at Pakistan for having supported the Taliban for seven years.

Khan speaks fluently and charismatically, his audience listening with rapt attentiveness. Just as he singles out poverty and ignorance as the worst problems in Afghanistan, it begins to rain. Then it pours, the first substantial rainfall in Herat in more than four years of drought. "*Allahu akbar!*" some men shout out in ecstatic joy, staring out the windows at the big drops drumming onto the school's tin roof. It is a moving moment. Khan exclaims, "And look what happens: our children are going back to school, and Allah gives us rain for our crops."

After the ceremony, hardly anyone notices that all the women leaving the school have put the *burqas* on again. The religious police detain and take away four Iranian journalists, for having illegally photographed the women's faces. The cultural drought in Herat continues.

My interpreter Yovid manages to hand my written request for an interview to the emir. Two days later, Khan's *chef de cabinet*, Sahid Yussufi, takes me to the ruler's residence. "Right here, another one of those American cluster bombs exploded this past weekend," Yussufi, a portly man in his thirties, tells me as we drive through a park in the outskirts of town. "A family at a picnic: the father is dead, the mother and her two daughters lost their legs." Yussufi is visibly angry at the U.S. Air Force. "And now they do not even remove the unexploded bombs!" Yussufi does not conceal his outrage over what he perceives as backtracking on the promises made by Americans and Britons. "Empty, just plain empty," he says bitterly.

We arrive at a splendid 1970s bungalow, located on a mountain slope overlooking Herat. Next to the villa is a large swimming pool, and a park stretches down into the valley. A mere two hundred yards above the residence, guarded by soldiers, is the guesthouse occupied by CIA agents. Next to enormous antennas, two men watch us with binoculars from a balcony.

"Whatever you do, do not ask His Excellency about the Americans up there, that would make him angry," Yussufi advises me as we walk up to the terrace. The view encompasses the entire plain, from the *musalla* minarets in the west to the army barracks in the east that were destroyed by American fighter jets and Cruise missiles. Burned-out tanks and armored vehicles are scattered across the slope below us. Yussufi points at a spot further up in the mountains. "That is where the only Al Qaeda training camp in western Afghanistan was located. It was a very secret place; only the top Taliban and Arabs had access to it." Here, too, Cruise missiles and B-52s have done a thorough job, leaving behind only rubble too risky to approach as it is littered with countless mines and unexploded cluster bombs.

The *amir sahib* is not home yet. Instead, I am greeted by Sar Wary, the emir's court painter. With pride, he presents his murals that hang throughout the bungalow. They depict the Lion of Herat, walkie-talkie in hand, directing his artillery in the mountains. Wary has painted more than 150 paintings in his life, but tells me, "When the Taliban took Herat they destroyed all my paintings that showed faces. They said my art was un–Islamic. After that, I was only allowed to do flowers and landscapes."

Outside, the emir's brown Toyota Land Cruiser races up the slope's serpentine road, followed by some thirty pickup trucks at high speed, loaded with armed fighters whose beards and turbans fly in the wind. "We have to wait a bit longer," Yussufi explains. "The mujahideen council has been summoned to an urgent meeting." About fifty battle-hardened commanders gather on the ground floor, punctuating the meeting with repeated cries of "*Allahu akbar!*" To my surprise, I recognize a familiar face among the guests, the oldest son of Sibghatullah Mujaddedi, the first post-communist Afghan president and still an important power broker. As the head of the religious Naqshbandi order, members of the Mujaddedi family have for centuries been the kingmakers in Kabul. On the sidelines of the war council, I strike up a conversation with a younger mujahed named Sahid, a Tajik not from Herat but from the Panjshir valley north of Kabul. He claims to have commanded two hundred men in the Northern Alliance. "I have come to Herat in order to speak to Ismail Khan," says Sahid, who is yet not willing to disclose what he wishes to speak to the emir about. Since joining the mujahideen in their struggle against the Soviets at the age of sixteen, Sahid has served with several different warlords. Under General Massoud's command he conquered Kabul in 1992, only to switch sides to his Pashtun archenemy Hekmatyar. "In the meantime, I fought as a mercenary for Azerbaijan against the Armenians in Karabakh," Sahid remembers. "They were paying a lot of money to war-experienced Afghans."

After the Taliban's rise to power, he once again joined Massoud, acting as one of his liaison officers in Russia. "We received arms from the Russians and transported them to our positions in the North." Sahid carries a notepad and a Thuraya satellite phone instead of a gun, and comes across as a good organizer, but remains silent about what he has been doing since the end of the war. "Business," he says vaguely. Noticing the two men watching us with binoculars from the CIA headquarters, we step behind a tree. "The Americans would like to find out if any Iranians have gathered here, too," Sahid whispers. "The Iranians helped us the most in the war against the Taliban. Of course, we do not reject their help now, either." Sahid also expresses what has become an all too familiar view in the region. "We Afghans know very well that the Americans did not come here to help us—they are here because they need Afghanistan to get access to the oil and gas at the Caspian Sea."

The war council is adjourned, and Khan is finally ready for an audience. "Do not forget to address His Excellency as 'His Excellency'!" the *chef de cabinet* urges me a final time. Khan enters the room with a slight shuffle, but his handshake is firm. We sit on a soft couch while a servant brings pistachios and tea.

Khan does not seem surprised that Herat, just as in the nineteenth-century Great Game between Russians and Britons, finds itself again in a geopolitical crossfire. "For ages, Herat has been a very special city, famous for its trade. It occupies a key position between Central Asia and Pakistan. The plans for a pipeline through our province show this—this is a very exciting project for us," Khan says, acknowledging that it would help improve relations between Afghanistan and its neighbors Turkmenistan and Pakistan. "If at all possible we will realize this project."

Khan diplomatically plays down his relationship with Iran. "The Iranians are good neighbors, nothing else," and points out that the two countries share a four-hundred-mile-long border, which is crossed by traders every day. Khan concedes that "Iran supported the struggle of the mujahideen, as did other countries," but dismisses charges that he received arms from Iran as late as this past year. "We had twenty-three years of war, so we have enough arms down here and do not need any new ones."

Khan feels his fighters are in complete control of Herat, making it the safest city in the entire country for citizens to move about freely without fear of bandits. His soldiers strictly enforce a ten o'clock curfew, stopping drivers with assault rifles and demanding that night's password. Herat is prey mostly to gangs of stray dogs that howl long into the night.

"It pains me to see how helpless my nation is at present," Khan says, sipping on tea. "It is a disgrace to be dependent on outside help." And while not a single dollar of the billions in aid promised by the international community has reached Herat, nobody in his town, Khan believes, would want to give Iran a role in Afghan politics. "After the experiences the Russians and the Pakistanis made with us, every neighbor should know that it does not pay to meddle with our affairs." As to whether this is equally true for the American troops, Khan answers cautiously. "I do not see the Americans as invaders or occupiers. I do not want to judge them by their deeds in the past. Lately, they have played a positive role in the fight against the Taliban and Al Qaeda." To retain its good reputation, Khan insists, the United States would now have to begin with Afghanistan's reconstruction, and leave the country as soon as all the terrorists have been defeated. "If they stay on against the will of the Afghan people, they could meet the same fate as the Russians did." His words do not sound like a warning, but like well-intentioned advice.

*   *   *

Several months after my meeting with Khan, I find myself in a convoy of dark Lexus limousines racing through the streets of Kabul. The city has changed dramatically since my last visit right after the war. Many new shops have opened, women walk the streets without the cover of a *burqa,* and countless huge off-roaders belonging to the UN and NGOs creep, through the heavy, bumper-to-bumper traffic. Kabul has become terribly over-crowded. Over the summer of 2002, hundreds of thousands of refugees have returned from Pakistan. The twenty or so different ethnicities that exist in Afghanistan mingle freely in the capital. I spot tall, fierce-looking Pashtuns, fairer-skinned Tajiks, blond-haired Nuristanis, Mongol-looking Hazaras, and many others.

In the backseat of the Lexus at the head of this convoy is Ahmed Massoud, the fifteen-year-old son of the legendary mujahideen leader. He has allowed me to accompany him to his initiation as Afghanistan's future leader. Dressed in a beige suit, he nervously shifts around on the leather seats, his hands crumpling his *pakoul,* a flat-brimmed felt cap. Today, September 9, is the one year anniversary of the assassination of his father, the "Lion of Panjshir."

Shortly before the terror attacks in New York and Washington, two French-speaking men arrived at the Northern Alliance headquarters at Khoja Bahauddin, disguised as television journalists seeking an interview with Massoud. No sooner had the talk begun than the men, now suspected to have been Al Qaeda terrorists, set off a bomb hidden in a battery belt. One of the assassins was killed instantly, the other attempted to flee but was captured and killed. Massoud was severely injured and died within minutes. To keep his death temporarily secret from nervous Northern Alliance troops, the body was flown by helicopter to a hospital in Tajikistan. Nobody had any idea that his assassination would be only the first act in a much greater drama.

At his father's funeral in his birthplace of Jangalak in the Panjshir Valley north of Kabul the then-fourteen-year-old Ahmed, his only son, declared, "I want to be the successor of my father." So far, he has largely been shielded from politics, though, spending his time at the family home in Panjshir and at a school in the

Iranian city of Mashhad. Behind the scenes, though, he is being groomed as a child regent.

The convoy reaches the Kabul stadium, where the main ceremony for the anniversary of Massoud's death is to take place. Thousands of people are milling around on the square in front of the arena. Units of the International Security Assistance Force (ISAF) guard the entrance gates in armored vehicles. An ISAF helicopter hovers above the crowds. Since the end of the war, some five thousand peacekeepers from twenty-two nations enforce law and order in Kabul. The Afghan government has repeatedly urged the antiterror coalition to enlarge the ISAF contingent and also to station the peacekeepers in other parts of the country. Outside the capital, the situation is still very unstable, especially in the southeast where clan feuds keep flaring up. So far, the ISAF leadership has reacted cautiously to the Afghan requests. It is concerned that an overstretched peacekeeping force might be drawn into armed conflict. The Bush administration has dropped its initial opposition to expanding the ISAF, but it is still unwilling to commit any of its eight thousand ground troops to the peacekeeping mission. Cleaning up and creating order after a war is a job the Americans are more than happy to leave to their European allies.

Several of the forty state-of-the-art police cars given to the Afghans by the German government have taken up position around the stadium. Today, Kabul has been placed on high security alert, in expectation of terrorist attacks. Only a few days earlier, a car bomb went off in a busy shopping street. More than thirty people were killed, and dozens were injured. At the time of the explosion, my translator and I were a mere three minutes' walk from the scene, which was covered with mangled bodies and severed limbs.

The terrorists used an insidious tactic to maximize casualties. They ignited a small explosive to drive the crowds toward the end of the street, where a much larger bomb lay hidden in the trunk of a yellow Toyota taxi. The detonation was so powerful that it shattered all the windows on the street. The attack shocked the city, as not since the Taliban takeover of Kabul in 1996 had a single incident caused the violent death of so many people. Government and international security forces warned of impending Al Qaeda attacks during the September 11 anniversary week.

Later that day, with the Afghan government reeling from the bomb attack, President Karzai barely survived an assassination attempt in Kandahar. He had traveled to the former Taliban stronghold to attend his brother's wedding. When he and Kandahar's governor left the governor's palace, they climbed into the presidential limousine. An Afghan soldier jumped forward and opened fire with his AK-47 assault rifle. Two bullets entered the car through the windshield, missing Karzai by only a few inches. One of the president's Afghan bodyguards was mortally wounded before his colleagues shot and killed the assassin. While Karzai's limousine sped off, his bodyguards from the U.S. Special Forces searched the streets for more suspects. The assassin, who apparently acted on his own, was later revealed as a Pashtun from a village near Kandahar, notorious for its Taliban sympathies. The threat of a coup d'etat rattled the country's most powerful cabinet members who gathered at the Intercontinental Hotel for frantic, late-night consultations. One minister, visibly shaken, told me, "If Karzai dies, that would be the end. Then the civil war would start all over again."

The next morning, President Karzai returned to Kabul. The tall Pashtun, dressed in a finely woven gray *chapan* robe, was flanked at the airport by dozens of American bodyguards wielding submachine guns. Karzai disappeared inside an armored Chevrolet Suburban. The convoy raced off, escorted by an armored U.S. military vehicle with a top-mounted machine gun. After Karzai's deputy Haji Qadier had been betrayed and murdered by his own Afghan bodyguards several months earlier, the Bush administration decided to provide U.S. Special Forces for Karzai's protection. Thus, the "new face of Afghanistan," as Western media are fond of calling the Ben Kingsley lookalike, is the world's only sovereign head of state to be guarded in his own country at the expense of the U.S. government. Many Afghans find it telling that Karzai is unable to find a dozen men from his own people whom he can trust with his life.

President Karzai immediately convened his cabinet for a special session. Government spokesmen were quick to identify remaining Al Qaeda and Taliban elements, supported by the Pakistani Interservice Intelligence (ISI), as the parties responsible for both attacks. The Pashtun warlord Gulbuddin Hekmatyar is seen as one of the prime suspects: from his underground hiding-place, the virulently anti–Western Islamic fundamentalist has repeatedly called for a jihad against the Karzai regime and the American forces in the country. Although more attacks were expected, particularly around the anniversary of Massoud's death, the government decided to proceed with the festivities.

On this bright autumn morning the tension around the stadium is palpable. The young Ahmed Massoud is a prime target for assassination, but if that scares him, he does not show it. Putting on his *pakoul,* he jumps out of the Lexus and races up the stairs to the VIP rostrum, his entourage of bodyguards and government officials struggling to keep pace. "He is a leader, just like his father," a puffing Afghan tells me while we scramble after the boy.

In an arena where the Taliban used to publicly execute wrong-doers, some ten thousand people, most of them soldiers and schoolchildren, fill the stands as well as the football field itself. Many girls are also present, and not one of them wears a *burqa.* People carry banners with prayers for the martyr Massoud, while the soldiers—many of whom are bearded invalids in improvised wheelchairs—wave miniature national flags and wear T-shirts emblazoned with Massoud's portrait.

Gathered on the VIP rostrum are the powers-that-be of the new Afghanistan: ministers and religious leaders, foreign diplomats, UN dignitaries, and high-ranking officers of the U.S. military and ISAF. Among the top power players present are Defense Minister Qasim Fahim, Foreign Minister Dr. Abdullah Abdullah, and former Interior Minister Yunis Qanouni, the triumvirate of close Massoud associates known as the "Three Panjshiris." Next to them, ex-President Burhanuddin Rabbani and Abdul Rasul Sayyaf, two of the country's leading Islamic fundamentalists, lean toward each other for a chat. Only President Karzai is missing, for he has traveled to New York for the ceremony of the September 11 anniversary. I am the only journalist in the VIP area, as the majority of the press and television media have gathered on the football field below. Ahmed Massoud sits down in the front row, where several political leaders have already taken their places. Some greet him with a jovial handshake, while others bow their heads deferentially.

Ahmed's uncle Wali Massoud, the guerilla leader's younger brother, looks on with pride. "I hope that the boy will one day succeed his father," he says. The slight, mustached man who served as chargé d'affaires at the Afghan embassy in London is today one of the savviest players in Kabul's ongoing power struggle, and a rival to President Karzai. The amiable and impeccably mannered Wali has just founded his own party, the Massoudist National Movement of Afghanistan. A more secular alternative to the Islamic party *Jamiat-e-Islami,* it purports to be the political home for all of Massoud's supporters who are eager to see his legacy preserved.

Wali is openly critical of President Karzai. "At the moment, Afghanistan is leaderless. Karzai is the president but he is not a leader." His opinion reflects a growing feeling in Afghanistan that President Karzai is incapable of rallying behind him the country's various political and ethnic forces. Even UN officials privately complain about Karzai's lack of organizational skills, seeing him increasingly as a figurehead for the media. While still popular with the common people, his power in the far reaches of the country is so limited that he has already been nicknamed "the mayor of Kabul." When Wali compares him with his deceased brother, Karzai predictably does not fare too well. "My brother knew the problems of the Afghan people; Karzai does not. All he thinks about is his own political career. But he provides no direction, and he has disappointed the hopes people placed in him at the *Loya Jirga* [grand council of leaders]."

Ahmed joins our conversation. His uncle puts his hand tenderly on the boy's shoulder. "Today is a sad day for me," Ahmed says. "I miss my father very much. But I am also very excited because in a little while I have to make a speech." The boy's voice has not yet broken, and his handsome face is still a child's, but his father's long and angular features already show through, especially his dark eyes. I ask him if one day he intends to walk in his father's footsteps. "I am still too young and inexperienced," he replies. "But if the people want me to I will be their leader."

Sitting next to us, Defense Minister Marshal Qasim Fahim has closely followed our conversation. The brutish-looking Panjshiri Tajik, Massoud's longtime second-in-command, is currently seen as the most powerful man in post–Taliban Afghanistan, commanding the loyalty of thousands of troops in arms. He slams his hand on Ahmed's back, thundering, "Yes, of course you will be the leader of Afghanistan, no doubt about it." Then he laughs sardonically. Flinching, Ahmed asks me if we could continue our talk later. "The boy does not feel comfortable talking about this in the presence of a certain man," his uncle Wali whispers.

Defense Minister Fahim is the most powerful member of the Panjshiri clan whom the American B-52s have bombed into power in Kabul. Unlike Qanouni and Abdullah, Fahim is a cunning militarist out to control the Afghan national army, whose recruitment and training is being overseen by the U.S. Army. Many political observers also see Fahim as the most pro–Russian member of the cabinet.

A few days prior to the Massoud anniversary, Russian Defense Minister Sergei Ivanov arrived in Kabul on a state visit. At a reception in the Intercontinental Hotel, the former mujahed Fahim praised what he called the "traditionally good relations between Afghanistan and Russia" as if neither the Soviet invasion nor the jihad had ever taken place. Overweight Russian officers and graying Afghan jihadi veterans, once mortal enemies, cordially sat next to each other. Defense Minister Ivanov shed an equally mild light on history, pronouncing the bloody war in the 1980s as "experiments of the past," and handed a gift to Fahim: a Russian sword. "We Russians give the sword only to brave officers," said Ivanov, and both men looked equally flattered. At that moment, my translator Baqi, himself a veteran of the anti-Soviet struggle, left the room in silent protest. "I am disgusted," he explained. "What is happening in there is immoral. It is an insult to the hundreds of thousands who were killed back then."

The ceremony in the stadium begins with a mullah reciting a prayer, followed by the singing of the national anthem. A giant portrait of Commander Massoud is unveiled. "Dear Massoud, we will follow your way," an inscription reads. Against a backdrop of red roses, the warlord resembles a saint, or an Afghan Che Guevara. This portrait only adds to the unparalleled quasireligious personality cult that has broken out in Kabul since the war. There is hardly a telegraph pole or taxi windshield that is not plastered with Massoud posters, often seriously obstructing the driver's view.

All of Kabul's political players now seek to claim the national hero's legacy for their particular goals. Prior to the festivities at the stadium, a two-day "International Conference for Massoud Studies" was held at the Intercontinental Hotel. Political leaders, academics, and associates offered lengthy eulogies and hagiographies on the martyr. At the conference's closing ceremony, the participants launched a project to nominate Massoud posthumously for that year's Nobel Peace Prize. The fact that Massoud contributed his share to the Afghan bloodshed by refusing to share power with his mortal enemy Hekmatyar in the early 1990s has been consigned to official oblivion.

"It was I who for twenty-three years fought by Commander Massoud's side," shouts Marshal Fahim during his speech in the stadium, to cheers from his troops. Fahim's speech is one of many in the socialist-style pageant, so I strike up a conversation with a senior UN diplomat, who wishes to remain anonymous. "This government is soon going to be in serious trouble," he says. "It is lopsided, with Panjshiri Tajik at the helm of all important ministries. The Pashtuns will not put up with that for long and if the U.S. troops ever pull out, there will be civil war again. Kabul is an island in the wild, uncontrollable ocean that is Afghanistan."

After the speeches are finished, Ahmed sits down alone on a chair by the giant portrait of his father. An assistant holds an umbrella to shield the boy's head from the sun as dozens of veteran delegations march past him, laying wreaths of plastic flowers at the foot of his father's portrait. Ahmed shakes hands with every fighter. Government members, including Marshal Fahim, soon join the procession. To mark the end of what is now clearly an oriental initiation ceremony, Ahmed addresses the people in the stadium and, via radio and television, the entire Afghan population. "Do not just mourn the loss but do look ahead and continue on my father's way," the boy exclaims in a moving speech, drawing cheers from the troops in the stadium. One could almost believe in this moment that Ahmed was much more than just a mascot of an increasingly shaky regime.

A few days after the ceremony, I drive through the southern parts of Kabul. The impression of a completely destroyed city, as seen from images of foreign television coverage, is misleading. The residential areas are laid out around several steep hills. North of this natural boundary, rows of houses are almost totally intact. Since most attackers, particularly the Pakistan-backed Hekmatyar mujahideen and the Taliban, fired at the city from the south, their grenades and missiles did not fall in the protective shadow of the hills. On the southern slopes, the sight is an entirely different one. Not a single building left unscathed, a barren wasteland of dismal ruins stretching out for several miles, reminding me of pictures of Dresden or Hiroshima in 1945. Bullet-riddled, pockmarked walls are covered with starbursts from shellfire. Roofs have caved in. Even thin telegraph poles were hit and snapped. Those left standing are covered with posters of Commander Massoud. In King Zahir Shah's pseudoclassicist palace, where the monarch used to throw glittering parties before his overthrow in 1973, swallows nest in shell holes today. Of the seven hundred thousand people who used to live in these areas of Kabul, only sixty thousand have remained, many of them seeking shelter in squalid cellars.

With so much of the country in ruins, Amin Farhang, the minister for the reconstruction of Afghanistan, is one of the most important political figures in Kabul. Working in an ugly, unfinished building across the street from the heavily fortified U.S. embassy, Farhang, an economist who for many years has worked as a professor at Bochum University in Germany, looks very tired. "As you can imagine, the reconstruction of this country is no easy task," Farhang says. "Apart from the economic and political sphere, reconstruction has to occur on a social and psychological level as well. After more than two decades of war, every Afghan is more or less mentally ill, and it will take years to wean people away from the Kalashnikov culture toward a civil society."

Farhang's primary concern, though, is that economic reconstruction is taking so long to get off the ground. Afghanistan's infrastructure—roads, schools, and administration—is in a shambles, as is the private sector, where hardly any jobs have been created over the past several months. "After the war the international community was all excited and promised us billions of dollars in aid," Farhang complains. "Soon after they started looking for excuses not to pay." Of the $1.8 billion the Afghan government was slated to receive in 2002, only $90 million has actually arrived. About $1.2 billion went to the UN and nongovernmental organizations, citing unsatisfactory political development and lack of security in the country. "To get security you need reconstruction first," says Farhang angrily. "It is the United States that keeps arming the regional warlords and waging a war on our territory, but you cannot reconstruct a country that is simultaneously being used as a target."

If there is any good news in Afghanistan, it is the resurrection of the Afghan pipeline route. "The pipeline project is a done deal. Some big oil companies want to get into business with us," Farhang says excitedly. "Finally, after years of waiting Afghanistan will become an important transit country for Central Asia." As early as a few months after the war, the energy ministers of Afghanistan, Pakistan, and Turkmenistan convened for several preparatory meetings. On May 29, 2002, President Karzai flew to Pakistan's capital, Islamabad, to join President Pervez Musharraf and Turkmen dictator Saparmurat Nyazov to sign a treaty authorizing construction of a $3.2 billion gas pipeline from Turkmenistan to the Pakistani port of Gwadar, with a projected capacity of about one trillion cubic feet of gas per year. At a later stage, a second parallel pipeline for oil is also planned. The nine-hundred-mile route runs through the Herat-Kandahar corridor, which was under Taliban control until the victorious U.S. campaign in Afghanistan.

After twenty-three years of war and destruction, the pipeline, which could generate as many as 12,000 jobs and up to $300 million in transit fees per year, represents hope for economic progress. However, the plans could also cast a murky light onto the Bush administration's objectives in its Afghan campaign following September 11, 2001. Besides Osama bin Laden's elimination, the enormous oil and gas reserves of the Caspian Sea, six hundred miles to the northwest of Afghanistan, appear as the great price in the battle over Kabul. Skeptics and critics of the U.S. campaign have repeatedly pointed out the American oil industry's interest in Afghanistan as a potential corridor for a pipeline from the Caspian Sea to the Persian Gulf. Transport routes through the volatile south Caucasus and politically isolated Iran now appear risky by comparison to the southeastern route through Afghanistan. Its great advantage lies in ending on the Pakistani shore, directly to the east of the congested Strait of Hormuz.

"Unocal is still interested in the project," Farhang says. "But right now, they are keeping a low profile. Because of their cooperation with the Taliban they have a bad reputation in the country." The minister also claims the U.S. energy giant ExxonMobil and the French company TotalFinaElf as other potential pipeline suitors. The Afghan government has not yet officially invited tenders for the project, but the $2 billion construction is likely to be financed by the Asian Development Bank, which is currently conducting a feasibility study for the industry.

Politically, the interests in the pipeline issue have not significantly changed. "Back then, Pakistan created the Taliban specifically in order to be able to build this pipeline, and the United States supported this," Farhang says. Pakistan, always in dire need for energy resources, also hoped the Taliban would pass on the $300 million to $500 million in transit fees and customs in exchange for support. As evidence of Pakistani-American collusion, Farhang recalls an incident in 1996 when the Pakistani interior minister took the U.S. ambassador on a tour of Taliban-controlled Kandahar and Herat. "Apparently, the American ambassador was very much impressed with the stability in the country, and he expressed support to the Pakistanis for their policy," Farhang says. "What an insult to the Afghan people. I won't ever forget that!" Now, he adds, the United States is pursuing the same self-serving economic goals as in the 1990s but with direct military intervention. "Politics is a business. The United States won't ever give up their military bases in Afghanistan. From here, they will control the entire region." Farhang remains convinced, though, that the United States will have competition. "The Russians and the Iranians will once again try to sabotage the pipeline project."

In my talks with managers of other oil companies active in the Caspian region, the Afghan pipeline project evokes as much skepticism as interest. Unless peace and security are ultimately guaranteed in Afghanistan, it will be impossible to secure foreign investment. None of the companies I interviewed for this book have confirmed any contact with the new regime in Kabul.

In postwar Afghanistan, the ties between politics and the petroleum business have become much easier to recognize. President Bush's special envoy to Afghanistan and member of the National Security Council, Zalmay Khalilzad, had previously worked for Unocal on an elaborate risk analysis for the Afghan pipeline. While serving in the Clinton administration, the Kabul-born diplomat argued strongly in favor of official recognition of the Taliban regime, even though its radical views and excesses were common knowledge. "I am confident that [the Taliban] would welcome an American reengagement. The Taliban does not practice the anti-U.S. style of fundamentalism practiced by Iran—it is closer to the Saudi model."[1]

Only after Unocal placed its Afghan plans on hold did the senior strategist at the conservative think tank The Rand Corporation condemn the Taliban. Today, few decisions are made in Kabul without Khalilzad's consent. In early December 2002, President Bush appointed him as the special envoy for the civil reconstruction of a postwar Iraq.

Robert Finn, the new American ambassador to Afghanistan, is likewise a Caspian oil expert. In 1992, the career diplomat

opened the U.S. embassy in Baku, and was present at the signing of "Contract of the Century" between Azerbaijan and Western oil companies.

Afghan President Hamid Karzai himself worked as an adviser
to Unocal. In 1997, he represented the American company in pipeline negotiations with the Taliban leadership. Today, the Pashtun
Karzai, who openly supported the Taliban until 1994, enjoys
Washington's firm backing. In a bid to strengthen his power, in
the spring of 2002 Karzai selected Djuma Mohammaddi to be the
minister of industry. Warmly recommended by the Bush administration, Mohammaddi worked for fifteen years for the International Monetary Fund in the United States, and led the Afghan
delegation in the pipeline negotiations with Turkmenistan and
Pakistan.

"It was Mohammaddi who kept pushing the pipeline project
with tireless commitment," says Mahfooz Nedai, his deputy in the
Ministry of Industries. "At one of the interministerial meetings in
Islamabad an argument broke out between us and the Pakistanis,
and the whole thing was on the verge of failing. But Mohammaddi
solved all contentious issues with his counterparts. He wanted the
pipeline at any price." For Deputy Minister Nedai, who at the
Afghan Loya Jirga in June ran for the presidency against Karzai,
the reason is simple. "Washington has sent their men into our government for good reason. The Americans have not come to Central Asia just for the terrorists."

In late February 2003, Mohammaddi, returning from pipeline talks with the Pakistani government in Islamabad, died in a
mysterious plane crash in Pakistan. A U.S. diplomat in Kabul who
wished to be identified only as "Bill" plays down the connections
between politics and Big Oil. "For America, Afghanistan has no
value in itself. There are no raw materials and as a transit country for a pipeline it is not particularly suitable, either." Bill
dismisses the idea that Unocal came to a different conclusion:
"Back then, Unocal's plans were based on a completely false
analysis of the political and social situation in Afghanistan. Just
take the security risks. To protect this pipeline you would need
an entire army." The only goal pursued in the U.S.-led military

intervention, the diplomat stresses, has been to rid terrorists in Afghanistan of their sanctuary. "All else is conspiracy theories. There was no and there is no master plan: not one American would have thought on September 10 that our troops would be here today."

Bill adds that U.S. forces had no intention of establishing permanent military bases in the country. "If we were to stay here after we have destroyed the Taliban and Al Qaeda, the Afghans would soon no longer view us as guests, but as occupiers. It is with good reason that our defense attaché is currently reading a book on Vietnam," he says, then quickly adds, "Of course, we will keep some advisers and trainers here for the Afghan army, like we did in Iran in the 1950s and 1960s when we needed the oil there. Ever since the Iranians woke up in November and suddenly saw our troops at their border, they have naturally been in shock." Bill points to reports of Al Qaeda fighters finding refuge in Iran. By channeling arms to Ismail Khan, the envoy believes Tehran is trying to set up a satrapy in Herat. "But that is not going to work. We do not recognize that Afghanistan is part of an Iranian sphere of influence." Bill sees the relations between Afghans and Iranians, due to Kabul's lack of interest, as being in bad shape. His words have the ring of the nineteenth-century Great Game. "Oh, the Great Game never stopped around here," Bill concurs.

Another U.S. diplomat in Central Asia I interview shortly thereafter insists that Washington does not pursue any economic interests in Afghanistan. "We were attacked. Up to that point we had not wasted a single thought on Afghanistan." The diplomat, whose responsibilities include Caspian energy issues, assures me he had not once been occupied with a north-south pipeline running through Afghanistan. "Not a single report did I or my colleagues write on this route. We have always concentrated on the east-west corridors."

His statement is inconsistent with a U.S. Department of Energy report, released only a few days before the terror attacks of September 2001, that cites, "Afghanistan's significance from an energy standpoint stems from its geographical position as a potential transit route for oil and natural gas exports from central

Asia to the Arabian Sea."[2] The U.S. diplomat acknowledges that Washington now has begun to look seriously at the possibility of an Afghan pipeline. "The U.S. government is prepared to cooperate with American companies who have such plans. After all, Unocal has shown that the pipeline is feasible and profitable."

Bagram airbase, headquarters of all U.S. and allied antiterrorist troops in Afghanistan, lies about twenty-five miles north of Kabul on the Shamali Plains. The tarmaced road leading to the base is in amazingly good shape, considering the number of troop and tank movements it has seen over the years. It was on this road that anti–Taliban forces, along with their American and British allies streamed south to Kabul in November 2001. They met with no opposition as the Taliban had already fled to Kandahar. It was not the first time Kabul fell into the hands of an attacking force without a fight. When General Sir John Keane entered Kabul on June 30, 1839, with an army of fifteen thousand men, not a single shot was fired. Afghanistan's ruler Emir Dost Mohammed had fled and finally surrendered in November 1840. Sir William Macnaghten, political officer in Kabul, wrote in a report to the governor general of India that "from Dan to Beersheba" all was quiet in Afghanistan.[3]

Yet only a year later, the British Empire suffered the worst military catastrophe in its history. Mutinous Afghans under the command of Dost Mohammed's son forced the British troops and their families to retreat from Kabul. With rebel forces hot on their heels, the Britons and Indians tried to reach the safety of a fort in the eastern town of Jalalabad. Only one man, the military doctor William Bryden, arrived there a week later. He was the sole survivor as the Afghans had shown no mercy. The massacre inspired Rudyard Kipling to write "The Young British Soldier," which ends, "When you're wounded and left on Afghanistan's plains/And the women come out to cut out what remains/Jest roll on your rifle and blow out your brains/An' go to your Gawd like a soldier."

The last army to invade Afghanistan and, more importantly, leave it relatively unscathed was led by Alexander the Great. All subsequent conquerors met with ferocious resistance. "The Affghan will bear poverty, insecurity of life; but he will not tolerate foreign rule," Sir John Lawrence, then the British viceroy of India, noted in the late 1860s. "The moment he has a chance, he will rebel."[4]

Security precautions are extremely tight at Bagram airbase. Visitors need to pass two "Afghan gates" guarded by local soldiers. Then I walk to the American gate, where a press officer picks me up in a sand-colored Humvee. We drive through a jumble of wooden barracks and other spread-out military installations. Bagram airbase is so huge that it is made up of four different "cities." One has been named "viper city" for all the snakes that the U.S. forces encountered on their arrival in December 2001. More than 3,500 American and allied troops are stationed at Bagram. A few days before my visit, the 82nd Airborne from North Carolina took over from the 10th Mountain Division from New York as the main contingent. Every few minutes, a C-17 transport plane lands or takes off on the Soviet-built airstrip, ferrying troops and materiel. Chinook helicopters take U.S. soldiers to remote operational areas in the mountains near the Pakistani border. At the far end of the airstrip, I see a group of Apache and Black Hawk battle helicopters.

It is dinnertime. I am allowed to walk to the canteen without a military escort. On the way, soldiers speed past me on "gators," lawnmower-type vehicles and the most common means of transport at Bagram. To protect themselves against the dust and rocks, the drivers wear dark goggles. Undaunted by the filthy air, other soldiers use their free time for a run. A group of Afghan men, dressed in rags, walks toward the exit gates. They are locals working on the base. Under close guard of several American GIs, the men look like a chain gang. I later ask a press officer about it. "We do not want them to get anywhere close to the sensitive equipment we have on the base," she replies.

Passing the fuel handlers' tents after dinner I notice two wooden street signs marking the crossroads between "Exxon Street" and "Petro Boulevard." I peek into the "morale tent" where soldiers watch horror films and shoot pool. In the media tent, a sparsely furnished yet power-supplied tent nicknamed

"Pressmenistan," Bagram-based wire reporters while away their days and nights, waiting for newsworthy stories to report. With Operation Enduring Freedom being phased out and attention focusing on Iraq, this is not exactly a dream job. "The military don't give us anything to report on," complains an Associated Press reporter who arrived from a posting in East Africa two weeks earlier. "If they don't become more cooperative, I will do a story on the Afghans who smuggle hash into the camp and sell it to the soldiers."

At the mention of illicit substances Jim, a cameraman for a twenty-four-hour TV news channel, pulls out a bottle of Uzbek vodka he claims to have bought from Afghan guards at the gate. In his mid-thirties, Jim has been stationed at Bagram for six months already but says he does not mind. "I was in the military for eleven years myself. One gets used to camp life that way." For fun, Jim and his colleagues keep scorpions they caught on the base in a terrarium inside the press tent. "We give them names. The fun part is to starve them and then watch them finish each other off." The journalists have painted the tarpaulin behind the terrarium with gravestones bearing inscriptions such as "RIP Charlie. He died with his sword in his hand."

That night, I find it hard to sleep on my camp bed. A massive sandstorm sweeps across the Shamali Plains, while military planes continue to take off and land throughout the night. Somewhere in the distance a mine goes off. The next morning, the sandstorm is still raging, at times reducing visibility to a few yards.

As I leave the tent for a walk, I cover my face with a scarf. In one section of the base, separated by barbed wire, I see brawny men who have adapted their outward appearance, right down to the beard and the *patou* blanket-*cum*-scarf, to their Afghan environment. They are part of a couple of hundred U.S. Special Forces fighters based here. Many of the commandos are recuperating in Bagram after weeks on special missions in the mountains. They bear the brunt of a military campaign that has effectively developed into counterinsurgency warfare.

Operating in teams of ten to twenty men, they pick alleged trouble spots, recruit and pay local allies, and set themselves up in a safe house. From there, the commandos search neighboring villages for remaining Al Qaeda and Taliban fighters or sympathizers to ferry them to Bagram or, in some cases, Guantanamo Bay, Cuba, for interrogation. Reconnaissance is vital, as the situation can change quickly. Their missions have had mixed results. Observers and locals criticize the heavy-handed kick-the-door-in tactics used by some overzealous units. U.S. soldiers have repeatedly mistreated innocent locals. Others have interrogated and frisked Afghan women in their homes, an ignominy in the eyes of ultraconservative Pashtuns. The Army is also investigating the cases of at least two Afghans who died in detention at Bagram. As a result, the soldiers have met with increasing hostility, repeatedly coming under enemy fire. Casualties are on the rise.

In the early summer of 2002, the U.S. military provoked an international outcry when combat aircraft bombed wedding parties in several villages, killing dozens of unarmed Afghan civilians. The pilots claim they had mistaken the Afghan wedding custom of shooting in the air for an attack. In one case, the military leadership acted on a tip from an Afghan ally who claimed terrorists were hiding in a village. In fact, the Afghan abused American firepower to settle his own scores with local rivals.

"We have made mistakes," concedes Colonel Roger King, spokesman at Bagram for all U.S. forces in Afghanistan. "Now, we will no longer launch attacks on a single source of intelligence because people have their own reasons for telling us things." King is aware of the potential growth of anti–American sentiment. "As of yet there is no groundswell of 'Americans go home!' but we try to minimize events that could lead to such sentiments."

King is also aware of accusations by the Karzai government that U.S. forces are fragmenting Afghanistan by continuing to recruit regional warlords as allies in the struggle against remnants of the Taliban and Al Qaeda. Supplied by the CIA with dollars and arms, these commanders have built up strong private armies and are often implicated in the flourishing drug trade. Since the U.S. troops' arrival in Afghanistan opium production has increased twentyfold, from 185 tons of opium in 2001 to 3,400 tons in 2002.

Although the Karzai government imposed draconian punishments for growing opium, poppy cultivation surged from 8,000 hectares in 2001 to 74,000 hectares a year later. Before the war, the Taliban regime had imposed and strictly enforced, albeit as late as July 2000, a ban on poppy cultivation.

"We are after terrorists," King explains. "We do not look for drugs or drug dealers. They are not in our charter. In this war there are several grades of bad: drug dealers are bad, but the Taliban are real bad." King concedes that the U.S. Special Forces have been instructed explicitly not to intervene in drug smuggling. "Only if the drug dealers are Taliban or are planning terrorist activities, then we intervene." King admits that many American allies in the country have blood on their hands. "There are a lot of people who have been involved in the drug business but it is seen as a separate issue." These warlords have been recruited not by the regular forces but by the CIA, King emphasizes, adding that the Army has no influence on the secret organization activities. The U.S. military would try to persuade local allies to give up drug smuggling, King insists. "We sit down with them, we drink green tea, and we show them alternative ways to make money." Like what? "Well, we pay them," King says, straight-faced.

All over Bagram, hundreds of tents are being replaced with buildings made of wood and concrete. "You improve your foxhole every day," Colonel King smiles. The construction activity reflects a remarkable shift in American policy. In the autumn of 2002, high-ranking officials in the Bush administration began commenting that U.S. troops should stay in Afghanistan for more than a decade. "For a long, long time," General Tommy Franks, head of the U.S. Central Command, answered when asked how long U.S. soldiers would remain in Afghanistan.[5] Previously, government officials had assured the public withdrawal would follow a defeat of all Taliban and Al Qaeda fighters. President Bush himself quipped that he "was not in the nation-building business."

"After September 11 we came here for the single grim purpose of removing the government that had allowed the attacks to happen and hunting down the people who did it," Colonel King explains. "Now we also look at how we can make life better for the Afghan people so they can stand on their own feet." Part of this new policy includes bolstering the central government in Kabul, and training a national army. The Bush administration appears to be acknowledging that a war on terrorism cannot be won by military means alone, but also, as European diplomats and regional experts have continually stated, needs to be accompanied by civil measures to create stability that will dry up the breeding ground for terrorism. "It is good to be engaged in the world," Colonel King says. "That has nothing to do with imperialism. Our mistake before was simply that we did not watch the people who then hurt us on September 11. Now, our engagement gives us more awareness."

King looks across to the landing strip where two Apache combat helicopters are about to take off into the sandstorm. "We have a whole country to turn around, that takes time. At McDonald's, you cannot make it from the microphone to the food counter in thirty seconds either, can you?"

After my talk with Colonel King, a soldier drives me back to the airbase's gates. Tim is a reservist from Georgia and badly misses his wife. As I had forgotten to arrange transport back to Kabul, he agrees to take me beyond the Afghan checkpoints to a pickup point for local taxi drivers. As we pull up, a group of Afghan boys gathers around the Jeep, laughing and shouting. Some start banging their hands against our doors and windows. Tim urges me to get out quickly. Suddenly, the boys manage to open the vehicle's back door, grabbing a toolbox and other loose items.

"Get the fuck out of there!" Tim shouts. He jerks up the hand brakes, reaches for his M-16 rifle and jumps out. Frightened, the children run away, dropping some of the stolen tools. Tim stops and reflexively points the barrel of his M-16 at the backs of the fleeing boys. By the time I get out of the car, Tim has lowered his rifle, apparently realizing just how bad all this looked. There is complete silence around us except for the Jeep's rattling engine. Dozens of Afghan men who have watched the scene glare at Tim. Cursing, the soldier jumps into the Jeep and races back to the base.

Whether the U.S. troops will succeed in their terrorist hunt or instead meet the same fate as the Soviet invaders will depend largely on Afghanistan's neighbor Pakistan, one of the most powerful regional Great Game players and my long journey's final destination.

The Cradle of Terror: Pakistan

At the Michni checkpoint, we jump out of the car and clamber up a rocky hill. Below us lies the Afghan-Pakistani border crossing of Torkham, where a seemingly endless line of trucks crawls up the serpentine mountain road that cuts across the barren, treeless slopes. Among them are several buses with the passengers' luggage piled on top. They are returning Afghan refugees. Two boys from a nearby village approach us and offer a quick geography lesson. "That mountain back there still lies in Afghanistan, the one on the right, too. But this mountain over here, that is already Pakistan." I search in vain for fences or any other border markers, but the pillars that are said once to have marked the border have long disappeared. Afghanistan and Pakistan are not really divided; they blur into each other.

We are standing at the Khyber Pass, the fabled gateway between Central Asia and the Indian subcontinent. For thousands of years, traders and their camel caravans have traveled through here en route from China to Europe. For many armies, from Alexander the Great to the British, the pass across the White Mountains served as an invasion route in either direction. The generals of the Great Game spent many sleepless nights deliberating how to protect or conquer this strategic passage. The new Great Game does not stop at the Khyber Pass, as the catalysts in the struggle for power and pipelines in Central Asia lie here in Pakistan. The country's might lies in its 148 million inhabitants, which make Pakistan the seventh largest nation on earth, as well as the most populated power on the fringe of Central Asia.

The lords of the Khyber Pass have for centuries been the warriors of the Afridi tribe, thought to be descendants of Alexander's troops and renowned for their smuggling skills and love of war. Even after the partition in 1947, following independence of the British crown colony of India, the Afridi and other Pashtun tribes asserted their autonomy in relation to the Pakistani state. To this day, no Pakistani policeman is allowed into the "tribal areas" in western Pakistan, where traditional tribal codes reign supreme. The only representative of the government's interests vis-à-vis the tribes is a "political agent" in the city of Peshawar. No wonder that the lawless tribal areas are a paradise for bandits, heroin producers, and arms smugglers. For foreigners, entry is usually strictly forbidden. Only by obtaining special permission and an armed escort of the Afridi clan, am I allowed to travel through the "Khyber Agency" to Peshawar, on the last leg of the Great Trunk Road from Kabul.

My gunman's name is Rasul. He has a black beard, a broad smile, and an expression that is both naive and deeply serious. Slung over his shoulder he has an AK-47 with two additional magazines, attached with sticky tape. "Enough ammo for one day," he grins. Rasul, who is thirty, has since his youth worked as a gunman in the Khyber Agency. His pittance of a salary supports his wife and eight children, the oldest of whom just turned fourteen.

"I use my rifle when we fight with other tribes," Rasul tells me. In the tribal areas, conflicts kill hundreds of people a year. The confrontations are often based on blood feuds or religious tensions between Sunnis and Shiites. Another source of conflict is the *pashtunwali,* the moral code of the Pashtuns, that obligates every man to take bloody *badal* (revenge) if he, his family, or his tribe have been insulted or treated unjustly. Most arguments are about *zar, zan,* or *zamin*—gold, women, or land. "Most often we fight to restore the *nang* (honor) of a family," Rasul tells me. "Especially if women are involved."

We get back in the car and drive to the small town of Landi Kotal, a notorious smugglers' nest. In a row of two-storied adobe buildings lining the roads, there are shops selling electronic goods such as stereos and television sets. One showroom is full of fire-arms, mostly fully functioning imitations of Kalashnikovs that the Afridis and other tribes produce in workshops throughout the area. The business has boomed for decades, due to the perpetu-ally high demand across the border. In Landi Kotal, too, many men, including some youths, casually carry automatic rifles. As in Af-ghanistan, the bearded men wear turbans and *shalwar kameez,* baggy trousers with tunics, sometimes covered by dark pocketed vests. The few women in the streets are covered with light blue silken *burqas.*

During the U.S.-led military campaign in Afghanistan, people in the tribal areas clearly sympathized with the Taliban. An esti-mated nine thousand men, some even brandishing old *jezail* rifles, spontaneously crossed the border to fight the jihad against the attackers. Today, many of them languish in Afghan prisons.

I ask the driver to stop but Rasul tells me not to leave the car. "Don't forget, Pakistani law counts for nothing around here! Many criminals from Pakistan escape to us. Those people don't joke around much, you see." I jump out to buy some fruits in a shop. The shop owner is friendly, and there is the distinct smell of hashish in the air. Holding the AK-47 in his hand, Rasul does not move from my side, and soon shoos me back to the car. As we leave the town, graffiti on a wall, in English, says, "Long live Osama bin Laden!" Below it, children play football with an aluminum can.

Somewhere in the barren mountains near Landi Kotal, bin Laden's trail has gone cold. Most Western intelligence agencies agree that in December 2001 bin Laden and his fighters probably escaped from the eastern Afghan mountain fortress of Tora Bora to the Pashtun tribal areas where he remains hidden in a secret and barely accessible location. American B-52s bombed the wrong escape routes, and Special Forces hunters relied too much on ineffective Afghan allies. According to witness accounts, sev-eral groups of high-ranking Taliban and Arab Al Qaeda fighters came across the mountains from Afghanistan in the last days of Operation Enduring Freedom. I ask Rasul what he thinks happened to them. "If they are good Muslims, they are our guests. We give them food and shelter." Pashtun hospitality, *melmastia,* requires that.

Hospitality cannot be denied to anyone, even a criminal, and a host will make it a point of honor to sacrifice his life for a guest if necessary. "This is our tradition," says Rasul. "Besides, Osama is not a criminal but a hero. The Americans killed many innocent people in Afghanistan." Only after long negotiations with tribal leaders was the Pakistani army allowed in late 2001 to deploy troops along the 850-mile-long border with Afghanistan. Some sixty thousand soldiers are currently stationed here, equipped by the Pentagon with helicopters and military vehicles. Together with U.S. Special Forces, they guard the border and comb villages for suspects. Tension with locals is common, as among them are many supporters of the one-time mujahideen leader Hekmatyar who, probably also from a hiding place within the tribal areas, has called for a jihad against the Afghan government and the American troops.

We leave the Khyber Agency through a stone gate and reach Peshawar, capital of the Northwest Frontier Province (NWFP). Dating back to the Moghul era, the name Peshawar means "border town," which is what Peshawar still is today. During the CIA-backed jihad against the Soviet invaders in Afghanistan in the 1980s, the city became a hodgepodge of mujahideen, intelligence agents, journalists, and humanitarian organizations that took care of the millions of Afghan refugees. Arriving in Peshawar, British secret agent Tom Carew, a former SAS soldier, was disgusted. "The whole town was full of dusty, dirty, amputee beggars, speckled with scabs and sores, as well as being knee-deep in donkey shit and dust."[1]

Today, Peshawar has a wild Central Asian air to it. The streets around the hulking Bala Hissar fortress are one huge Pashtun bazaar. Bicycles, oxcarts, motorcycles, horse-drawn carriages, motorized rickshaws, and ramshackle cars all compete for space with garishly painted and richly decorated trucks. The city's once giant refugee camp east of the city has since been disbanded, and its inhabitants returned to their Afghan homes.

The former colonial British cantonment is in a tranquil part of the town with tree-lined boulevards, red brick villas and the army barracks. Here lives the journalist Rahimullah Yusufzai, who has seen more of the Taliban and Al Qaeda than any other outsider. The middle-aged Pashtun was the first to interview Taliban leader Mullah Omar in the spring of 1995. Later, Yusufzai also met twice with Osama bin Laden in his Afghan training camps for interviews that were published worldwide. In May 1998, bin Laden invited him and a few other journalists into his camp near Kandahar for an improvised press conference for the public launch of his jihad against the United States. "He was very friendly and modest, almost to the point of being shy," Yusufzai remembers, along with bin Laden's soft hands that spoke of the millionaire's son sheltered life, devoid of physical labor.

Yusufzai recalls that Taliban leader Mullah Omar was outraged by the press conference. "The next day, bin Laden was called to Kandahar and severely reprimanded. Omar shouted, 'There can be only one ruler in Afghanistan, and that is me. You are our guest, but do not get us into trouble with the Americans.'" The notion that Al Qaeda had free rein in Afghanistan is untrue, Yusufzai believes, adding that bin Laden was dependent on the Taliban and was unable to make any major moves without Omar's permission. Bin Laden's second interview with Yusufzai required a green light directly from Kandahar. "In the West people do not realize this. Bin Laden was a refugee who had a few fighters by his side, that was it. The Taliban always made fun of all his talk about jihad." Convinced that bin Laden survived the American attacks and is alive today, Yusufzai believes, "One day he is going to come out from his hiding place, if only because he is crazy about publicity."

As Afghanistan and Pakistan blur into each other geographically and ethnically, their history is likewise inseparable. This is partly attributable to the Durand Line, which the British arbitrarily drew in 1893 as the official border between British India and Afghanistan. Cutting directly through the Pashtun areas, the border was adopted by Pakistan after the crown colony's independence in 1947. However, no Afghan government has ever recognized it, and many Pashtuns envisage a "Great Pashtunistan" stretched across the Durand Line. Yet not only Afghan irredentism has caused Pakistani statesmen to keep an eye on its western neighbor. The homeland for the subcontinent's Muslims has also felt threatened by the more powerful India. The two countries have already fought three wars over the divided province of Kashmir, which is claimed by both sides. The conflict has intensified because of a Muslim rebellion ravaging the Indian-administered part of Kashmir since 1990. Terrorist attacks and the brutal responses by Indian security forces have claimed tens of thousands of lives. New Delhi accuses Islamabad of bankrolling the insurrection and training Islamic militants to infiltrate India.

The Kashmir conflict is inextricably linked with Pakistan's policies in Afghanistan. The small, wedge-shaped country cannot afford to also have a hostile neighbor on its western border, as it would run the risk of being smothered between two zones of instability. In an effort to gain "strategic depth," Islamabad has therefore tried, particularly during the past three decades, to exert massive influence on Afghan developments, which was rarely in the interest of the people of the Hindu Kush.

The man who for thirty years pulled strings behind the scenes in Afghanistan is General Naseerullah Babar. Born in 1928 and educated at a British boarding school, the former Pakistani interior minister is considered the "godfather of the Taliban." Without Babar's backing, their victorious whirlwind campaign in the mid-1990s would have been unthinkable.

Babar first meddled in Afghan affairs in 1973, after Mohammed Daoud had overthrown his cousin King Zahir Shah in Kabul and established a left-leaning, anti–Islamic regime. With calls for a Great Pashtunistan growing louder once again, the Daoud regime was potentially dangerous to Pakistan. In an effort to destabilize it, Babar, who was then governor of NWFP, brought Afghan Islamist Professor Burhanuddin Rabbani and two of his most outstanding students, Ahmed Shah Massoud and Gulbuddin Hekmatyar, to Peshawar. With the knowledge of only a handful of conspirators, including then-president Zulfiqar Ali Bhutto, Babar set up secret military camps to train the young men and several dozen other Afghans as guerrilla fighters. The curriculum for Massoud and Hekmatyar, then still friends, included the use of assault rifles and battle tactics. Babar then sent the talented Massoud to the Panjshir valley for a bloody partisan attack on Afghan government forces. Daoud got the message and became more accommodating.

A triumphant Babar then secretly took his young mujahideen to Islamabad and introduced them to the U.S. ambassador, and a successful yet ultimately tragic alliance was born. After the Soviet invasion of Afghanistan in 1979, the Americans knew exactly whom to send into battle against the Red Army. Babar, who created the mujahideen, no longer wielded any influence on the $3 billion covert CIA operation, as his longtime friend General Mohammed Zia ul-Haq had come to power in a coup d'état, executing Bhutto and sending Babar to prison for six years. A ruthless military dictator suited the U.S. government because Pakistan had become a frontline state in the Cold War. Washington allowed the pan-Islamist Zia and his secret service, the Inter-Service Intelligence (ISI), to funnel American dollars and weapons only to the most radical jihadis, especially Hekmatyar. When the Soviets began to withdraw their troops in 1988, Zia was killed in a mysterious plane crash, along with the head of the ISI, four generals, and the U.S. ambassador. All the men who knew everything about CIA activities in Afghanistan were dead.

After Zia's death, Pakistan returned to a democracy with Benazir Bhutto, daughter of the national hero, becoming the first elected woman to lead a Muslim country. However, actual power in the increasingly corrupt regimes of Bhutto and her rival Nawaz Sharif remained concentrated in the hands of the army and the ISI. After the collapse of the Soviet Union, the generals, with many pan–Islamists amongst them, sought to extend Pakistani influence to the newly independent Muslim republics of Central Asia. Apart from obvious trade opportunities, these countries were sitting on enormous oil and gas reserves, badly needed by energy-starved Pakistan. As in the nineteenth century, the one country offering access to the Central Asian steppe was Afghanistan, which at the time had descended ever further into chaos and civil war. As the Pakistani stooge Hekmatyar looked less likely to prevail over his foes and stabilize the country, Islamabad began looking for new allies. In the spring of 1994, General Babar, by now Bhutto's interior minister, heard for the first time about the Taliban.

"It is not true that Pakistan created the Taliban. They were an indigenous Afghan movement," General Babar, now retired, tells me at a lunch in Peshawar. "Of course, we started supporting them when they became more powerful." Tall and stately, the seventy-five-year-old Pashtun exudes a powerful authority. In his right hand, he holds an officer's stick made of bamboo. His left shoulder drops slightly, the result of a shrapnel injury in the 1971 war against India. Babar acknowledges that he provided the first impetus for the Taliban's mind-boggling string of military victories in the mid-1990s, with an idea that many of his colleagues in government deemed sheer madness at the time. With the help of several ISI officers, he assembled an aid convoy of thirty trucks that were to drive from the south Pakistani city of Quetta via Kandahar and Herat to the Turkmen capital of Ashkhabad, directly across territory controlled by murderous mujahideen militias. Prime Minister Bhutto liked the idea and traveled to Turkmenistan to meet with the Uzbek warlord Rashid Dostum. Accompanied by the U.S. ambassador and five other Western diplomats, Babar flew to Herat, without notifying the Afghan government in Kabul, in a bid to recruit local mujahideen commander Ismail Khan for the convoy project. Khan and Dostum agreed to let the trucks pass through their fiefdoms, without any idea of the consequences.

In late October 1994, the trucks disembarked, with several ISI officers and two young Taliban commanders on board. Near Kandahar, some of the city's militia leaders blocked their way, demanding money. Urged on by Babar, Taliban leader Mullah Omar, whose fighters only controlled a few villages, decided to free the convoy with force. In the course of the fighting, the Taliban gained control of Kandahar. Surprised by their own success and their immense popularity with the masses, they turned toward Kabul, with full Pakistani backing.

"Our support was only moral and diplomatic," Babar insists, eating a bowl of mutton soup. "We did not train the Taliban. They needed no training. Nor did we provide any equipment or weapons. They got all that from other warlords who joined them." Babar carefully avoids the issue of money, knowing that many of the warlords were only convinced to join the Taliban with the help of generous bribes, which were paid for by Pakistan and Saudi Arabia. Many Afghan eyewitnesses also reported that Urdu-speaking army and ISI officers took part in the Taliban campaigns.

Challenged with this contradiction, Babar concedes that Pakistan also provided material support. "We gave them satellite phones and set up a phone network so that they could communicate and coordinate their actions." At the same time, young Afghan refugees who were studying in radical Islamic *madrassas* by the tens of thousands were encouraged to return to their country and join the Taliban ranks. Many of those madrassas were run by the extremist party Jamiat-e Ulema, whose leader Maulana Fazlur Rahman had entered a governmental coalition with Bhutto and Babar. That way, the regime in Islamabad also rid itself of many of the militant men who were becoming a social problem for Pakistan.

"I was in charge of the whole operation," Babar boasts, the pride in his success prevailing over his efforts to conceal any wrongdoing. "I often met with Mullah Omar, he was a good man." I ask Babar, who in the 1990s would sometimes refer to the Taliban as "our boys," whether he ever felt that they were too extreme in their views and policies. "No, they were not. They were good people who created peace and stability. Afghanistan is a tribal country where you need tribal leaders and laws."

Apart from "strategic depth," what did he hope to get out of supporting the Taliban, I ask Babar. "The talk about strategic depth is nonsense," Babar replies angrily. "We wanted a stable and peaceful neighbor in the West. We realized that Afghanistan is a perfect corridor for goods from Central Asia. Those countries needed an Asian outlet, especially for oil and gas. We wanted to take advantage of that." He explains how desperately Pakistan needs energy resources, and how it could at the same time profit from being a transit country for a gas pipeline to India. "The pipeline from Turkmenistan would have been a blessing for the region but for that we needed peace." According to Babar, the United States fully supported the Pakistani Taliban policy from the very beginning. Shortly before the fall of Kabul in September 1996, he took the U.S. ambassador Tom Simmons on a tour of Kandahar and Herat for meetings with Taliban leaders. Although the extreme policies of the new rulers, especially with regard to women, had long been known, Babar recalls that "the ambassador was delighted by what he saw. I even took him shopping in Herat."

There was only one problem with an Afghan pipeline carrying Turkmen gas to Pakistan: the Taliban and the Bhutto government were more inclined to use the Argentinian company Bridas, which competed for the project with Unocal. Bridas seemed the more suitable partner for the pipeline construction because it did not need any loans from international financial institutions, whose first requirement would be international recognition of the Taliban regime. Lobbying hard for Unocal, U.S. ambassador Simmons had heated arguments with Bhutto over her support for Bridas. In early November 1996, the Pakistani president sacked her government on charges of corruption, which many Pakistanis believe was the result of American pressure. The new government, led by Nawaz Sharif, turned its back on Bridas and declared its support for Unocal. Islamabad's official recognition of the Taliban regime soon followed.

Three years later, Sharif was overthrown by his top military commander, General Pervez Musharraf, who declared himself the chief executive officer. Familiar with military dictatorships and fed up with the rampant corruption under democracy, most Pakistanis, including the political parties, welcomed the takeover by Musharraf, who promised to hold democratic elections soon. Instead, he tightened his control on the country and named himself president. Pakistan, already under American sanctions for pursuing its nuclear program, became increasingly ostracized internationally.

September 11, 2001 changed all that. Once again, Pakistan became a frontline state, this time in the war on terrorism. Within days, the Bush administration pressured Musharraf to withdraw his support for the Taliban regime and side with the United States. Bush's infamous dictum of "you are either with us or you are against us" left no room for neutrality. Overnight, Musharraf purged the most pro-Taliban generals in his army and the ISI.

"The Americans blackmailed Musharraf. He had no choice but to drop the Taliban," says Babar, who saw his entire Afghan policy collapse. "Musharraf was still a major when I became a general. He is a very mediocre soldier. And now look at the state Afghanistan is in today. Again the government is weak and the warlords are strong. It was better under the Taliban," he says bitterly, and with that, our lunch talk is over.

What Babar and other Islamist strategists leave behind in their pursuit of "strategic depth" is a history of bloodshed in Afghanistan, as well as a mess in their own country. In Kabul, India has gained influence, and the new Tajik-dominated Afghan government is suspicious of any further interference from Islamabad. Pakistan itself is now beset with Islamic militants who threaten to make the country practically ungovernable. Outraged by Musharraf's opportunist betrayal of their Muslim brethren in Afghanistan, (his new nickname, "*besharraf*," is Pashtu for "man without honor") the militants have vowed to assassinate him.

Underground organizations have given refuge to the Taliban's top echelon and, according to intelligence sources, Al Qaeda cells are firmly ensconced in Pakistan. They are blamed for several deadly terrorist attacks after the Afghan war, targeting foreigners and Pakistani Christians. In the southern city of Karachi, the country's economic center and social hotbed, bombs were thrown at the American consulate and a bus carrying French engineers, resulting in dozens of deaths. American journalist Daniel Pearl was abducted and brutally murdered. Some Al Qaeda terrorists such as September 11 mastermind Khalid Sheikh Mohammed have been arrested, but others remain at large. Musharraf has reacted by outlawing several of the most radical Islamic groups, either by detaining their leaders or putting them under house arrest. At the same time, he has vowed to curb Islamic militants in the Pakistan-administered sector of Kashmir and to prevent them from crossing over to the Indian-controlled area for attacks.

Musharraf did so only after intense pressure from the Bush administration following an attack by Islamic terrorists on the Indian parliament in New Delhi on December 13, 2001. An outraged Indian government moved nearly one million troops to the line of control that divides Kashmir. The Musharraf regime responded in kind, leading to heavy exchanges of artillery fire and threats of mutual nuclear obliteration. Only in mid-2002 did the adversaries tone down their saber-rattling and withdraw some of their divisions.

On a journey to the idyllic *Azad Kashmir* (Free Kashmir), the Pakistan-administered sector, from all appearances it looked as though the army had, insofar as it was possible, sealed the line of control in order to prevent militants from infiltrating the neighboring country. Underground jihadis I met with complained that the Musharraf regime was forcing them to suspend their incursions into the Indian sector. They also confirmed that training camps had been disbanded and their leaders had been told to keep their heads low. "But the jihad never ends," one of the militants told me. "Once our commander tells us to resume the struggle we will cross the border again and fight."

Since the beginning of the war on terrorism, the United States has propped up the Musharraf regime by lifting sanctions and granting Pakistan abundant financial aid. While in 2001 the country received less than $5 million for narcotics control and humanitarian assistance from the United States, Islamabad received a whopping $701 million a year later. Taken from the Emergency Response Fund, the lion's share of the money was spent on military measures and border control. For 2003, some $305 million has already been earmarked for Pakistan, a figure that is likely to increase during the course of the year. At the same time, Washington has persuaded the World Bank and the International Monetary Fund to remit some $1.3 billion of Pakistan's debt and postpone the payback deadline for additional loans totaling $12.5 billion.[2]

While Washington has been practically silent on Musharraf's undemocratic regime, the nuclear program, and human rights abuses, there have been dissenting voices. Ambassador Peter Tomsen, special envoy to Afghanistan from 1989 to 1992, oversaw the last phase of the CIA-funded covert operation against the Soviet Army and the communist regime in Kabul. Before my journey to Pakistan, I met with Tomsen in the Washington, D.C., suburb of McLean, Virginia, a Republican party stronghold, with his neighbors including such heavyweights as Donald Rumsfeld, Colin Powell, and, until recently, Dick Cheney. "This neighborhood votes Republican but as a diplomat one has to swing both ways," Ambassador Tomsen laughs.

"I have played the Great Game in that region for thirty-two years," Tomsen says with a mischievous grin. "It never ends, only the players change. Recently, the United States has become more involved." When the Soviets invaded Afghanistan in 1979, Tomsen served in the political section of the American embassy in Moscow. "We warned the Russians not to attack the country but in reality we wanted them to step into that trap." During the 1980s, Tomsen was based at the U.S. embassy in Beijing, in charge of purchasing Chinese arms for the Afghan mujahideen. "We bought whole warehouses of weapons and shipped them to Karachi." In 1989, as President Bush's special envoy to Afghanistan, the Pennsylvanian coordinated all covert support for the mujahideen at an estimated cost to American taxpayers of more than $3 billion. In his new capacity, Tomsen never traveled to Afghanistan itself but made twenty-one trips to Pakistan and seventeen to Saudi Arabia. There, he consulted with Prince Turki Al-Faisol, the head of Saudi intelligence, who was the key figure in the funding of Arab mujahideen such as Osama bin Laden. Later, Prince Turki was also instrumental in building up the Taliban.

"On my first trip to Pakistan, I realized that we supported the wrong people, militant Islamists," Tomsen remembers. "The ISI and the Saudis passed our weapons and money only to groups on the radical fringe, like Hekmatyar's. The CIA had no problem with that. I wanted our arms deliveries to be stopped, but at that time the Soviet Union seemed the greater of the two evils." In late 1991, the U.S. government and the doomed Gorbachev regime signed an agreement that both sides would stop their support for the opposing Afghan factions. Ironically, it went into effect on January 1, 1992, the day on which the Soviet Union ceased to exist.

With the Najibullah regime overthrown, Tomsen was charged with reopening the American embassy in Kabul. "But then the State Department decided to disengage and pull out of Afghanistan altogether," Tomsen recalls. "We stopped all assistance, including humanitarian aid." With the Soviet demise ending the Cold War, the people of Afghanistan were no longer of any use to Washington and left at the mercy of the radical mujahideen factions that the CIA had built up and unleashed. Their internecine warfare eventually led to the rise of the Taliban and Al Qaeda. "We should not have walked away like that, it was a mistake to abandon them," Tomsen admits.

Tomsen moved on to become ambassador to Armenia but remained involved in Afghan affairs. In June 2001, he was one of the last foreigners to visit Ahmed Shah Massoud at his headquarters in Badakhshan. Since Operation Enduring Freedom, Tomsen has regularly returned to Kabul where, in his view, Washington is once again supporting the wrong people. "Those unsavory warlords we used against the Taliban are thugs. We should have stopped paying them after the bombing ended—but we still have not. Has it helped us? No." Recalling that the allied forces failed to catch or kill any significant number of important Taliban and Al Qaeda, Ambassador Tomsen accuses the American allies of working for the Pakistani secret service. "And the ISI continues to support the Taliban network. They know every inch of the border region, so I am sure they know each and every one of Osama's movements." Describing the Pakistani army and the ISI as a "poisonous establishment," Tomsen charges Musharraf with playing a double game to ensure his political survival. "Musharraf lies to us, just like Saddam Hussein. He assured us that he would stop the Islamic militants in Kashmir, but he does not live up to his word."

One promise Musharraf has kept after three years is to hold elections as a prelude to handing over a limited share of his power to a new civilian government. In the days leading up to the elections on October 10, 2002, the atmosphere in Peshawar is charged. Every evening, great crowds of bearded men gather at party rallies, marching through the streets to the sounds of drums, waving flags, and holding banners and burning torches. However, the campaign rallies are not nearly as exuberant as they were in the 1990s, for the prevailing mood is one of cynicism. Most people doubt that Musharraf is serious about handing back even a limited amount of power. In April, he held a controversial referendum to have himself confirmed as president for an additional five years. No other candidates were allowed. While authorities claimed that a 60 percent turnout produced a 97 percent approval rate, human rights and monitoring groups accused Musharraf of rigging the vote. Unperturbed by growing criticism, Musharraf consolidated his power in August by single-handedly changing the 1973 constitution: A new army-dominated National Security Council would oversee any elected government. The amendments also allow Musharraf to dissolve Parliament and to appoint Supreme Court judges.

These measures further strengthened the dominant role of the military in Pakistan. Men in uniform have ruled the country for most of its tumultuous fifty-six-year history, and every year the armed forces devour about $2.5 billion, or nearly one-fifth of the national budget. Additionally, the military enjoys many institutional perks and privileges that keep it above the jurisdiction of civilian courts. It owns several of the country's largest industrial enterprises, as well as the best farmland in the Indus valley. Former or active military officers run most nationalized economic assets, such as shipping ports, the postal service, railroads, and the telecommunications authority. Because of its lack of accountability to any civilian authority, the military has effectively carved out a state within a state where corruption is rampant.

To prevent any serious challenges to his regime, Musharraf then neutralized the main democratic parties, the Pakistan Muslim League (PML) and the Pakistan People's Party (PPP), by threatening to have their respective leaders, Sharif and Bhutto, arrested if they returned from exile to run for office. A further 40 percent of the parties' nominees were barred by a new rule that requires candidates to hold a four-year college degree, disqualifying about 98 percent of the population. At the same time, intelligence agencies privately pressured politicians to form a pro–Musharraf "King's Party" for a rubber-stamp parliament that would legalize the military putsch and serve as a fig leaf vis-à-vis the West.

The only other political party allowed to campaign freely is the United Action Council or Muttahida Majlis-e-Amal (MMA), an alliance of six Islamist parties. United for the first time, they have found a common denominator in an openly anti–American platform. "Down with Bush!" shouted Maulana Samiul Haq, one of the coalition's leaders, at a political rally. "This is a war between Islam and American infidels!"[3] The black-turbaned Haq runs the *madrassa* Dar-ul-Uloom Haqqania, where several Taliban leaders and thousands of other Afghan and Pakistani holy warriors studied the Koran. Another MMA leader is Maulana Fazlur Rehman, whose party Jamiat-e Ulema Islam (JUI) has founded most of the estimated ten thousand *madrassas* in the Pashtun-populated provinces. Roughly a third of all Pakistani children, mostly from poor families, attend these Koran schools, where they are fed and lodged free. They receive a purely religious education and sometimes military training from mullahs, many of whom have been influenced by a mixture of Saudi Wahhabism and the equally orthodox and pan-Islamic Indian Deobandism.

The *madrassa* graduates enter Pakistani society with a vastly different view of the world from that of students of the rundown state schools and the upper middle-class English-style schools. Massive social confrontations seem inevitable in a country where only 15 percent of the 148 million inhabitants are literate. One way to stave off simmering conflicts would be for the government to make secular education mandatory at *madrassas*. Musharraf has refused to encourage this, as he is seeking to curry favor with the Islamists who despise him for his about-face on Afghan policy.

Things run smoothly on election day. Turnout is low, but much less violence breaks out outside poll stations than many observers had feared. While the army remains in its barracks, international observers complain about the government's surreptitious backdoor machinations that fall just short of outright vote-rigging. In Peshawar, copies of an open letter appear at the bazaar and in refugee camps. Writtten in both Urdu and English, it claims, "Pakistan, the fort of Islam, has become an American base where Muslims are being killed. Musharraf backs Bush in his fight against Islam. Without Musharraf's support America would not have dared to set foot in Afghanistan. I call upon you to come forward and get rid of him." The letter is signed by "your brother, Osama bin-Mohammed bin-Laden," though the request at the bottom of the page to "please photocopy this and pass it on" makes the letter seem a fake.

Early next morning, my translator Iftikhar calls my hotel room to wake me up. "Get up!" he shouts into the phone. "The Islamists have won the elections!" The parties that constitute MMA have never in the history of Pakistan collected any more than 5 percent of the popular vote. Confined to NWFP and Baluchistan, they would get a maximum of two or three seats in the national parliament. In this election, however, the one-time fringe party had won fifty-two seats in the 342-member national parliament, making the MMA the third largest political force in Pakistan. Even more impressive, the MMA won the majority of seats in the provincial assemblies of NWFP and Baluchistan.

After a hurried breakfast, I jump in a taxi with Iftikhar to Nowshera, a small town east of Peshawar where MMA supporters are rumored to be staging a huge victory rally. On the way, I notice hundreds of cars decorated with the green MMA party flag. Their drivers honk and wave at each other in solidarity. In Nowshera, an unkempt market town with a few dilapidated former colonial buildings lining the main road to Islamabad, some five thousand supporters have gathered in a large open field. They are addressed by Qazi Hussain Ahmed, who is perhaps the most powerful of the MMA's leaders. His party, the Jamaat-e Islami, has played a role in Pakistani politics for decades and established strong ties with the ISI during the Afghan jihad. The geography professor is seen as one of the more moderate MMA figures, but that does not show today. "This is a revolution!" cries the white-bearded Ahmed. The crowd responds with a jubilant roar and shouts of "*Allahu akbar!*" I ask a group of Pashtuns standing near me why they voted for the MMA. "We hate America, that is why!" they answer at once. "America is evil. We want their military out of our country."

After the rally, Ahmed and his entourage move on to a mosque for midday prayers. Through loudspeakers, the imam's service is transmitted into the streets where hundreds of faithful kneel in rows. Their bodies move up and down in rhythmic prayers. In search of a delicious glass of fresh pomegranate juice that street vendors sell this time of year, I chance upon a gun shop. The showroom is filled with Kalashnikov and M-16 imitations that gunsmiths produce in workshops in the tribal areas. "Within ten days, an Afridi gunsmith can duplicate any given rifle he has never seen before," says the shop owner, lazing on a rope bed. He adds he will sell me an AK-47 for four thousand rupees, or roughly ninety dollars, a foreigner's rate. How is the business, now that there is no more civil war in Afghanistan? "We sell very few rifles to Afghans," he replies. "There are plenty of Pakistanis who buy them."

The loudspeakers fall silent. The prayers are finished. Outside the mosque, I approach MMA leader Ahmed for an interview. He agrees, asking me to follow his Toyota Land Cruiser to his home on the edge of Nowshera. We arrive at a sumptuous house, enclosed by high walls and guarded by the party's militia force, young men in camouflage fatigues who appear unarmed. In the garden, a tent made of bamboo poles and yellow oriental quilts has been erected for supporters. As we enter the compound, dozens of men, teenagers, and grizzled farmers come forward to greet and hug their idol. Young men, green bandanas emblazoned with Koran verses wrapped around their heads, shout slogans and raise their clenched fists in the air. One man places a wreath of plastic flowers around Ahmed's neck. With hugs and repeated exchanges of "*Salaam aleikum!*" ("peace be with you"), Ahmed patiently greets every one of his supporters, from the wretched-looking poor to the well-groomed dignitary, only occasionally readjusting his characteristic *karakur* felt hat and black vest.

Over a cup of tea and sweet cake, I ask Ahmed what policies the MMA alliance stands for. He answers in impeccable English, betraying his academic background. "Our program is very simple. This country has been based on Islamic ideology, and therefore its government should work according to Islamic injunctions." Does that mean the imposition of *sharia* law? Ahmed removes his glasses and sarcastically replies, "Ah, here comes yet another Western journalist keen to write that all we want is chop off women's hands. Look, I have traveled a lot in the West and I know how much you people misunderstand *sharia* law. It is really about preserving human dignity." Ahmed explains that his party should not be compared to the Taliban, whose discrimination against women and nationwide ban of television had been too extreme. "All in all, however, we supported them because they were just and sincere people who brought peace to Afghanistan." Ironically, Ahmed's opponent in the Nowshera constituency was none other than Taliban mentor Naseerullah Babar. Running on a ticket of Benazir Bhutto's party, the former interior minister had lost to Ahmed by a huge margin.

"Many people in Pakistan feel that the United States disturbed the peace and targeted innocent people in Afghanistan," Ahmed continues. "The American government had no proof that the Taliban had anything to do with what happened in New York on September 11, 2001." Ahmed led tumultuous street protests against American bombing and against Musharraf, which landed him in prison for four months. "The Americans have a hegemonistic attitude. They try to impose their cultural values on us. In fact, the United States is waging a war against Islam."

The sixty-year-old Ahmed recalls that during the Indian struggle for independence from Britain, people looked to America for inspiration and support. "For us, the country was a haven of liberalism and anticolonialism. Now they have become as imperialist as the British. But they make no effort to look for the reasons why they are hated so much. The United States should change its foreign policy because it is not in their interest, as September 11 has shown. " On my way back to Peshawar, I have to remind myself that Ahmed is one of the more moderate Islamists in Pakistan.

Musharraf's election has backfired. With most votes going to parties that oppose his rule, the ballot has resulted in a net loss of power for the dictator. Yet, the Islamists' victory paradoxically strengthens his hand vis-à-vis Washington, enabling him to portray himself as a secular bulwark against a greater Islamic evil. In a major effort at damage control at home, Musharraf delays the summoning of parliament for five weeks in order to give his agents time to induce parliamentarians to defect to the King's Party. By early December, they have managed to cobble together a majority coalition for a pro-army prime minister, Mir Zafrullah Khan Jamali. In his inaugural speech, the fifty-eight-year-old pledges to continue with Musharraf's policies. The general remains squarely in charge, and the army continues to be the most powerful party in the country.

In the freewheeling NWFP and Baluchistan it is the MMA that forms the provincial governments. Its power is limited to banning indecency on cable television, local newspapers, and the notoriously graphic cinema billboards in Peshawar. The extremists might also outlaw the widespread sale of postcards with sultry Bollywood film stars, and impose mandatory prayers for all public servants. Most importantly, the new local rulers might discreetly obstruct the antiterrorism work of U.S. Special Forces along the border to Afghanistan. Local security forces are now more likely to turn a blind eye to the harboring and possible regrouping of Taliban, Al Qaeda, and Hekmatyar fighters.

In late 2002, a serious dispute breaks out between Washington and Islamabad after the Pakistani government denies American forces in Afghanistan the right to cross the border into the tribal areas in pursuit of suspected militants. The move comes after American warplanes bomb a Pakistani village where Pashtun gunmen were believed to have hidden after an attack on a U.S. army patrol on the Afghan side. In a similar incident only a few days later, Pakistani and American forces exchange heavy machine-gun fire in the Waziristan tribal area.

These are only the first signs that the U.S. troops' self-image of "liberators" is far from being shared by most people in the region. Ultimately, this growing hostility against the American presence in Central Asia might decide the new Great Game's outcome.

Angry Young Men: An Epilogue

Years ago, long before I first traveled to Central Asia, I met "Major Black Man" in the West African country of Sierra Leone. The tall man, who was exactly my age, was a fighter in the Revolutionary United Front (RUF), one of the most feared rebel groups in Africa, which gained notoriety by chopping off limbs of thousands of civilians during the country's ten-year civil war. Working as a reporter for the London *Daily Telegraph,* I had ventured across the front lines to the rebels' positions in the bush. After some time, the RUF commander allowed me to proceed to the rebel-controlled diamond fields, the civil war's main spoils. During the ten-hour car drive on muddy tracks through the bush, I talked with Major Black Man, one of my armed escorts, about his reasons to fight for the RUF. He told me of the abject poverty in which he had grown up, of hunger and illness, and that he had never had a chance to go to school. "I had no hope and I was angry, so angry," Black Man said. "My life was shit and it was going to be short anyway. So I took up a gun to have a bit of fun before I die. I have nothing to lose."

What makes a man a terrorist? On my travels for this book, I often thought of Black Man's words when I met other angry young men who, with nothing to lose but their seemingly value-less life, were prepared to fight for whatever their leaders told them was worth the fight. One of them was the twenty-year-old Ahmed I once met in an Internet café in Tashkent, the capital of

Uzbekistan, whose dictator Islam Karimov has become the Bush administration's latest ally in the new Great Game over power and pipelines in Central Asia. Over a cup of tea Ahmed told me that he had just been released from prison after serving a three-year sentence for allegedly belonging to an Islamic terrorist organization. "The guards beat me every day," Ahmed said. "It was awful but I never stopped praying to Allah." The group the young Muslim belonged to was a religious Sufi order, which, he insisted, had nothing to do with terrorism. "But maybe in the future my brothers and I have to defend ourselves and fight." How did Ahmed feel about the arrival of American antiterror troops in Uzbekistan? "They only make things worse. They don't help us, the people, but only the government. I hate America."

Ahmed's angry words reflect a dangerous trend throughout Central Asia that could ultimately decide the new Great Game's outcome. The region's impoverished populaces, disgusted with the United States' alliances with their corrupt and despotic rulers, increasingly embrace militant Islam and virulent anti–Americanism. Since the Bush administration has been using the September 11 terror attacks as an excuse to pursue policies seen by many outside the United States as arrogant, aggressive, and outright imperialist, the change in perception could not be any more drastic. At the end of the Cold War in 1989, America was admired and loved by the Soviet-oppressed peoples of Eastern Europe not only as the leader of the West but as the champion of democracy, civil liberties, and cultural progress. This cultural appeal was perhaps as powerful, albeit more subtle, a weapon in the struggle with the Soviet Union as NATO's military might. Young Czechs, Poles, and Hungarians, even if they had never heard of the Bill of Rights, craved American rock music and blue jeans.

Today, the United States has lost most of its cultural attractiveness in the ex-Soviet countries of Central Asia and their neighbors, and it is widely hated for its politics. To be sure, some of the resentment is motivated by envy of American wealth and most young men in the region still dream of obtaining a U.S. visa and a green card, although the Bush administration's massive post-September 11 curtailment of civil liberties, particularly those of Muslim immigrants, frightens some. Worse, many people in the region have come to realize that the democratic and liberal values Americans enjoy at home are often missing from U.S. foreign policy. They resent the immoral opportunism with which Washington courts the region's dictators, such as Azerbaijan's Aliyev, Kazakhstan's Nazarbayev, and Pakistan's Musharraf. Many Muslims also perceive Bush's war on terror, rightly or wrongly, as a brazen cultural crusade against Islam.

While the war on terror has allowed the Bush administration to massively extend American influence in Central Asia, this influence all too often relies on the mere projection of power. Though military and intelligence action may be an effective short-term way to obliterate identified terrorist groups such as Al Qaeda and to discourage "rogue states" from sheltering them, it cannot eradicate terrorism as such and might instead make it easier for terrorist groups to recruit new fighters. Final victory in the war on terror cannot be achieved through military means alone but must be accomplished through a multipronged approach of military, political, and economic measures that also target the social roots of terrorism. While B-52s and Cruise missiles inspire fear and hatred, the building of roads, schools, and hospitals would win people's hearts and minds. Why has the Bush administration not provided sufficient funds to engage in such nation-building in Afghanistan, instead continuing to support regional warlords who tear the country apart and are deeply implicated in the heroin trade? Why has the Bush administration not helped the Musharraf regime in Pakistan to secularize the country's tens of thousands of Koran schools that continue to churn out America-hating Islamic militants? These are just two randomly chosen examples of the many myopic U.S. policies in the region that are bound to eventually backfire terribly, as did the CIA's arming of Islamic mujahideen like Osama bin Laden in Afghanistan in the 1980s.

Why do so many people hate America so much? Whoever seeks to root out anti-American terrorism cannot ignore this core question. Sadly, the few debates of this issue since the

September 11 outrage have not led to many honest answers. "They hate our freedom and democracy," President Bush, at his Manichean best, has repeatedly stated. While this may be true for some Al Qaeda figures, most America haters have better reasons.

In late March 2003, American forces invaded Iraq, in what is the latest war of the new Great Game over oil. The troops quickly seized the vast oil fields in the south before pushing north to Baghdad to remove the regime of Saddam Hussein from power. Regardless of its eventual outcome, the Iraq war will have enormous repercussions on the entire region, seriously undermining America's hopes of victory in the war on terror. While ostensibly waged to disarm Iraq of its alleged weapons of mass destruction, Operation Iraqi Freedom underscored the fact that the new Great Game over oil fields and pipelines in Central Asia gives but a foretaste of future energy wars over the world's remaining oil and gas resources.

In Iraq, the Bush administration has for the first time put into practice its new doctrine of "preemptive self-defense" against countries that could one day pose potential terrorist threats to the United States. Most international lawyers see the invasion of Iraq, a sovereign Arab country, as a violation of the UN Charter of 1945, which prohibits aggressive military action unless provoked by an attack or authorized by the UN Security Council. With Washington unable to show compelling evidence of Iraq's ties to Al Qaeda, it was unable to secure the backing of neither the UN nor NATO. Supported only by its ally Britain and a small "coalition of the willing," the United States invaded Iraq more or less unilaterally and against public opinion in most countries across the world. In going it alone against the explicit opposition from many countries, most notably Russia, China, France, and Germany, the Bush administration managed to alienate longtime allies and to squander even the last remnants of worldwide post-September 11 solidarity with America. Relegating the UN (and all nations that constitute this organization) to what it called "irrelevance," the Bush administration has further consolidated the new post–Cold War world order best described as *Imperium Americanum*.

While there can be no doubt about the tyrannical nature of Hussein's regime, its military removal at the cost of thousands of lives is similar to taking a baseball bat to a hornet's nest. Rather than miraculously spreading democracy in the Middle East, as the Bush administration would have people believe, the war is more likely to worsen regional instability. Furious at their own despotic leaders' cooperation with the United States, radical Islamic groups in Egypt, Jordan, and Saudi Arabia could attempt to rise in revolt. With Afghan Taliban fighters already joining forces with the mujahideen of warlord Hekmatyar in a jihad against America, more violence could soon erupt in Pakistan and Afghanistan. "Before the war in Iraq there was one Osama bin Laden; now there are one hundred," Egypt's President Hosni Mubarak succinctly put it.

By opening the Iraqi Pandora's box, the Bush administration also puts at risk the few successes in the war on terror. The invasion and possible occupation of a Muslim country, resented as yet another attack on Islam and an imperialist bid to control the region's oil reserves, will inevitably fill the ranks of Al Qaeda in the region, increasing, not decreasing, the threat of September 11-style terrorist attacks in the United States and Europe.

American arrogance of power will not fail to affect relations between the United States and its main rivals in the new Great Game: Russia, Iran, and China. Long before the diplomatic rift over Iraq, those countries suspected that the Bush administration was using its war against terror in Central Asia to seal the American Cold War victory against Russia, to contain Chinese influence, and to tighten the noose around Iran. Faced with Bush's verdict that "those who are not with us are against us," the regimes in Moscow, Beijing, and Tehran became increasingly worried about what they perceived as an aggressive U.S. foreign policy aimed at "full-spectrum dominance," i.e., worldwide control of political, economic, and military developments. In what reads like a deliberate allusion to Lord Curzon's famous "chessboard" dictum, President Jimmy Carter's national security adviser Zbigniew Brzezinski argued as early as 1997 that "America is now Eurasia's arbiter, with no major Eurasian issue soluble without America's participation or contrary to America's interests. How the United States both manipulates and accommodates the principal geostrategic players on the Eurasian chessboard and how it manages Eurasia's key geopolitical pivots will be critical to the longevity and stability of America's global primacy."[1]

The arrogance and hubris expressed in such words infuriate the conservative power circles in Moscow who loathe the prospect of a long-term American military presence in Russia's strategic backyard. For them, the much-lauded post-September 11 "strategic partnership" between Russia and the United States is hardly more than a tactical teaming-up whose raison d'être is the common struggle against terrorism. Former KGB officer Putin's pragmatic *salto occidentale* appears to be but a back-against-the-wall maneuver in a game whose rules Russia no longer sets, destined to attract Western investment until a reinvigorated Russian economy once again allows for a more dominant foreign policy. The clearest indications of the Kremlin's cunning double game are Russia's intense cooperation not only with Hussein's Iraq but also with the two other countries in the "axis of evil," North Korea and Iran.

While Russia and the United States continue to argue over the routes of pipelines, the new Great Game need not necessarily be a zero-sum game. Washington would in fact have good reasons to cooperate with Moscow in the energy field because Russia, sitting on about fifty billion barrels of oil and the world's largest gas reserves, could help allay the America's oil dependence on the Middle East.

Yet faced with the Bush administration's outright refusal to listen to the Kremlin's objections to the invasion of Iraq, Russia is now more likely to join forces with China in undermining American global supremacy. With its economy increasingly dependent on oil imports from the Middle East and Central Asia, China in particular will assert its interests in those regions even more vigorously in the future. Iran, another Great Game adversary that some hawks in Washington have already singled out as Washington's next target in the preemptive war on terror, is also likely to step up its actions against U.S. interests and pipeline plans in the Caspian region, Afghanistan, and possibly Iraq. Contrary to the Bush administration's hopes that Operation Iraqi Freedom will discourage "rogue states" from acquiring weapons of mass destruction, Iran (like North Korea) might come to see the possession of nuclear bombs as the sole effective defense against a possible American attack.

By spilling over the Central Asian borders into Iraq, the new Great Game over oil has entered its crucial stage. However vehement the denials by the Bush administration, its true intention in Iraq clearly is to turn the country into a strategic oil supplier for the U.S. economy and America's new ally in the Middle East, as an alternative to Saudi Arabia. What is at stake behind the rhetoric of disarmament and human rights is nothing less than the control over the earth's remaining fossil reserves, as envisaged in the May 2001 Cheney report on U.S. national energy policy.

Iraq sits on an astronomic 112 billion barrels of crude, the world's second largest oil reserve. Before the war, Iraq legally exported about two million barrels a day as part of the UN "food for oil" program. Most of its production facilities were in dire need of technical modernization, but the UN sanctions kept foreign investors out. Once U.S. troops bring the country firmly under American control, there will be no shortage of corporate suitors for drilling concessions. Iraq's light, low-sulfur oil, considered to be of supreme quality, often lies right under the surface, allowing for production costs as low as two dollars a barrel.

With the help of $20 billion of investment in new and existing facilities, Iraqi oil output could soar within a few years to seven million barrels a day, roughly a tenth of global consumption. Abundant supply on the world market would lead to a long-term oil price drop, which is just what lagging Western economies need. "When there is a regime change in Iraq, you could add three to five million barrels of production to world supply [per day]," Bush's then-economic adviser Larry Lindsey bluntly stated as the U.S. war aim in September 2002. "The successful prosecution of the war would be good for the economy."[2]

The only possible alternative to Saudi Arabia as a "swing supplier," Iraq has become the linchpin in the U.S. strategy to secure and diversify cheap oil supply while breaking the clout of the Arab-dominated oil cartel OPEC. Lest foreign investors in Iraq be burdened by production limits, a new U.S.-installed government in Baghdad could go as far as pulling the country out of OPEC. Soon, the block of non-OPEC producers, including Russia and the Caspian countries, would churn out enough oil to bust the cartel by undermining its high-price agreements.

In the wake of geostrategic moves, oil corporations are jockeying for the best deals in a post-Hussein Iraq. While it seems absurd that President Bush would launch such a costly military campaign to obtain a handful of lucrative contracts for his Texan oil friends, it is not difficult to imagine that a post-Hussein regime bombed into power by B-52s would favor American suitors for Iraqi oil fields. After meeting with managers of ExxonMobil and ChevronTexaco, Ahmed Chalabi, the leader of the dubious CIA-backed Iraqi opposition, promised that "American companies will get a big shot at Iraqi oil."[3]

A few days later, Lord John Browne, CEO of British Petroleum, which pioneered the discovery of oil in Iraq in the early twentieth century, publicly warned the Blair government that British oil companies would lose out against their American competitors if London did not participate in a war on Iraq.[4]

Oil interests also partly accounted for the antiwar positions of France, China, and particularly Russia. Energy companies from all three countries had concluded with the Hussein regime a number of multibillion-dollar oil contracts, which they feared a new Iraqi government indebted to Washington would declare null and void, only to offer them to U.S. companies. More strategically, the Russian government abhorred the thought that a "liberated" Iraq would flood the world market with cheap oil, reducing the market share for Siberian oil. The Russian state budget, which is financed almost entirely through oil and gas export revenues, has been calculated in expectation of an oil price of twenty-three dollars per barrel. To make matters worse, high production costs in Siberia could cause Western oil corporations (whose capital Russia tries to attract) to invest in a re-opened Iraq instead. "Our budget would collapse," Aleksei Arbatov, deputy chairman of the Duma's defense committee, described the consequences.

No matter how many soldiers and civilians have so far died in Iraq and other Great Game battlefields for the sake of brazen energy imperialism, they won't be the last. With the industrialized world's addiction to oil growing unabated, more energy wars are a realistic prospect. As the planet's remaining oil reserves are going to last for only a few more decades, the struggles over access and profits between countries and multinational corporations are fast becoming fiercer, and they continue within the societies of oil-rich countries. In Kazakhstan, Nigeria, Venezuela, Sudan, Angola, the Arab sheikhdoms, and many other countries sudden oil wealth has led to corruption, economic decline, political oppression, revolutions, or civil wars. "We are drowning in the excrement of the Devil," the Venezuelan OPEC founder Juan Alfonzo once said of an oil boom's dire side effect.[5]

The fallout of energy imperialism will be felt in the United States and Europe in the shape of floods of refugees and oil price shocks, which will force governments to further increase costly overseas military commitments. In the long run, though, the vulnerability of oil infrastructure in volatile regions makes it virtually impossible to secure energy supply purely by military means. As part of a foresighted security policy, political leaders would be well advised to dilute our nefarious dependence on petroleum through the promotion of renewable energy technologies, which the task of climate protection against the global greenhouse effect urgently requires anyway.

Nearly a hundred years ago, on August 31, 1907, the first Great Game ended when Russian foreign minister Count Alexander Izvolsky and the British ambassador Sir Arthur Nicholson signed a secret treaty in St. Petersburg in which both countries defined their imperial interests in Central Asia. The Russian government accepted that Afghanistan lay in the British sphere of influence. In turn, London pledged never to challenge the Tsar's rule over the rest of Central Asia.

How long the new Great Game is going to occupy the strategists of the early twenty-first century, and if it will be possible to
end it as peacefully, is anyone's guess. As I write these final lines,
CNN is showing pictures from Baghdad of "collateral damage"
after a Cruise missile attack. An anguished Iraqi man stands in
the street, holding in his arms the mangled, blood-covered body
of a small boy. Seconds later, the news report is interrupted by
commercials for SUVs and painkillers.

Acknowledgments

T his book would have been impossible to write without the
help and encouragement of many wonderful people to whom
I would like to express my gratitude and appreciation:

Alec Russell and Paul Hill on the foreign desk of the London *Daily Telegraph* and all other newspaper and magazine editors who paid for my travels to obscure countries across the
globe.

Professor Odd Arne Westad and my other teachers at the
London School of Economics, who gave me the intellectual tools
for my work.

Clare Conville and Emma Parry, my agents in London and New
York, who believed in me and shared their excitement for this book
idea with all the right people.

Morgan Entrekin, Toby Mundy, Brando Skyhorse, and Bonnie
Chiang at Grove Press and Atlantic Books who have accompanied
this book's genesis with enthusiasm, erudition, and patience.

Sebastian Allison, Aziz Alpysbaev, Ben Arris, Imran Aslam,
Ian Bremmer, Dr. Siv Bublitz, Jens Dehning, Robert Ebel, Elena
Egereva, Fiona Hill, Abdullah Jan, Dieter Jarzombek, Muniba
Kamal, Byrd Leavell, Adam Lebor, Steve Levine, Dr. Amir Logh-
many, Anthony Loyd, Ahmed Rashid, Andrew Rearick, David
Rennie, Simon Retallack, Alexander Rondeli, Laurent Ruseckas,
Natalie Sabanadze, Harald Schumann, David Stern, Alex Todorovic,
Vartan Toganyan, Peter Verheijen, Marcus Warren, Rahimullah

Yusufzai, Anara Zhaxymuratova, and many other friends, companions, and colleagues who have all supported this book project in their own ways.

Sheikh Miraghajan from Kabul and the many kind people in the Caucasus and Central Asia who showed me true hospitality in their houses.

Yovid from Herat and all other interpreters and guards who helped me understand people and who got me safely out of unpleasant situations.

Igor from Sochi and the countless car mechanics in the Caucasus who managed to keep my old beloved Citroen CX-25 Turbo-diesel running.

Benjamin Paarmann who fact-checked this book with great skill and resourcefulness, and Charlotte Pattenden who proofread the manuscript with admirable attention to both detail and overall context.

Abdul Aziz Samandar, my friend and travel companion in Afghanistan, who showed me his country like no one else could have, and who taught me the meaning of respect.

All my gratitude and love goes out to my mother, my brother Ralf, my friend Matthias, and Laila, without whom there would have been no home to return to.

New York
April 2003

For comments and more information, visit the book's website *www.newgreatgame.com,* or send an e-mail to *Lutz@Kleveman.com*

Notes

The Devil's Tears: An Introduction

1. The expression "New Great Game" was first coined by the Pakistani journalist Ahmed Rashid. See *Taliban: Militant Islam, Oil and Fundamentalism in Central Asia* (Yale Nofa Bene: New York, 2000).
2. Quoted in Rashid, id., p. 145.
3. The best sources for energy statistics are the International Energy Agency, Paris, *www.iea.org,* and the U.S. Department of Energy, *www.eia.doe.gov.*
4. Quoted in *The Guardian,* October 23, 2001, p. 19.
5. *www.whitehouse.gov/energy.*
6. Quoted in *New York Times,* October 14, 1998.
7. Quoted in Dekmejian, Hrair and Hovann H. Simonian, *Troubled Waters: The Geopolitics of the Caspian Region* (Palgrove MacMillan: New York, 2001), p. 30.

Pipeline Poker: Baku's Oil Boom

1. Maclean, Fitzroy, *Eastern Approaches* (Penguin Books: London, 1991), p. 32.
2. Dumas, Alexandre, *Gefährliche Reise durch den wilden Kaukasus, 1858–1859* (Erdmann: Stuttgart, 1995), p. 131 (author's translation).
3. Yergin, Daniel, *The Prize: The Epic Quest for Oil, Money and Power* (Simon & Schuster: New York, 1992), p. 56.
4. Ibid., p. 133.
5. Ibid., p. 183.

6. Ibid., p. 337.

7. Mehdi, Amineh Parvizi, *Towards the Control of Oil Resources in the Caspian Region* (New York, 1999), p. 127.

8. Brzezinski, Zbigniew, *The Grand Chessboard* (Perseus Book Group: New York, 1997), p. 129.

Stalin's Legacy: Georgia

1. Quoted in *Moscow Times,* May 20, 2002.
2. Quoted in *International Herald Tribune,* April 29, 2002, p. 8.
3. Quoted in *New York Times,* August 15, 2002.
4. Quoted in *Moscow Times,* September 20, 2002.

Bandits and Oil Barons: Chechnya

1. Gall, Carlotta, and Thomas de Waal, *Chechnya: A Small Victorious War* (MacMillan: London, 1997), p. 127.
2. *Moscow Times,* May 21, 2002.
3. Gall, op. cit., p. 60.

The Big Pipeline: Decision in the Villa Petrolea

1. Quoted in *New York Times,* September 19, 2002.
2. Quoted in *Wall Street Journal,* October 8, 2002.
3. Quoted in *Moscow Times,* September 20, 2002.

The New Oil Dorado: Kazakhstan

1. Hersh, Seymour M., "The Price of Oil," in *The New Yorker,* July 9, 2001.
2. *New York Times,* December 11, 2002.
3. Hoffmann, David, "The Politicisation of Oil," in Ebel, Robert and Rajan Menon (eds.), *Energy and Conflict in Central Asia and the Caucasus* (Rowman & Littlefield: Oxford, 2000), pp. 55–77.
4. *New York Times,* November 16, 2002.

The Waking Giant: China

1. Maclean, op. cit., p. 122.
2. Meyer, Karl and Shareen Brysac, *Tournament of Shadows: The Great Game and the Race for Empire in Asia* (Counterpoint Press: London, 1999), p. 329.
3. Quoted in Hopkirk, Peter, *The Great Game: The Struggle for Empire in Central Asia* (Kodansha America: New York, 1994), p. 334.
4. Quoted in ibid., p. 463.
5. Quoted in *New York Times*, December 16, 2001, p. 1.
6. Ibid.
7. Quoted in *New York Times*, September 13, 2002, p. 6.
8. Quoted in *Jane's Intelligence Review*, March 1, 2002, p. 47.
9. Quoted in Hopkirk, op. cit., p. 455.
10. *New York Times*, July 3, 2002, p. 1.

Persian Trump Cards: Iran

1. Hersh, op. cit.
2. Kemp, Geoffrey, "U.S.-Iranian Relations," in Ebel, op. cit., p. 155.
3. BBC Business News, October 4, 2002.
4. Quoted in Mehdi, op. cit., p. 113.

Stalin's Disneyland: Turkmenistan

1. Quoted in *Wall Street Journal*, July 25, 2001, p. 2.
2. *The Economist*, August 2, 2001.
3. Rashid, op. cit., p. 280.

The Yankees Arrive: Uzbekistan and Kyrgyzstan

1. U.S. Department of State, Bureau of European and Eurasian Affairs Fact Sheets 2002.
2. Rashid, Ahmed, *Jihad: The Rise of Militant Islam in Central Asia* (Yale University Press: New York, 2002), p. 135.
3. Quoted in Hopkirk, op. cit., p. 442.
4. Quoted in ibid., p. 444.

5. Maclean, op. cit., p. 74.
6. Quoted in *New York Times,* December 7, 2002, p. 12.
7. Radio Free Europe, Central Asia Report, December 29, 2002, Vol. 2, No. 47.

Pipe Dreams: Afghanistan

1. Quoted in *The Washington Post,* October 7, 1996.
2. Quoted in *The Guardian,* October 23, 2001.
3. Hopkirk, op. cit., p. 237.
4. Meyer, op. cit., p. 156.
5. Quoted in *International Herald Tribune,* August 29, 2002.

The Cradle of Terror: Pakistan

1. Carew, Tom, *Jihad: The Secret War in Afghanistan* (Mainstream Publishing: London, 2001), p. 49.
2. U.S. Department of State Account Tables—budget estimate FY 2003.
3. *Newsweek,* October 21, 2002, p. 39.

Angry Young Men: An Epilogue

1. Brzezinski, op. cit., pp. 194–195.
2. Quoted in *The Observer,* November 3, 2002.
3. Quoted in *Washington Post,* September 15, 2002.
4. *The Guardian,* October 30, 2002.
5. Quoted in Hoffmann, op. cit., p. 67.

Bibliography

Anderson, Jon Lee. *The Lion's Grave: Dispatches from Afghanistan* (Grove: New York, 2002).

Barudio, Günter. *Tränen des Teufels: Eine Weltgeschichte des Erdöls* (Klett-Cotta: Stuttgart, 2001).

Brzezinski, Zbigniew. *The Grand Chessboard* (Perseus Book Group: New York, 1997).

Carew, Tom. *Jihad: The Secret War in Afghanistan* (Mainstream Publishing: London, 2001).

Croissant, Michael P. and Bülent Aras, eds. *Oil and Geopolitics in the Caspian Sea Region* (Praeger Publishers: Westport, CT, 1999).

Dekmejian, Hrair and Hovann H. Simonian. *Troubled Waters: The Geopolitics of the Caspian Region* (Palgrave MacMillan: New York, 2001).

Dumas, Alexandre. *Gefährliche Reise durch den wilden Kaukasus, 1858–1859* (Erdmann: Stuttgart, 1995).

Ebel, Robert and Rajan Menon, eds. *Energy and Conflict in Central Asia and the Caucasus* (Rowman & Littlefield: Oxford 2000).

Elliot, Jason. *An Unexpected Light: Travels in Afghanistan* (MacMillan: London, 1999).

Engdahl, F. William. *Mit der Ölwaffe zur Weltmacht: Der Weg zur neuen Weltordnung* (Böttiger Verlag: Wiesbaden, 2000).

Gall, Carlotta and Thomas de Waal. *Chechnya: A Small Victorious War* (MacMillan: London, 1997).

Goltz, Thomas. *Azerbaijan Diary: A Rogue Reporter's Adventures in an Oil-Rich, War-Torn, Post-Soviet Republic* (M. E. Sharpe: New York, 1999).

Hopkirk, Peter. *The Great Game: The Struggle for Empire in Central Asia* (Kodansha America: New York, 1994).

Kaplan, Robert D. *Eastward to Tartary: Travels in the Balkans, the Middle East, and the Caucasus* (Random House: New York, 2000).

———. *Soldiers of God: With Islamic Warriors in Afghanistan and Pakistan* (Vintage Books: New York, 2002).

———. *The Ends of the Earth: From Togo to Turkmenistan, from Iran to Cambodia, a Journey to the Frontiers of Anarchy* (Vintage Books: New York, 1997).

Kipling, Rudyard. *Kim* (Penguin Books: London, 1994).

Maclean, Fitzroy. *Eastern Approaches* (Penguin Books: London, 1991).

Mehdi, Parvizi Amineh. *Towards the Control of Oil Resources in the Caspian Region* (New York, 1999).

Meyer, Karl and Shareen Brysac. *Tournament of Shadows: The Great Game and the Race for Empire in Asia* (Counterpoint Press: London, 1999).

Pleitgen, Fritz F. *Durch den wilden Kaukasus* (Kiepenhuer & Witsch: Cologne, 2000).

Roy, Olivier. *The New Central Asia: The Creation of Nations* (I. B. Tauris: London, 2000).

Scholl-Latour, Peter. *Das Schlachtfeld der Zukunft: Zwischen Kaukasus und Pamir* (Goldmann: München, 1994).

Rashid, Ahmed. *Taliban: Militant Islam, Oil and Fundamentalism in Central Asia* (Yale Nofa Bene: New York, 2000).

———. *Jihad: The rise of militant Islam in Central Asia* (Yale Univesity Press: New York, 2002).

Yergin, Daniel. *The Prize: The Epic Quest for Oil, Money and Power* (Simon & Schuster: New York, 1992).

Index